# TAKING MONEY SERIOUSLY

# Taking Money Seriously
## and
## Other Essays

DAVID LAIDLER
*University of Western Ontario*

The MIT Press
Cambridge, Massachusetts

© by David Laidler, 1990

This book was printed and bound by
BPCC Wheatons Ltd, Exeter in Great Britain.

*Library of Congress Cataloging-in-Publication Data*

Laidler, David E. W.
  Taking money seriously and other essays/ by David Laidler.
    p.    cm.
  Includes bibliographical references.
  ISBN 0–262–12148–4
  1. Money.   2. Monetary policy.   I. Title.
HG221.L243   1990                                    89–13609
332.4—dc20                                           CIP

# Contents

# Preface

A number of principles have guided me in selecting papers to be reprinted in this volume. First and foremost I have tried to produce a collection which has certain coherent threads linking its chapters, even if this does mean that there is sometimes a certain overlap among their arguments. Secondly, I have included a number of papers which have appeared either in journals whose major readership is regionally concentrated (e.g. *The Canadian Journal of Economics* or *Australian Economic Papers*) or in edited volumes initially aimed at a rather narrow audience (e.g. the Canadian Macdonald Commission Research Series) in the hope that the proportion of the material included here which is new to the average reader will be reasonably high. Finally, I have put a high premium on pieces that are non-technical and easily accessible. Several of the essays reprinted here—e.g. Chapters 1, 3, 4, 7 and 8—were originally written for non-specialist audiences; and, in selecting others for inclusion, I have tried to match their level of exposition. Hence, though I hope that this book will be of interest to my fellow academic monetary economists, I believe that all of it will be comprehensible to any student who has worked through an intermediate level textbook such as Parkin and Bade's *Modern Macro-economics* (2nd edn. 1988, Philip Allan). Teachers might therefore find it a useful source of supplementary readings on topics, a little outside of the contemporary mainstream, for undergraduate and beginning level graduate courses in macro- and monetary economics.

All of the essays reprinted here have been subjected to a little editing before reprinting. Errors have been removed where they have been found, and the balance of material between text and footnotes has been adjusted to ensure that the latter contain only genuine asides rather than important matters of substance. Also, particularly in the cases of Chapters 3 and 9, small amendments to the text have occasionally been made to remove references to events or debates that might be hard for an undergraduate reader (who was still in primary school when these, the oldest essays reprinted here, were first written) to recognise. I have not, however, attempted to rewrite large sections of papers in order to imbue them with a spurious timeliness, as will be apparent, for example, to anyone reading the final section of Chapter 7 which is firmly rooted in Canadian policy issues of the mid-1980s. Nevertheless, editing even one's own work is time-consuming. I am therefore grateful to the University of Western Ontario for an appointment to a Research Professorship during the academic year 1988–9 which enabled me to prepare this volume for publication.

No one can write anything without the help and advice of colleagues and students, and I would like to express my gratitude to the following, without thereby implicating them in the views I express: Paul Anglin, Clarence Barber, Olivier Blanchard, Russell Boyer, Reuven Brenner, Karl Brunner, Victoria Chick, Robert Clower, Alan Coddington, Laurence Copeland, Anthony Courakis, Keith Cuthbertson, Michael Darby, Jurgen Eichberger, Martin Evans, John Flemming, Pierre Fortin, Joel Fried, Milton Friedman, Jo-Anna Gray, Paul Gomme, Dieter Helm, Zvi Hercowitz, Steven Holland, Seppo Honkapohja, Peter Howitt, Jerzy Konieczny, Peter Jonson, Lars Jonung, Axel Leijonhufvud, Brian Loasby, David Longworth, Alvin Marty, Thomas Mayer, Bennett McCallum, Allan Meltzer, Patrick Minford, Johan Myhrman, Robert Nobay, Michael Parkin, Don Patinkin, David Peel, Edmund Phelps, Baldev Raj, Charles Rowley, Cillian Ryan, Thomas Rymes, John Sargent, Thomas J. Sargent, Ronald Shearer, Jeffrey Sheen, Hans-Werner Sinn, Gregor Smith, David Soskice, Franco Spinelli, George Stadler, Stafan Viotti, and George Zis.

The essays reprinted here have the following origins: Chapter 1, 1988 Presidential Address to the Canadian Economics Association, *Canadian Journal of Economics* 1988; Chapter 2, the 1983 Harry Johnson Lecture, *Conference Papers* supplement to the *Economic Journal* 1984; Chapter 3, revised version of 'The Welfare Costs of Inflation in Neo-Classical Theory—Some Unsettled Questions' presented at a 1976 IEA Conference on inflation, and published in Erik Lundberg (ed.), *Inflation Theory and Anti-Inflation Policy*, London, Macmillan, 1978 (an Italian translation of an earlier version of this paper appeared in the *Rivista Internazionale del Scienze Sociale* April–June 1978); Chapter 4, *Banca Nazionale del Lavoro Quarterly Review* 1986; Chapter 5, *The Manchester School of Economic and Social Studies* 1988; Chapter 6, paper prepared for a conference held at the Free University of Berlin on *Monetary Theory and Monetary Policy: New Tracks for the 1990s* September 1988 and forthcoming in the proceedings of that conference to be edited by Stephen Frowen, London, Macmillan; Chapter 7, the 1986 Joseph Fisher Lecture in Commerce, *Australian Economic Papers* 1986; Chapter 8, J. Sargent (ed.), *Post-war Macroeconomic Developments*, Vol. 20 of Research Studies prepared for the Royal Commission on the Economic Union and Development Prospects for Canada (the Macdonald Commission)—Toronto, University of Toronto Press; Chapter 9, presented at the 1976 University of Paris-

Dauphine Conference, *Zeitschrift fuer Wirtschafts-und Sozialwissenschaften* 1979; Chapter 10, presented at the 1985 George Mason University Conference on Deficits—J. Buchanan, C. K. Rowley and R. D. Tollison (eds.), *Deficits*, Oxford, Basil Blackwell, 1987. I am grateful to the following editors and publishers who first printed these essays for permission to include them in this volume: (Ch. 1) the editors of the *Canadian Journal of Economics—Revue Canadienne d'Economique*; (Ch. 2) the editors of the *Economic Journal*; (Ch. 3) Messrs Macmillan, London; (Ch. 4) the editors of the *Banca Nazionale del Lavoro Quarterly Review*; (Ch. 5) the editors of the *Manchester School of Economic and Social Studies*; (Ch. 6) Messrs Macmillan, London; (Ch. 7) the editors of *Australian Economic Papers*; (Ch. 8) the University of Toronto Press, Toronto; (Ch. 9) Messrs Duncker and Humblot, Berlin; (Ch. 10) Messrs Basil Blackwell, Oxford.

David Laidler
May 1989

# Introduction

Monetary economics has made progress over the years, but not in any easily mapped fashion. It has moved in fits and starts along a path with many detours. Along the way it has often discovered excellent and powerful ideas, but it has almost as often mislaid others which are just as useful. I say mislaid, rather than lost, because useful ideas are resilient, and have a way of turning up again (sometimes in new disguises) when they are needed.

It would be possible to illustrate this general characterisation of the development of monetary thought by referring to a large number of episodes chosen from the last two and a half centuries, but it will suffice here to refer to the last two decades. Twenty years ago 'monetarism' was at the height of its academic influence—its effect on policy came later, as is usually the case in these matters—but new ideas, developed in the early 1970s and seeming at first merely to be elaborations of monetarist notions, in due course undermined that influence. Those new ideas, which formed the basis of what we call 'new-classical economics' were good ones to be sure, but, in the process of developing them, their proponents often seemed to lose sight of older, equally good, ideas. The essays reprinted in this book represent one economist's efforts to sustain and develop further those older doctrines, to explore their relationship to newer lines of thought, and to argue their continued policy relevance.

Monetarism was, as I have argued in much greater detail elsewhere (Laidler 1982), based on two analytic devices, namely an empirically stable aggregate demand-for-money function, and the expectations-augmented Phillips curve. The former relationship was thought to ensure that variations in the quantity of money would have an important influence on the behaviour of nominal aggregate demand in the economy, and the latter to ensure that variations in nominal demand would have mainly real consequences in the short run, but would be absorbed by the price level in the long run. These ideas have run into two sets of problems. First, during the 1970s the stability of the demand for money turned out to be less robust than its proponents had hoped. Second, and from the point of view of monetarism's academic influence far more important, the theoretical analysis of the expectations-augmented Phillips curve pioneered by Robert E. Lucas (1972) has, as it has evolved, led to the conclusion that variations in the quantity of money cannot have interesting real consequences. According to new-classical doctrine, money can still cause inflation, but anticipated inflation is not important, and unanticipated fluctuations in money are unlikely to be significant and long lasting enough to be dominant causes of the cycle.

There is no need to go into details about new-classical analysis here. Its nature is explored in Chapter 4 of this collection. Suffice it to note that to treat the expectations-augmented Phillips curve as the aggregate supply curve of a competitive Walrasian economy characterised by certain informational imperfections was to treat a monetary economy as one in which money had no means of exchange role to play; and to assume that, within that economy, agents formed expectations 'as if' equipped with a 'true' model of it with which they could process all 'relevant' information, was to imply that, in an economy where money-supply data are available on a weekly basis, changes in that variable would be quickly anticipated and therefore harmless. Thus was 'monetarism' with its slogan 'money matters', transformed into a framework in which money hardly mattered at all. New-classical economics pays no more than lip-service to money's means of exchange role. Nor of course did the 1960s vintage monetarism from which it grew, which is why that monetarism was so easily undermined by new-classical ideas when its microfoundations were explored.

Money matters because monetary exchange is an alternative institution for co-ordinating economic activity to the Walrasian market. This theme is taken up in the first two chapters of this collection, which thus explore an alternative extension of monetarist ideas to that which the mainstream of monetary economics developed in the 1970s and 80s. Chapter 1 deals with the connections between the existence of the institution of monetary exchange and the informational problems and price stickiness which seem to be required if any simple macroeconomic model is to produce the significant monetary non-neutralities which characterise real-world economies. It argues that all three phenomena stem from the same source, namely the costs of generating and processing information that arise in an economy which lacks a Walrasian auctioneer who obligingly performs such services at zero cost. It also argues that to postulate such nominal stickiness as a starting-point for macro-modelling is not to attribute 'irrationality' to economic agents.

Chapter 1 stresses the importance of a precautionary demand for money in a non-Walrasian world, as does Chapter 2 from a somewhat different perspective. Chapter 2 argues that the monetary 'buffer stock' effects stemming from the interaction of precautionary money holdings and price stickiness lie at the root of many of the apparent instabilities that have plagued empirical studies of the aggregate demand-for-money function. It also explores the implications of these ideas for the role of interest rates in the transmission of monetary shocks, and for critiques of monetarist ideas based on the observation that the quantity of money, far from being a variable whose value is given from outside the economy, is in fact determined within it as a by-product of the credit-creating activities of the banking system. Hence Chapter 2 deals with two important issues in the debate about the continued empirical relevance of monetarist ideas.

Chapter 3, printed in its present form for the first time in English here, discusses the costs of inflation. Monetarist analysis of these issues, epitomised by Friedman's (1969) essay, *The Optimum Quantity of Money*, was always vulnerable to the criticism that the costs to which it pointed seemed small relative to the amount of fuss being made about the problem. This apparent contradiction gave, as the date of the first version of this essay (1976) should make clear, an early impetus to my concerns with money's means-of-exchange role. If inflation leads to an increase in the consumption of 'shoe-leather' in our rather prosperous economies, we might take a rather benign view of it. If it threatens to undermine the exchange mechanisms upon which that prosperity depends, it is an altogether more serious matter.

Now the ideas expounded in the first three chapters of this book are certainly not new-classical, but I regard them as potential complements to, rather than substitutes for, the best elements in new-classical thought. As I remarked earlier, the problem with the last two decades of monetary economics has not been that new-classical ideas are bad. The insistence of Lucas *et al.* on the importance of the equilibrium analysis of maximising behaviour has been extremely salutary. The problem has been only that these good ideas have been pushed too far to the neglect of other good ideas. This theme is developed in Chapter 4, which is an extended critique of new-classical economics. Chapter 5 may be regarded as a sort of brief technical appendix to preceding arguments, particularly some of those set out in Chapters 2 and 4. This, the only essay in this collection where any algebra (albeit of the simplest sort) is used, explores the differences and similarities between the simple textbook-style models that emerge from new-classical analysis on the one hand and the 'buffer stock' money approach on the other.

The second half of this collection is devoted to the discussion of policy issues. There has been no parallel as yet in the policy field to the downgrading of money that has taken place in the more purely analytic literature of monetary economics. Even so, economic doctrines usually have their policy impact with a time-lag, and one which abstracts from money's role in the mechanism of exchange could be particularly dangerous if it got loose among politicians and bureaucrats, for the simple reason that it accords no useful role to governments in the management of money. The *raison d'être* of monetary policy-making institutions must be the existence of some public good or natural monopoly element in the monetary system. A body of theory which treats money as a pure store of value does not readily yield insights into this matter, but one which focuses on the role of monetary institutions in fostering exchange does. Chapter 6, then, uses ideas set out earlier to defend the discussion of monetary policy as an academically respectable exercise, and the existence of publicly regulated institutions to execute it as socially desirable.

Chapter 6 argues that monetary policy is important but makes no concrete recommendations about its conduct. Discussions of this issue are to be found in Chapter 7 and propound a somewhat weakened form of the monetarist doctrines of the 1960s. Both the theoretical arguments of earlier chapters, and much real-world evidence, lead to the conclusion that institutional evolution is of the essence in the monetary system. That being the case, the quasi-constitutional rules for the conduct of monetary policy which were much favoured twenty years ago, by this author among others be it said, simply are not feasible. Though, as I argue, there is still much to be said for steadiness in the conduct of policy, and for the authorities refraining from discretionary interventions which they do not have knowledge to design efficiently, these aims cannot be locked in place once and for all by some legislative fiat. Rather, because they must be pursued against a shifting institutional background, their importance must be continually reaffirmed through public debate if policy is to be kept on track.

In the world we live in, the institutions through which political choices about monetary policy are exercised are overwhelmingly national in scope. At the same time, real economic activity is becoming increasingly internationalised. Hence any discussion of monetary policy issues must recognise its international dimension. Chapter 8 is a survey of debates about international monetary issues which stresses the need to maintain the viability of the international economy in the face of the fragmentation of responsibility for monetary policy among individual nation states. It concludes that, whatever enthusiasts for one system or another might argue, there is little to choose between fixed and flexible exchange rates as far as the performance of the real economy is concerned, but that, so long as the inflation rate is a matter of legitimate political concern, there must be a preference for a flexible-rate regime. The theme of the interdependence of political and monetary jurisdictions is also central to Chapter 9. Though this discussion of currency unions dates back to 1978, the topic is once more fashionable as British economists debate the merits of entering the European Monetary System, and I trust that the arguments there developed, though rather old, will nevertheless be found of some interest.

Only under a flexible exchange-rate regime can different choices about monetary policy made in different political jurisdictions be reconciled with one another without disrupting the real economy. That was the essential message of Friedman's celebrated 1953 essay on this topic, and the fact that it emerges in the discussions of Chapters 8 and 9 of this collection simply serves to confirm the continuity of the ideas expounded here with earlier monetarist doctrine. The last chapter of this collection provides yet another treatment, in the context of a particular policy problem, namely the United States' fiscal deficit, of this same link between domestic political processes and international monetary institutions. It argues that the latter, far from imposing constraints upon policy choices, are themselves objects of such choices. Hence this chapter reiterates in a specific context the underlying theme of the policy section of this book, namely that the very fact of money being the basis of the economy's exchange mechanism renders the design of monetary institutions and the conduct of monetary policy a matter of political choice.

Now the arguments developed in this book were certainly inherent in the monetarist ideas of the 1960s. They represent a viable line of inquiry rather different to that in fact taken by the new-classical economics which most commentators would regard as a natural development of those same monetarist ideas; but this does not make the choice between new-classical ideas and those stressed here an 'either/or' matter. New-classical ideas have been taken too far perhaps; but, as I have already said, many of them are still good ideas. Even so, the notion that money's essential function is that of means of exchange, and that this renders the nature of monetary institutions important to an economy's performance, are good ideas too. If the publication of these essays helps to remind readers of that, and prompts some of them to explore further the implications of those ideas for monetary theory, then it will have served a useful purpose.

# 1

# Taking Money Seriously

## Introduction

There are many parallels between the 'Keynesian revolution' and the 'monetarist counter-revolution', but surely the strangest of them is this: both were set in motion by economists who were convinced of the central importance of money to the economic processes they were investigating, and both ended up evolving views of the world in which money has but a minor role to play. This parallel did not arise entirely fortuitously. Whatever Keynes may have intended, what came to be called Keynesian economics soon came to rely on a version of Walrasian general equilibrium analysis in which market mechanisms exist and function independently of the behaviour of the supply and demand for money; and monetarism took over the same theoretical foundations.[1]

In this chapter I shall argue three points: that such Walrasian analysis does not permit money to be taken seriously; that if we do take money seriously, in the sense of regarding monetary exchange as an alternative, instead of a supplement, to Walrasian mechanisms for co-ordinating economic activity, many of the apparently anomalous rigidities upon which predictions about money's importance appear to hinge can be understood as the outcome of maximising behaviour; and that if we also take money seriously, in the sense of paying attention to the empirical evidence we have on the nature of the economy's demand-for-money function, we find that some of it does indeed point to the desirability of looking at monetary exchange in just this way.

## Money in Keynesian, Monetarist and New-Classical Economics

In the economics of Keynes, as in classical economics, money was a means of exchange; and textbook macroeconomics even now refers to 'transactions' and 'precautionary' motives for holding money, which are said to

1

derive directly from that role. However, when monetary economists adopted Walrasian general equilibrium, in its IS–LM guise, as their basic vision of economic activity, they adopted a model which could not generate such motives internally. Whatever the vocabulary of the monetary economics that developed after the publication of the *General Theory*, its logical structure came to treat money as an asset pure and simple; and the emphasis which Hicks (1935) and Keynes (1930, 1936) placed on money's role as a short-term speculative asset represented an important contribution to monetary economics precisely because it laid the foundations for a theory of the demand for money as a store of value and because such a conception of money was the only one which could be accommodated comfortably within a Walrasian frame of reference.

The monetarist counter-revolution was an attempt to change perceptions about empirical phenomena, not to create a new theoretical structure. It therefore did nothing to interrupt the process, already close to completion in the 1950s, of integrating monetary theory with Walrasian value theory.[2] The further this process was pushed, the more did the representative model of a monetary economy come to resemble one of a barter economy in which there happened to exist a peculiar asset called 'money' whose 'real' (i.e. 'utility'-yielding) quantity varied in inverse proportion to its price in terms of goods. The utility in question was said to arise from money's role as a means of exchange, of course, but there was no such role for it to play within the logical structure of the representative macro-economic model. Though that model was undoubtedly useful as a starting-point for empirical work, it was also very vulnerable to theoretical criticisms such as I have been summarising here. Clower (e.g. 1965, 1967), Hahn (e.g. 1965) and Tsiang (e.g. 1966), for example, had all articulated them by the mid-1960s, but though the end of that decade saw much interest in the microeconomic foundations of monetary economics, this particular line of argument was to become, and indeed remain, something of a minority taste among macroeconomists. The reason for this was the success of new-classical economics.

The original aim of Robert E. Lucas and his collaborators was to provide a microfoundation for monetarist predictions about the short-run non-neutrality of money, and Friedman's (1968) long-run 'natural unemployment rate' hypothesis. The nature of that endeavour initially attracted attention to the supply side of the economy in general and the labour market in particular; only later (though surely inevitably) were new-classical economists forced to face up to the fact that the Walrasian framework with which they continued to work does not provide an internally coherent justification for the existence of money. Their resolution to this difficulty has taken two forms. Some, the proponents of what Hall (1982) has called the 'new monetary economics', have pushed the money as a store of value view to new limits, and have concluded (correctly as far as the world described by their model is concerned) that, if money is dominated in rate of return (as it is in the real world) no one would hold it unless the Government compelled them to do so.[3] Others, notably Lucas (e.g. 1984), have reintroduced money's means of exchange role into a dynamic, but still essentially Walrasian, model in the shape of an arbitrary 'cash in advance' constraint which derives directly from the work of Clower and Tsiang (though the rescue of Walrasian style macroeconomics was hardly what the latter intended that idea to accomplish).

Protagonists of the approaches in question would no doubt argue that they are still exploring matters of logic, and that their theories should not yet be expected to meet the test of empirical relevance. Even so, the widespread adoption of these approaches has opened up a yawning gap between theoretical and applied work on monetary issues. In either type of new-classical model, monetary shocks can cause price-level fluctuations, but their assumptions of competitive equilibrium and rational expectations ensure that the amount of real harm which results is trivial. Setting aside issues of superneutrality, it is the fundamental prediction of new-classical theory that only unanticipated changes in the money supply have consequences for real variables. Early work by Robert J. Barro (e.g. 1978) seemed to confirm that prediction, but later investigations by Frederick Mishkin (e.g. 1982) have called those results into question on econometric grounds. Furthermore, given the amount of information available in the real world about the behaviour of monetary aggregates, and the speed with which it becomes public, it is impossible to account for the magnitude of observed cyclical fluctuations in real income and employment in such terms.

This is the basic message of the work of Boschen and Grossman (1982) which exploits the simple fact that, with money supply data published weekly, the correct real-world counterpart of 'unanticipated money' must be the measurement-error component of those published data, and finds that, while this error has no discernible effect on real variables, publicly announced fluctuations do appear to have such influence. This failure of a key prediction of the new-classical model is one reason why new-classical economics, mainly at the prompting of Kydland and Prescott (1982), is in the process of spawning 'real business-style theory' as an alternative, completely non-monetary, explanation of economic fluctuations.[4]

'Keynesian' arguments about the minor relevance of money for the behaviour of prices, output, and employment were, of course, very different from those of new-classical economics. They involved assertions about the existence of liquidity and investment traps, and of sociological influences on money wages and prices so strong as to swamp the effects of conventional market forces. Monetarism rebutted these arguments with empirical evidence about particular functional relationships and also about broader based associations among the quantity of money, the price level, and output. Such evidence continues to accumulate, and those of us concerned with applied problems in general, and policy issues in particular, remain convinced that, in the real world, 'money matters' as much as ever.

To support this proposition, let me present two scatter diagrams of data taken from the FRB St. Louis *International Economic Conditions*, annual edition, June 1987. Figure 1.1 plots the relationship between average inflation rates ($\dot{p}$) and average nominal-money-less-real-income growth rates ($\dot{m}-\dot{y}$) for eleven countries over the period (roughly) 1970–85. Figure 1.2 plots the year-by-year relationship, for each of those same countries, between the deviation over a two-year period of real-income growth from its long-run average value ($\hat{y}$) and the deviation in the first of those years of nominal-money growth from the average value prevailing over the previous three years ($\hat{m}$). These scatters reveal two empirical relationships central to monetarist doctrine, namely a long-run one between money growth and inflation, and a short-run one between changes in money growth and subsequent real-income growth.[5]

The inflation/money growth relationship appears to be the stronger of the two, but Figure 1.2 nevertheless indicates that changes in money growth rates significantly increase the probability of subsequent variations in real-income growth. Brunner and Meltzer (1987) have recently recanted their view that monetary shocks are the dominant impulse driving economic fluctuations in the light of their reading of the evidence

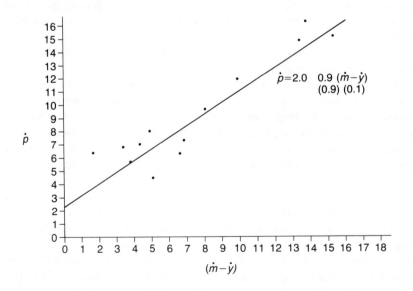

**Figure 1.1**   Average Inflation and Growth Rates

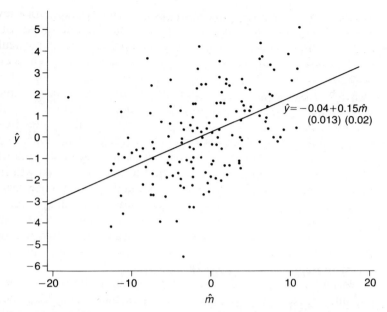

$$\hat{y}= -0.04+0.15\hat{m}$$
$$(0.013)\ (0.02)$$

**Figure 1.2** Changes in Money Growth and Deviations of Real-Income Growth from Trend

generated by the 1970s and 80s, and are now more inclined to take an eclectic view of the mechanisms underlying the cycle, such as has long been advocated by Leijonhufvud (e.g. 1986). The data I present here certainly leave room for a substantial non-monetary component among the factors driving the cycle, but they are also consistent with the view that monetary impulses, if not dominant, have nevertheless remained systematically important over the very period in which popular opinion would have it that monetarism was being discredited.

I should note here that Parkin (1987) uses data related, but by no means identical, to mine to argue that the new-classical 'unanticipated money' explanation of fluctuations in real variables is valid after all. The logic of his argument requires us to accept the assumption that the fluctuations of relative commodity price in the early 1970s reflected purely supply-side influences, and were independent of monetary shocks. It also requires us to ignore the arguments of Boschen and Grossman (1982), and to treat monetary changes which were not foreseen at the beginning of a calendar year as remaining unanticipated throughout the year. Though given these premises its logic is impeccable, not everyone will find Parkin's argument compelling.

In any event, I do not present the above data as 'proving' anything about the real world. Rather my intention is to show that the 1970s and 80s have generated no crucial empirical experiment that would force an impartial observer to abandon monetarist doctrine. The rise of new-classical

economics has been based on theoretical arguments, not empirical, and it
is surely ironical that a body of doctrine, whose immediate motivation was
to provide a tight theoretical rationale for monetarist generalisations about
the short-run empirical importance of money for real variables, has ended
up re-establishing the classical doctrine of 'neutral money' on firmer
theoretical foundations than ever. As I shall now go on to argue, new-
classical economics, despite its great theoretical clarity and rigour (I judge
it here by the standards of macroeconomics) is at best unhelpful, or at
worst downright misleading, in empirical applications because its models,
even those which employ a cash-in-advance constraint, do not encompass
the basic facts of economic life that require economies to make use of a
means of exchange in the first place. They do not take money seriously
from a theoretical point of view, and that is why they cannot take it
seriously empirically.

## Money and Alternative Market Mechanisms

New-classical concerns with the microfoundations of macroeconomics did
not arise in an intellectual vacuum. Lucas's (1972) paper grew out of his
earlier contribution (with Leonard Rapping) to the celebrated (1970)
Phelps *et al.* volume on the *Microfoundations of Employment and Inflation
Theory*. Moreover, the late 1960s and early 70s saw widespread efforts to
find a satisfactory microfoundation for the theory of money *per se*. I have
already alluded to the work of Clower, Hahn, and Tsiang, and mention
ought to be made too of the contributions of Hicks (1967), Leijonhufvud
(1968), Niehans (1971), Brunner and Meltzer (1971), Ostroy (1973),
Melitz (1974), Howitt (1974), Goodhart (1975), Jones (1976), and Alchian
(1977) among others. Certain common themes ran through this otherwise
heterogeneous collection of work. All of it drew attention to the enormous
costs of generating and processing the information needed to co-ordinate
the activities of individual agents in that complicated set of social
arrangements we call an economy, and all of it argued that the institution
of monetary exchange should be understood as a device to deal with them.[6]
Such ideas have many antecedents in classical economics, because, for two
hundred years at least, it was recognised that a barter economy would be so
costly to operate that it could hardly be expected to exist outside of the
economist's imagination, except in extremely primitive (at least in material
terms) societies.

Within the Walrasian economy from which the contributors to the
above-mentioned literature were trying to escape, information and
incentives sufficient to co-ordinate the activities of otherwise isolated and
self-interested agents are provided by the structure of relative prices.
These have to be equilibrium prices because only in their presence can

agents come to market secure in the knowledge that what they bring with them will be just sufficient to purchase what they wish to take away. Furthermore, if we assume that supply and demand for every good and service always match, perhaps it is also harmless to assume (it is certainly usual) that the Walrasian market is a place where agents can costlessly find willing trading partners as well. Now the information and co-ordination problems which the 'market' solves in this Walrasian story include those with which 'money' deals in traditional accounts which begin with the inconvenience of barter. That is why monetary theory based on Walrasian general equilibrium analysis either treats money as an asset pure and simple, or has to introduce monetary exchange in an apparently arbitrary fashion by appealing to a cash-in-advance constraint. It is also why the lines of inquiry opened up in the literature to which I have referred above still deserve the attention of monetary economists.

The Walrasian auctioneer solves the problem of co-ordinating economic activity by performing three distinct tasks: setting market clearing prices, informing agents about them, and bringing suppliers and demanders together so that trades can go through. In contrast, the adoption of a common means of exchange in an initially non-Walrasian barter economy simplifies co-ordination problems but does not eliminate them. Long transactions chains are ruled out if agents with something to sell take money in exchange, and, when it comes to buying, offer money. It takes two parties to strike a single bargain, however; and even in a monetary economy, agents offering specific goods or services for sale still have to find someone who wants to buy them, agents offering money in exchange for specific goods or services still have to find sellers, and buyers and sellers have to find a mutually acceptable price. Some degree of market uncertainty, and associated search and transactions costs, which would be completely absent from a Walrasian set-up, therefore remain in money-using economies.

Some contributors to the literature to which I referred earlier, notably Howitt (1974, 1979), have found it helpful, and realistic, to note the existence of specialised agents, dealers or middlemen, who play a key role in coping with these remaining co-ordination problems. These dealers (who may or may not also be producers) act as specialised traders, located at specific places and open for business at specific times. They hold inventories of goods ready for sale, and set their prices too. Consumers are thought of as coming to these dealers' places of business during working hours, purchasing goods from them, and (if the dealers are also producers) as selling factor services to them as well. Monetary exchange, in the view of market mechanisms to which I here refer, is an institution which naturally complements the dealer. If sellers are specialised in the sense of offering for sale a well defined class of goods, then it is clearly sensible to think of them being willing to take in return a commonly acceptable means of exchange, and as posting their prices in terms of that means of exchange too. Moreover, dealers must buy goods to replenish their inventories, and producers must pay the suppliers of their inputs. It is also sensible to expect that these trades will be mediated by money.

Now note that this vision of the trading process amplifies traditional accounts of how monetary exchange deals with the inconveniences of barter by cutting down on long transactions chains and saving 'shopping time'. In a dealer economy, a consumer wanting something specific does not have to search the market for some other agent who has it for sale. It will suffice to go to the right dealer. Money does little to save the consumer's shopping time in this view of the world. Its main function is to simplify the act of exchange *per se* (though of course the combined effect of dealer-mediated trade carried on which money is to reduce the many inconveniences of barter). This point is of some theoretical importance, because it is possible to conceive in principle of an economy which replaces the Walrasian auctioneer with dealers and monetary exchange in one of his three roles, that of bringing buyers and sellers together, but maintains that entity to set market clearing prices and to keep agents informed of them. For certain theoretical purposes, such as investigating the evolution of a means of exchange from an initial situation of barter in an economy in which search costs are important, a set-up that ensures the existence of equilibrium prices and grants agents access to information about them is particularly attractive. Moreover, a money-using economy in which equilibrium prices always rule, but in which the auctioneer's capacity for conveying information to agents about market clearing prices is limited to telling them about their selling prices, has a familiar new-classical aspect, becoming in effect Lucas's version of a cash-in-advance economy.

A model of this type, though, is unusually artificial, even by the standards of macroeconomics. Dealers are not just a useful fiction like the auctioneer: they exist; and it is awkward to work with a system which relies on both entities simultaneously, one to justify the existence of money and the other to set prices and inform agents about them. Once they are introduced, it is natural to have dealers set prices, and also, along with their customers, collect and process the data on which market activities are premissed. If prices are set by individual dealers, however, they may differ for the same goods at different places in the economy. Though consumers may not have to spend time looking for suppliers of what it is they want, they will nevertheless find that it pays to search for a favourable price. Dealers too face problems which would not arise in a simpler world. Presumably they wish to maintain their prices at market clearing values, but they must devote resources to calculating those values. Sales volume will convey some information about whether prices are right or not, but if consumers are shopping around, it will have a stochastic character. Price setters who start off with the right price must therefore distinguish between random fluctuations in sales and those which signal a lasting shift in demand, and respond only to the latter.

All this gives money a more complicated role to play than it has in a simple cash-in-advance economy. If consumers find it worth while to shop around for favourable prices, the timing of their transactions, as well as those of dealers, becomes stochastic. They will therefore find it convenient to hold inventories of goods to smooth out discrepancies between the timing of acts of consumption and purchase. Dealers too will need inventories of goods in stock to absorb discrepancies between sales of goods and purchases from suppliers, whether these arise from random sources or from the possibility that it takes time to solve signal extraction problems before prices are changed. Where trade is carried on by money, however, movements of goods inventories must involve complementary fluctuations in the pattern of cash inflows and outflows, and these in turn must be absorbed by an inventory of cash balances (or, depending upon the sophistication of the economy and the costs of trading in financial markets, of liquid assets). In short, if we dispense with the auctioneer entirely and have prices set endogenously, we create a world in which a precautionary demand for money becomes of the essence.[7]

## *The Precautionary Demand for Money and Price Stickiness*

The traditional textbook model of the precautionary demand for money begins with individual agents who inhabit an economy much like that sketched out above. The model takes it for granted that transactions are mediated by money, and that, because of market uncertainty, agents face a stochastic pattern of cash inflows and outflows. It also takes the existence of other financial assets for granted, and argues that, if there are costs of transforming other assets into cash, agents not only use money as a means of exchange but also hold a 'buffer stock' of cash to reduce the frequency with which they incur the costs of trading other assets for means of exchange in order to permit their transactions in markets in goods and services to go through. Such a model leads to a conventional formulation of the 'long run' demand-for-money function, in which the demand for real balances rises with some scale variable measuring the real volume of market activity and falls as the opportunity cost of holding money rises.[8]

Now it is of the very essence of a demand for precautionary balances that, in the individual experiment, its value should fluctuate around an average or target level as the agent encounters those unpredicted fluctuations in the pattern of payments and receipts against which the balance is held in the first place; and such an approach to modelling the demand for money also enables us to predict the existence, in the market experiment, of a reduced (or quasi-reduced) form equation describing the short-run behaviour of real balances which displays the key characteristic of what we call (misleadingly if this explanation of the phenomenon is correct) the 'short-run demand-for-money function', namely a lagged dependent variable on its right-hand side, or, more generally, strongly serially correlated residuals. However, as I have shown elsewhere (see Chapter 5), a necessary (not sufficient) condition for this result to arise in the context of a 'buffer stock' model of the demand for money is that there exist a degree of price stickiness in the system; and, of course, the existence of price stickiness also produces just the kind of short-run non-neutrality which, I have argued above, provides a strong empirical incentive to take money seriously.

It is a commonplace that price stickiness can arise, quite mechanically, from inertia in expectations, from the existence of nominal contracts of significant length, or indeed from price-setting agents facing non-trivial costs of changing them; it is also a commonplace that the twin assumptions of Walrasian equilibrium and rational expectations which underpin modern new-classical monetary theory rule out this phenomenon. However, if we take the proposition that monetary exchange reduces, but does not eliminate, uncertainty from market transactions, we are led not only to postulate the precautionary model of money holding referred to above: we are also led to take a more benign view of price stickiness assumptions, whether we motivate them in terms of systematic expectational errors or in terms of institutional rigidities. Precautionary money holdings and price stickiness both arise from the same source, namely the informational imperfections that characterise an economy in which activity is co-ordinated by monetary exchange.

Consider in this context the rational-expectations idea. The proposition that maximising agents will make full use of all information economically available to them is irresistible, but how much information is that? The typical new-classical model does not contain an explicit analysis of the costs and benefits of information. It assumes that agents have access to certain data and computational techniques but not to others, and that they fully exploit the information with which they are endowed. This is of course a simplifying assumption, quite justifiable for certain analytic purposes, but it nevertheless produces models which behave 'as if' the marginal cost of information rises in one step from zero to infinity, and in which scarcity of information occurs because the marginal cost of acquiring it becomes infinite before some theoretically ideal maximum amount of information (that which would guarantee the achievement of full Walrasian equilibrium) is reached, and not because more information is to be had at a finite price. One can easily accept the rational-expectations idea while simultaneously denying the relevance of this special case, and, from a more general viewpoint, that idea does no more than compel us to think of agents gathering and utilising information up to the point at which the marginal cost to them of acquiring it equals the marginal benefit that its possession confers.[9]

In a money-using economy, the marginal benefit from acquiring information must be the reduction in transactions costs that agents achieve by being better informed. Such a reduction will be achieved by a closer matching of cash receipts and cash outlays so as to avoid the need to engage in costly trade in financial assets; but, as we have seen, the precautionary demand for money arises precisely from its capacity to reduce those same costs. If information enabling agents better to match up their cash inflows and outflows is to be had at zero marginal cost, they will of course acquire it, use it, and hold a smaller precautionary balance than they otherwise would; but if it comes only at rising marginal cost, and if money holding is a cheap buffer against the consequences of ignorance, those agents' decisions will, as a matter of rational choice, be based on less information than the economist looking into the economy from the outside would regard as available to them. Moreover, as Galbraith (1988) has shown, such 'economically rational' expectations are capable of generating serially correlated errors which agents do not find it worthwhile to eliminate.

Information gathering and money holding do not exhaust the avenues open to agents wishing to reduce the costs imposed upon them by the existence of a stochastic element in the time pattern of their payments and receipts. The nominal price at which they stand ready to deal is a variable under agents' control, and the effects on their cash flow of fluctuations in demand and supply which they encounter may be reduced by varying it. However, haggling over prices in and of itself takes time and trouble which can be avoided if agents enter into contracts with one another to deal at pre-set prices, or, in the absence of continuing relationships among specific agents, if sellers simply state prices at which they stand ready to deal over non-trivial time intervals. Price flexibility in goods markets, then, may be viewed as a means of reducing transactions costs in asset markets, albeit a costly one. The degree of nominal price flexibility in an economy should be higher, the higher are the costs of its substitutes, namely information and money holding; and the existence of precautionary money holdings should be associated, not only with a degree of ignorance on the part of agents, but also with markets characterised by a degree of nominal price stickiness.

In a money-using economy the extent of the gaps between complete price flexibility and the amount which actually characterises markets, and between 'all available' information and the amount gathered and utilised will, moreover, vary. I am referring here not only to the possibility of exogenous technical progress in communications and data processing, though in a secular perspective these matters are surely important: I am also thinking of the endogenous responses of agents to variations in money's effectiveness in mitigating the consequences of ignorance and inflexibility. If money holding is a cheap and reliable buffer, then agents will find that it pays to remain relatively uninformed about the processes affecting the variability of their net receipts, and will be relatively unwilling to undertake any costly measures that might render them either more predictable or controllable. If, on the other hand, money holding itself is a costly or unreliable source of insulation from such uncertainty, then the expenditure necessary to acquire and utilise extra information is more likely to be made.

Both the costs of using money as a buffer against market uncertainty and its reliability in that role, have to do with the behaviour of the general price level. As is well known, expected changes in money's purchasing power are an important component of the opportunity cost of holding it. If money holding's capacity to act as a buffer against costly consequences of market uncertainty and inflexibility is available only at a high price, agents have a strong incentive to minimise those costs by other means. Hence, the foregoing argument suggests that anticipated inflation both discourages money holding and encourages expenditure on information and the maintenance of price flexibility on the part of agents. From the private point of view, such a response is presumably optimal, but from a social perspective it is wasteful. It involves devoting real resources to the reduction of costs which would, in conditions of price stability, have been offset by holding money; and, so it is usual to argue, once we leave a commodity money world, real balances are, on the margin, socially cheap (indeed perhaps free) to provide. Therefore, instead of admiring the sophistication which the inhabitants of economies characterised by monetary instability seem to develop about market processes, as we so often seem to, we should deplore it as the product of a wasteful expenditure of effort induced by irresponsible policy.

It is worth drawing explicit attention to the fact that the informational problems encountered in a monetary economy of the type I am discussing here are rather different from those met up with in a new-classical system. There, sellers are presented gratis with all available information about their own market, in the shape of a given money price for their output, but have to extract an estimate of the general price level (in order to compute a relative price) from other data. With endogenous price setting, the information most needed by agents concerns the state of the market in which they are dealing. Data on the general price level are not irrelevant here, but it is hard to believe that they are of primary importance relative to local factors such as the tastes and incomes of potential customers, the prices of particular inputs, and the prices of close substitutes and complements for whatever it is that is being produced and sold. Hence the fact that agents apparently do not make use of readily available information about the money supply, so puzzling to a new-classical economist, is easily reconciled with the rationality postulate in an economy with endogenous price setting and information that is costly on the margin.[10]

However, the degree of priority given by agents to generating information about the general price level's behaviour will itself be endogenous. Anticipated changes in the price level influence the cost of obtaining money's services, and unanticipated changes reduce the quality of those services—while, crucially, the extent to which price-level variations are anticipated or unanticipated will itself depend upon the resources agents devote to gathering data on the matter and analysing them. Fluctuations in the price level thus create incentives to acquire expertise not just about local market conditions but also about the monetary system. The larger those fluctuations, the more productive (privately) does it become to gather the latter kind of information and to act upon it.

There is, though, an externality here. Monetary instability encourages individual agents to acquire information and to gain flexibility, so that they may vary their own prices to counter its effects. Such price flexibility tends to be self-generating however, because the more other prices vary the more does it pay the individual dealer to maintain and utilise the capacity to vary his own. To give one example of this phenomenon, Holland (1988) has shown, over the period 1965–86, that the degree of wage flexibility in the USA has systematically increased in response to the intensity of price-level fluctuations.

Both positive and normative aspects of these matters deserve more attention than can be given to them here. Suffice it to note that monetary instability which affects expenditure flows without generating price fluctuations should, as Friedman (1984) conjectured and recent work by Hall and Noble (1987) appears to confirm, increase agents' holdings of money; though also that to the extent to which monetary instability begins to generate price-level fluctuations it will reduce the usefulness of money holding.

Whether this last effect in turn will lead to a smaller or a larger demand for money is an open question. Klein (1977) produced a model in which matters could go either way, but his evidence that a reduction in the level of services yielded by a unit of real balances would lead to an increase in the quantity of them held was subsequently overturned by Laidler (1980). Moreover, in Klein's model there was no substitute for 'money services', and I conjecture that, to the extent to which it is possible to substitute for these by devoting resources to generating information and flexibility, a substitution out of money as price fluctuations increase becomes more likely. If this is indeed the case, then, at the level of the economy as a whole, these tendencies reduce money's usefulness; and so, as Keynes (1936, p. 269) long ago noted, price flexibility may not be quite the unmixed blessing that economists sometimes think it to be. One of its effects is to undermine the capacity of money balances to act as a substitute for costly information gathering and processing. It is perhaps not surprising that the political popularity of replacing decentralised and largely unregulated monetary exchange with alternative, *dirigiste* schemes for co-ordinating economic activity tends to be greatest in periods of monetary instability.

## Some Implications for Macro-Modelling

The foregoing analysis has implications for how we should model price-formation mechanisms in general and expectations mechanisms in particular. The new-classical assumption that economic agents understand the structure of the economy and use that understanding to make optimal forecasts of the variables which concern them was never intended to be taken literally. Rather its proponents would have us think of agents as operating by 'rule of thumb', and discarding rules which systematically mislead them until they find one that works 'as if' its forecasts were being generated by a correct model of the economy they inhabit.

But how close to a 'correct model' need a rule of thumb be for agents to be satisfied with it? It would presumably suffice if its forecasts produced no systematic errors with consequences costly enough to make it worth agents' while to devote resources to reducing them. Economies in which money is cheap to hold and stable in its purchasing power give fewer incentives for simple and potentially erroneous rules to be weeded out. They are, therefore, likely to be inhabited by agents whose 'rational expectations' about the price level are subject to a higher variance, and are less robust in the face of changes in the pattern of shocks impinging on the economy, than those with a history of inflation and monetary instability. A simple example (based on the assumption that monetarist analysis is broadly correct) will illustrate some possible implications of such a view.

In a small open economy operating a fixed exchange rate on a world economy characterised by price-level stability, the rule of thumb that tomorrow's price level will be close to its average value over some past period will give essentially the same prediction as one which has it moving in proportion to the nominal-money/real-GNP ratio, or indeed as the forecast of some more complex 'true' model of the economy. An economist modelling such an economy would have equal predictive success by attributing to its inhabitants any of the above means of forecasting price-level behaviour. If those inhabitants were using the first rule of thumb, however, they would be ill equipped to cope with the adoption of flexible exchange rates and unstable discretionary monetary policy. They might discover a more general rule in due course, but, as Parkin's (1977) analysis suggests, the economist modelling the transition between regimes would be in trouble if he ignored the learning process and simply attributed his version of the 'true' model to them at all times. At the same time, if agents did learn to monitor the money supply, and as a consequence adopted a rule of thumb a step closer to the 'true' model, then they would have little problem in forming expectations relevant to a transition back to a fixed rate or some similar stable regime, and neither would an economist in predicting their behaviour.

It is a mistake to treat 'expectations' as purely psychological phenomena when engaged in macro-modelling. What proximately matters for the way economies function is not what people expect but how they act, and agents who have new information, understand its significance, but are not free to act upon it, may as well be ignorant. Nominal rigidities may be the result of desirable resource-economising arrangements in an economy in which cash balances efficiently and cheaply buffer agents against the consequences of any imbalances in money flows which those rigidities may provoke; but they can cause real problems if circumstances change so as to reduce money's capacity to play that role. To return to the previous illustration, under a fixed exchange rate the success of the simple rule of thumb that the price level will tend to maintain a stable average level will encourage agents to engage in fixed nominal-price contracts for significant time periods. Moreover the length and rigidity of those contracts will have more to do with uncertainties about conditions in the market for the particular item being traded, than with the likely course of the purchasing power of money. Under a discretionary monetary regime, when price-level behaviour becomes an issue, we might expect to find shorter contracts and more indexing, even though these involve more transactions costs. Moreover the transition from the fixed rate to discretionary policy would likely be more difficult than the reverse change, because of this contrast in institutional starting-points.

Now I do not intend the particular piece of elementary conceptual history running through the preceding paragraphs to be taken literally. I do, however, intend to be taken seriously the general message which it illustrates: namely that it is dangerous uncritically to model agents' behaviour on the assumption that they form their expectations using the same model of their economy as the economist who studies them. Maximising agents ought not always to be expected to act like that. Rather they will utilise only the information which the history of their economy has provided them with an incentive to acquire. Properly understood, however, this argument does not lead to the conclusion that new-classical analysis is always and everywhere misleading. Economies in which agents' rules of thumb are consistent with the processes driving the behaviour of critical variables will look very much as if they are inhabited by well informed rational agents of the textbook variety. Those rules of thumb are likely to be rather sophisticated in economies where the incentives to develop them have been strong, and the institutional flexibility needed for agents to respond quickly to new information is also likely to be present in such economies. Furthermore, ignorance and nominal rigidities, which characterise economies with a history of monetary stability, will be quite irrelevant to predicting their behaviour so long as that monetary stability prevails. New-classical models should cope rather well with data generated by either type of economy.

Our analysis also warns us, however, that models which postulate that agents act 'as if' they understand the structure of the economy are unlikely to work well during transition periods, particularly those which involve a reduction in money's capacity to provide a cheap hedge against ignorance and inflexibility. If agents' rules of thumb mimic in their predictions the economy's true structure only in a particular policy environment, but create systematic errors in another, then agents will have to experience those errors and the costs they impose before they can be expected to begin to correct them. Far from being ruled out by the postulate of rational behaviour therefore, systematic error would seem to be required by its application to learning processes. Hence, instead of refusing to take seriously explanations of particular historical episodes which rely on systematic errors on the part of agents, or price rigidities which are 'irrational' in prevailing circumstances, we should look askance at any account of the onset of instability that does not pay due attention to these phenomena. Moreover, because the period over which any individual is in a position to take important economic decisions (about such things as pricing policies, for example) is a good deal shorter than a lifetime, and because the intergenerational transmission of knowledge is an uncertain process, we should not rule out either the possibility of 'errors' being repeated. A good deal of older work on business-cycle history, and related topics, might regain respectability from this observation.

Now, though the idea that old rules of thumb and institutional arrangements persist in new environments with which they are incompatible might help us understand the earlier stages of episodes of monetary instability, we must also recognise that the later stages will surely be characterised by the discovery and adoption of new ones. It is much easier to draw attention to the problem of how to enbed an account of learning in an economic model than it is to solve it. Let me simply observe here that attempts to model agents' learning processes 'as if' they were econometricians seeking information about the economy by statistical induction seem to me to be of limited usefulness. Many of my colleagues would probably be delighted to see me proven wrong here, because if we could formulate an empirically robust theory along such lines, it would enable us to use the postulate of rational maximising behaviour to cope with transition periods as well as with times of stability and hence to extend the area of experience to which new-classical analysis can usefully be applied.[11]

There are two interrelated problems here. First, on my reading of the history of our discipline, economic knowledge seems to evolve by a process much more akin to that which Karl Popper characterised as 'conjecture and refutation' than any other. In saying this, I do not wish to support a naïve view of scientific method which has it that the individual economist advances an idea and then sets out disinterestedly to try to refute it. Rather the process is a social one in which self-interested agents defend their own ideas and attack those of others in a highly competitive environment. Furthermore, and this brings us to the second problem alluded to above, there is an inherently creative and hence unpredictable element to the process of conjecturing hypotheses about how the economy operates. It is only if we envisage an end to the development of *qualitative* economic knowledge, so that learning need only be concerned with *quantitative* matters, that techniques of statistical inference will enable us to model all relevant aspects of learning satisfactorily. However, there is considerable comfort to be found in this, at first sight, nihilistic observation. Rymes (1979) and, more recently, Sargent (1984) have drawn our attention to the fact that it is all too easy to be led into an essentially vacuous type of economic determinism if we push ideas of rationality and foresight too far. To introduce an inherently unpredictable element into our vision of economic life, in the shape of a postulate about how learning takes place, enables us to avoid this particular trap. Perhaps it is the social scientist who believes that everything can and must be explained as the outcome of carefully calculated rational behaviour who is the real nihilist in this instance.[12]

## Predictions about the Demand for Money

Now the vision of market mechanisms underlying the foregoing arguments focuses on money's means-of-exchange function and argues that money holding should be viewed as an essentially precautionary phenomenon. To the extent that this rather specific view of money's role in economic life gets support from empirical work, those arguments are strengthened and begin to lose their predominantly a priori character. Empirical work on the aggregate demand-for-money function began in earnest in the late 1950s as a result of a change in the basic question which monetary economists asked. Instead of 'why do people hold money?' the issue became 'given that they do, what determines how much they will hold?', and Friedman's (1956) bold postulate that the aggregate demand for money was a stable function of but a few arguments was the starting-point in settling it. The 'money-as-if-a-consumer-durable' approach adopted in much empirical work yielded large dividends in quantitative knowledge by modelling the aggregate demand-for-real-balances function as the sum of the demand functions of individual agents who treated money as a source of purely private-utility-yielding services. It ignored the nature of those services, not because they had not been analysed, but because the empirical questions being asked did not seem to require that attention be paid to them.

Even so, it was soon pointed out, notably by Fried (1973a), Dutton and Gramm (1973), Karni (1974), Diewert (1974), and Phlips (1978) that models of the demand for money which incorporate brokerage fees, as precautionary models inevitably do, may rather easily be made to yield the prediction that the demand for money should depend upon the real-wage level. The key step here is to characterise this 'fee' as representing the time that agents must spend to turn other assets into cash.[13] This prediction was confirmed by evidence presented in the last four of the above-mentioned studies, and has more recently been confirmed again by Dowd (1985). Also, as Fried stressed, when the prediction in question is combined with the observation that, at the level of the economy as a whole, real income and real wages tend to move together, it implies that regressions which include only the former variable will yield an upward-biased estimate of its coefficient. This argument is important because it reconciles the characteristic prediction of precautionary demand models that the income elasticity of demand for money is below unity with the frequent occurrence of empirical estimates of this parameter in the region of unity. Lucas (1988) has recently shown that a particular function characterised by a unit elasticity, namely that first proposed by Meltzer (1963), is still discernible in United States data, and shows how such a function may be interpreted as arising from the structure of an (almost) Walrasian economy—that is, one characterised by market clearing prices, limited information, and an exchange mechanism which imposes a cash-or-credit-in-advance constraint. Hence, it is important to the arguments advanced in this paper to be able to reconcile such evidence with the precautionary model of the demand for money.[14]

Evidence that it pays empirically to take explicit note of money's means-of-exchange function has thus long been available, but while it seemed possible to obtain good empirical performance from simpler functions which ignored this detail, this evidence had little impact. We can no longer be confident that it is safe to ignore the role money plays in the economy when we model the demand for it. Problems of empirical stability are neither illusory nor confined to recent data. Closer inspection of already well-analysed historical time series has revealed shifts in what initially seemed to be stable relationships. Recent work on these matters has exploited ideas about money which stress its means of exchange role. Thus, Bordo and Jonung (1987), invoking the essentially classical analysis of Knut Wicksell (1906) as a starting-point, have investigated the effects of such institutional factors as better communications, easier access to banking facilities, and so on, on the demand for money, and have found them to be systematically important. Such explanations of specific shifts in the demand-for-money function seem both plausible and natural in the light of the arguments presented earlier. Bordo and Jonung's work thus gives us further cause to treat money's means-of-exchange role, and the closely related precautionary nature of money holding, as being of considerable empirical relevance.

I noted earlier in this chapter that the dynamics of the 'short-run demand-for-money function' may be derived from postulates about the degrees of price stickiness and expectational sophistication prevalent in the economy. Thus the precautionary approach to modelling the demand for money enables us to explain this aspect of the empirical evidence without resort to postulates about portfolio adjustment costs or measurement error, but as a natural characteristic of a monetary economy. Furthermore, in this view, short-run instability in velocity can be explained as the consequence of variations in price stickiness and informational character-istics, both between economies and over time. Such an approach to this important empirical problem once more follows immediately from the vision of money's role in the economy advanced above, a vision which has proved to be a fruitful foundation for empirical work on the demand for money.

The work in question, usually referred to as 'buffer-stock modelling', is not, of course, without its critics. Thus Milbourne (1988) has recently prepared a careful survey of much of the literature to which I am here alluding, and points to three types of problem. First, he notes, correctly, that some models rely on the dubious assumption that nominal money is a completely exogenous variable to generate their predictions. The assump-tion in question is certainly helpful to exposition, but fortunately it is not essential, as work by, for example, Gordon (1984) shows. Second, Milbourne argues that there are severe econometric problems with attempts to test buffer-stock ideas using single-equation techniques. Not everyone—not, for example, Carr, Darby and Thornton (1985)—accepts this criticism, but that work which follows the lead of Bergstrom and Wymer (1974) and Jonson, Moses and Wymer (1976) in taking a complete model approach to estimation is in any event immune to it. Finally Milbourne notes, citing Cuthbertson and Taylor (1986), that when it is combined with the new-classical version of the rational-expectations idea, which treats information and data processing as free goods, the 'buffer stock' approach runs into real empirical difficulties because the data appear to reject the restrictions on parameter values implied by the resulting model. However, more recent work by Cuthbertson and Taylor (1987), which was not available to Milbourne, shows that this problem may be dealt with by attributing what we might term 'sensible', rather than fully rational, expectations to agents. The arguments of this chapter strongly suggest that the existence of a significant precautionary element in the demand for money is likely to be incompatible with any extreme categorisation of expectations, and hence to gain support from these more recent results.[15]

A number of other predictions about the demand for money follow from the ideas set out in this essay. For example they imply that we should not think of the individual's precautionary demand for money as being underpinned by a stochastic pattern of payments and receipts generated by some exogenously given structure. Far from being exogenously given, this stochastic pattern is, if only within limits, controllable. Its dispersion can be reduced by devoting more resources to gathering market information, and by devoting more resources to maintaining the capacity to act flexibly in the market. Moreover, the incentive to devote resources to these ends varies systematically with the cost of holding money. When this cost is high, resources will be devoted to reducing the dispersion of cash flows, and vice versa. Hence *movements along* a demand-for-precautionary-balances function derived on the assumption of a given structure of information will be accompanied by systematic *shifts* of that function. Note also that those shifts will not be reversible to the extent that information, once acquired, or new contractual arrangements once put in place, are durable. Ratchet effects in the demand-for-money/interest-rate relationship, which figured prominently in the empirical work on the alleged instability of the US demand-for-money function surveyed by Judd and Scadding (1982a), might repay further investigation in the light of this argument.

The foregoing analysis also suggests that complications, in the form of interdependencies among agents' money holdings, might arise in getting from the individual- to the market-demand curve for money. Such interdependencies will exist in principle because a time-and-trouble cost of obtaining cash in exchange for other assets is basic to any model of the individual's precautionary demand for money. The cost to any one agent, however, of obtaining cash will surely vary with the amount of cash which other inhabitants of the economy hold. The more money held by others, the lower will be, to any particular agent, the costs of finding a willing cash buyer for some other asset; and, therefore, the less money will that agent hold. Thus, as the nominal interest rate rises, and each individual reduces cash holdings, the fact that all other agents simultaneously do the same produces forces which offset, though not of course entirely, this negative movement. The aggregate demand-for-money function will, then, be more steeply sloped with respect to the rate of interest than will be the sum of the individual relationships.[16]

Now this last prediction can hardly be tested directly. To do so we would need data in which the opportunity cost of holding money varied for an individual while it remained constant for the rest of the economy. However it might be indirectly tested by noting that cross-section data on the demand for money as a function of real income tells us something about how an individual's money holdings vary when those of all other agents remain constant, while aggregate-time-series evidence on the same relationship tells us about the same relationship when the money holdings of others are simultaneously changing. The externality just discussed would be held constant in the former case and at work in the latter, so the cross-section income elasticity of demand should be the higher of the two. The general presumption about income effects is that cross-section studies yield lower parameter estimates, so it is not without interest that the only systematic survey of evidence on this question of which I am aware (Feige and Pearce 1977) does in fact find cross-section estimates to be higher on average. The difference here is not statistically significant, and the work surveyed did not pay attention to brokerage-fee effects, so one should not make too much of this result. Even so, the question is surely worth more detailed examination than it has so far received.

## *Conclusion*

Now it can be argued that the predictions about the demand-for-money function discussed above, both those which have been tested and confirmed, and those which for the moment remain conjectures, are of rather minor importance. So indeed they are as far as the demand function itself is concerned. They represent at best rather small embellishments to our knowledge of this relationship. However, I have taken the time to discuss them here, not because of what they tell us about the appropriate empirical specification of the demand-for-money function *per se*, but because of what their empirical confirmation suggests, or would suggest, about the motives underlying the behaviour which that function summarises.

As I have remarked above, where trading at false, and perhaps sticky, prices set on the basis of less than 'all available' information is of the essence, serially correlated fluctuations in output and employment, not to mention prices and real balances, naturally arise. In such a world, money is significantly non-neutral, and monetary policy is important. Though it was at one time taken for granted that any satisfactory macroeconomic model would display such characteristics, the recent fashion for building upon Walrasian microfoundations has undermined any consensus about such matters. I have argued in this chapter that an alternative, non-Walrasian vision of the workings of the economy can be used to defend a traditional approach to macroeconomic modelling, and that a precautionary view of money holding is central to that vision. Thus, if evidence that the precautionary model of the demand for money has explanatory power over real-world data makes a trivial difference to our beliefs about the

properties of the demand-for-money function, it ought nevertheless to
have a profound effect on the way we think about the workings of market
economies. That is the most important reason of all for taking money
seriously.

## Notes

1 The parallels between the Keynesian revolution and the monetarist counter-
revolution were analysed by Johnson (1971) in a lecture whose occasionally *ad
hominem* character should not distract its reader's attention from its underlying
seriousness. The standard reference on the distinction between 'Keynesian
economics' and 'the economics of Keynes' is Leijonhufvud (1968).

2 The publication of the first edition of Patinkin's *Money, Interest and Prices* in
1956 was of course a major landmark here.

3 Hall cites papers by Black (1970) and Fama (1980) as being key contributions
here, but the contributions to this literature which have attracted most attention are
probably those of Wallace (1981) and Sargent and Wallace (1982). Note that
Bennett McCallum (1983) criticises this stream of the literature, particularly that
part of it which explicitly relies on Samuelson's (1958) 'overlapping generations'
framework, for neglecting money's means-of-exchange role, and (1987) shows how
adapting an 'overlapping generations' model to accommodate this phenomenon
changes its properties. Wallace (1988) provides a non-technical survey of the 'legal
restrictions' theory of money which remains useful despite the fact that it
systematically ignores any work that is critical of the approach.

4 Another reason for the current popularity of real-business-cycle theory is the
finding of Nelson and Plosser (1982) that the time path of United States real income
is satisfactorily characterised as a random walk. This finding, however, seems
fragile, if work by John McCallum (1988) and Pierre Perron (1987) is taken into
account.

5 The data utilised in Figures 1.1 and 1.2 are for the following North American
and European countries and time periods: USA 1971–85, Germany 1974–85,
Canada 1970–84, UK 1970–84, Italy 1971–84, Japan 1971–84, Sweden 1971–85,
Spain 1971–83, Switzerland 1970–85, Belgium 1970–84, and the Netherlands
1971–84. France is omitted because of a major break in its money supply series. In
each case the money supply is 'narrow' money, real output is GNP, and the price
level is the GNP deflator. Each scatter has plotted with it the relevant least-squares-
regression line, with the standard error of its coefficients given below them in
parentheses. The possibility that the money–growth–output relationship is the
result of 'reverse causation' can never be completely ruled out, though the
plausibility of this explanation is reduced by the time-lag inherent in Figure 1.2.
Historical analysis of particular episodes, such as that employed by Friedman and
Schwartz (1963) on the Great Depression, or Howitt (1986b) on more recent
Canadian experience, seems to me to provide the best means of countering this line
of argument.

6 Brian Loasby has drawn my attention to the strong similarities between such
a treatment of money, and Coase's celebrated (1937) analysis of the firm as a social
institution. To discuss this insight here is beyond the scope of this essay, but the
parallel is well worth following up.

7 The analysis of the preceding two paragraphs draws rather heavily on
arguments which I set out in Laidler (1975). The reader's attention is drawn to

papers by Leijonhufvud (1973) and Jonson (1976a) which also explore these and related aspects of money's 'buffer stock' role. See also Chapter 2.

8 A particularly simple version of such a model was developed by Weinrobe (1972) and forms the basis of my own exposition of the precautionary motive in my book on the *Demand for Money* (Laidler 1985, 3rd edn), where the reader will also find references to other, more complex, treatments of this topic.

9 When we put matters this way, it becomes clear that we are dealing with ideas first advanced in Stigler's seminal (1961) paper on the 'economics of information' and discussed in the context of monetary economics by, among others, Brunner and Meltzer (1971) and Laidler (1975 Ch. 1). Brunner and Meltzer took up this theme again (1987) and developed it along lines very similar to those I am following here.

10 Thus, anyone seeking a microeconomic story about inflation–unemployment–output interaction to complement the monetary economics I am here expounding should look to the work of Phelps (1970, 1972) as a starting-point, rather than to the 'aggregate supply curve' analysis of new-classical theory.

11 Recent examples of this type of analysis include Marcet and Sargent (1987) and Howitt (1987).

12 An emphasis on the limits of rationality as a foundation for economic analysis is a pervasive theme of 'post-Keynesian' macroeconomics. See Chick (1983) and Foster (1987) for examples of work along these lines. Note also that new-classical economists are not ignoring this problem, at least as it arises in the context of transitions in the state of knowledge. See, for example, Lucas (1986) for a penetrating discussion of the issues involved, a discussion in which, let it be emphasised, he shows himself to be extremely sympathetic to the notion that there are limits to the explanatory power of the rationality postulate.

13 Of course brokerage fees also play a prominent role in Baumol (1952) and Tobin (1956) transactions demand roles; those models concentrate on money's means-of-exchange role, and hence are close to the spirit of the approach to monetary economics that underlies this essay. Indeed, Clower and Howitt (1978) may be regarded as an exploration of how the Baumol–Tobin model should be modified in the context of a non-Walrasian economy.

14 Note that Svensson (1985) and Hartley (1988) introduce a precautionary element into the demand for money in a version of Lucas's system by altering the timing with which information is made available to agents and by permitting cash to be used in a wider (but overlapping) range of markets than credit is. They thus attribute to cash the capacity to generate market 'flexibility' of a type first analysed by Goldman (1974). All this analysis treats the provision of information as exogenous, and hence differs crucially from the approach taken here; but it nevertheless represents a step towards closing the gap between Lucas's approach to the analysis of money and that advocated in this chapter.

15 Even so, the ideas under discussion here are difficult to test directly and definitively, because, as Milbourne's survey suggests, only a properly specified complete macro-model provides an appropriate vehicle for investigating them. There is obviously much room for debate about what such a model would look like, and hence considerable scope for creating alibis for particular results.

16 I discuss this externality in Chapter 3. Note that it bears a strong family resemblance to the externalities in search processes that produce the multiple equilibria which characterise the models of Diamond (e.g. 1984) and Howitt (1985), and which have been analysed more generally by Drazen (1987).

# 2

# The 'Buffer Stock' Notion in Monetary Economics

Not the least of Harry Johnson's contributions to our discipline was the series of survey papers on aspects of monetary economics that he produced during the 1960s and 1970s. It is no exaggeration to say that the way in which the literature of monetary economics is organised even now follows the design which Johnson first set out (in 1962) and built on in the subsequent decade. Nevertheless, the subject has not stood still, and one of the more interesting developments of the last few years has involved the introduction of what has been variously described as the 'disequilibrium money', 'shock absorber' or, as I prefer to call it, the 'buffer stock' notion into monetary economics.

The development of this line of thought was getting under way before Johnson's untimely death, much of it indeed under the auspices of his own research programme at the LSE. Even so, this did not happen early enough for the relevant ideas to be put in their proper niche by Johnson himself, and the buffer-stock approach is not yet fully integrated into the mainstream of monetary economics. Much of the relevant literature is empirical, concerned with modelling particular aspects of the monetary experience of specific countries: hence it is fragmented, and contains few papers which attempt a coherent account of just what this approach is and how it relates to other approaches to monetary analysis. Although essays by Goodhart (1982a, b), and Judd and Scadding (1982a) contain important discussions of these issues, to the best of my knowledge only Jonson (1976a) and Knoester (1979a) have devoted entire papers solely to this central issue, and these are relatively inaccessible and hence less widely known than they deserve to be.

In this chapter, I shall attempt to give a brief account of the essentials of this approach. First I shall sketch out its microeconomic background, and then I shall discuss those theoretical characteristics which differentiate it from the new-classical analysis of Robert E. Lucas Jr. and his associates, as well as from the conventional 'Keynesian' approach to monetary economics. Last, but by no means least, I shall argue that it yields simple theoretical insights into important empirical and policy-related issues which are troublesome for alternative approaches. In short, my tribute to Harry Johnson on this occasion involves me in the dangerous business of trying to emulate him, by offering a survey of a new and interesting body of analysis. I hope that my failure to match his standards of clarity and incisiveness in this lecture will not deter those who hear or read it from taking the subject-matter seriously.

## The Microeconomic Background

Exponents of the notion of money as a 'buffer stock', and of the body of macroeconomic analysis associated with it, imagine the typical economic agent to operate in what is commonly called a 'market economy', but markets in the everyday sense of the word are conspicuous, if not by their absence, then at least by their rarity in such an economy. Trade does not take place at one time and place, and at prices known to all agents; nor does it consist of a series of bilateral exchanges of goods and services between agents, each of whom is intent on consuming what he receives in each transaction. Instead, trade is multilateral with one party to each bilateral exchange typically accepting some asset, not because he desires it for its own sake, but because he confidently expects someone else to accept it from him in due course in exchange for something else.

The buffer-stock approach thus presupposes the existence of a system of monetary exchange. Such a system, considered as a social institution, is a substitute for the kind of Walrasian market which, more often implicitly than explicitly, provides the basis for so much macroeconomic theory.[1] Though barter transactions occasionally take place, and although trade credit arrangements also exist, the typical would-be buyer, whether a firm seeking labour, or a household seeking consumption goods, must as a matter of social convention offer in exchange money, or a credible promise to deliver money in the near future, in order to be able to transact. Moreover, given that there are costs to finding a buyer for assets when money is required, the individual agent might be expected to hold a fraction of his wealth in money as a 'temporary abode of purchasing power', to use Milton Friedman's phrase, even if it yields a lower explicit return to him than do other stores of value.

Theorising about the demand for money typically takes arguments such as these for granted, and answers questions about what determines how much money the individual agent will want to hold, and about how that quantity varies with its determinants. The relevant 'quantity of money demanded' here is not an entirely straightforward concept. The phrase does not refer to an amount of money which an agent will want to hold at each and every moment, but rather to an amount which he will want to hold on average over some time interval. The phrase 'quantity of money demanded' denotes, that is to say, the average or target value of an inventory, of a *buffer stock*, of cash balances.

The foregoing proposition is true even about the demand for money of an agent who is always able to fulfil his plans, and for whom trading activities bring no surprises, but it is also true about the demand of one whose income is subject to unforeseen variations, or whose expenditure is on goods the availability of which cannot be taken for granted, or the prices of which fluctuate unexpectedly.[2] To hold a buffer stock of generally acceptable purchasing power prevents, at least in part, surprises in markets where the agent is a seller from impinging upon his buying activities, and vice versa. Indeed the matter goes deeper: an agent's chances of being surprised in his market activity are not independent of the time and effort he puts into seeking and processing information relevant to those activities. If money holding enables him to endure the consequences of surprises at lower cost than would otherwise be the case, then money becomes a substitute for information. Thus the very existence of a monetary system which enables him so to protect himself will cause the agent to be more prone to surprises. Hence fluctuations in holdings of money about their target value are of the very essence of economic activity co-ordinated by monetary exchange.[3]

The individual agent's target demand for money might itself be expected to vary over time. The conceptual experiments that we perform at the level of the individual agent when teaching the theory of the demand for money usually involve the postulate that the agent is faced with some exogenous shift in one or more of the determinants of the demand for money—an interest rate, the price level, or the level of permanent income, say. We then trace out the consequences of that change for the agent's target holdings of nominal balances. Sometimes we complicate our experiment with an account of the effects of rising marginal adjustment costs on the path which money balances follow over time as they are brought towards that target level. When we do this, we refer to the target level as the 'long-run' demand for money, and to intermediate steps along the adjustment path as points on various, essentially Marshallian, short-run demand-for-money functions.

The experiments to which I have just referred are typical of the literature, but, in an economy characterised by monetary exchange, the windfall gains and losses which the agent experiences from time to time might well manifest themselves in unexpected variations in cash holdings. A discrepancy between actual and long-run target money holdings can just as well arise from this source as from changes in the arguments of the agent's long-run demand-for-money function, and there is no reason to believe that the response to such a discrepancy depends in any way upon what generates it. Given that a discrepancy exists, the agent will attempt to move towards a long-run target demand for money by altering the current rate of flow of expenditure on goods, services, and asset accumulation. That is to say, for the individual agent, a discrepancy between actual and desired cash balances will set in motion a real balance effect.[4]

I make no claim for any novelty in the microeconomic aspects of the buffer-stock approach to monetary analysis that I have just described. Apart from a few nuances of emphasis, mainly having to do with trade being a matter of monetary exchange rather than simultaneous barter, and with the characterisation of the agent's long-run quantity of money demanded as being a target or average-over-time value of an inventory, rather than a fixed amount observable at any moment, there is nothing in the last few paragraphs which is not a commonplace. Nevertheless, these apparently unimportant nuances, which so much of the literature of monetary economics ignores, form the basis of the buffer-stock approach.

## The Market Experiment, Equilibrium, and Disequilibrium

We are not concerned with the individual agent for his or her own sake in monetary economics. We are interested in macroeconomic phenomena, with the way in which changes in the money stock interact with the real side of the economy to influence income, employment and the price level, not to mention the balance of payments and the exchange rate in open economies.[5] The notion of an aggregate demand-for-money function is central to the analysis of these issues, and we study the individual agent mainly to get some insight into the nature of this aggregate relationship. Typically, indeed, that is all we do; and the aggregate function is often treated as being simply a scaled-up version of the demand function of some representative agent.

It is hard to deny that such a simple approach to studying money in the aggregate economy has been fruitful; but nevertheless, when we follow it, we play down the very properties of money stressed in the foregoing discussion of the individual agent. In particular we treat the aggregate demand for money as determining a quantity of cash balances which the economy as a whole will wish to hold, not just on average over time, but at any moment; and we also assume that market mechanisms somehow operate to ensure that the demand for money thus determined is kept equal to the quantity of money in circulation. There is no other way to justify the almost universal use of the quantity of money in circulation as the dependent variable in empirical studies of the demand-for-money function, regardless of the period of observation to which the data appertain.

The procedures to which I have just referred may or may not be safe, but to criticise them effectively we must show that the factors they ignore are important for the real-world phenomena about which monetary economics makes predictions. The buffer-stock approach claims that, in treating money 'as if' the economy had a well-determined stock demand for it which is realised at each and every moment, conventional treatments of monetary analysis do indeed leave out of account factors whose absence detracts from their empirical content.

The above criticism is levelled at both conventional 'Keynesian' macroeconomics and at the new-classical analysis of Robert E. Lucas Jr. and his associates. These two bodies of macroeconomics are very different from one another, and the latter has much less in common with the buffer-stock approach than does the former, as we shall see in due course. Nevertheless, both proceed 'as if' the observed demand and supply for money were always equal to one another. In the Keynesian approach it is interest-rate flexibility that guarantees this, and in the new-classical framework, general wage and price flexibility. In each case, however, the economy is treated as being always 'on' its aggregate demand-for-money function. It is this property of both types of model which the buffer-stock approach challenges; that is why it is sometimes referred to, somewhat misleadingly, as the 'disequilibrium money' approach.

The notions of 'equilibrium' and 'disequilibrium' that are creeping into the discussion had better be clarified. By 'full equilibrium' I mean a situation in which each agent is able to carry out all plans vis-à-vis buying and selling goods, services, and assets, and in which the ex ante expectations upon which those plans are based are fulfilled ex post. The buffer-stock approach is not differentiated from others merely by the suggestion that the world we live in occasionally might depart from such a full equilibrium state. Indeed that branch of new-classical analysis called 'equilibrium business-cycle theory' relies for most of its content on a careful analysis of the consequences of the last-mentioned condition being systematically violated across agents. The models which that theory generates are nevertheless 'equilibrium' models, in the more limited sense that all agents' ex ante plans are executed in markets where prices are free to vary in order to reconcile any initial inconsistencies among those plans before trading takes place.

Such equilibrium models are constructed so that all agents in them can and do at each and every moment achieve, among other goals, their target levels of money holdings. Once one begins to think of money explicitly as a buffer stock, it becomes a distinct possibility that such a notion of equilibrium might be too restrictive. It is of the very essence of such a stock that agents should expect, and even perhaps plan, to be away from desired average holdings of it from time to time; but, when they are, it might reasonably be argued that they are hardly 'out of equilibrium' in the sense of being unable to carry out their plans. Furthermore, an equilibrium business-cycle theorist would be unlikely to attach much significance to this point. An economy in which the supply and demand for money were equal to one another in the aggregate would behave in the same way, regardless of the state of individual money holdings, unless there were systematic distributional effects at work, and it is customary not to rely on such effects in macroeconomics. To put matters in terms of the well-known analysis of Archibald and Lipsey (1958), so long as the tastes of all agents *vis-à-vis* goods and money are identical, the aggregate demand for goods and money at any moment will be independent of the distribution of the money stock. Thus every agent can be 'off' his long-run demand-for-money function without there being any macroeconomic consequences, provided that the price level is such as to generate the appropriate aggregate quantity of real balances. Thus the equilibrium business-cycle theorist could argue that the buffer-stock idea is only significant for individual behaviour at best, and irrelevant for understanding events at the level of the economy as a whole.

The buffer-stock approach does not in any *a priori* way imply either the theoretical or empirical irrelevance of the idea of an equilibrium between the aggregate demand and supply of money. However, it does stress the possibility that, at certain times and places, and over certain time intervals, because time aggregation too could eliminate them, discrepancies between the actual and desired money holdings of individuals might not cancel out upon aggregation over agents.[6] More specifically, it asserts that the kind of quarterly and even annual macroeconomic data which we use in our empirical work are sometimes usefully analysed in such 'disequilibrium' terms and that, therefore, the above-mentioned defence of equilibrium methods of analysing such data is suspect. For this to be the case it is necessary that wages and prices be less than perfectly flexible, but this postulate is not sufficient to guarantee the relevance of the buffer-stock approach. I shall now take up these points in more detail.

## Price Stickiness and The Role of the Rate of Interest

The difference between the buffer-stock approach and the new-classical equilibrium economics concerns the interpretation of a simple stability experiment of the following kind.[7] Suppose a closed economy is initially in full equilibrium, in the sense defined above, and suppose, for the sake of simplicity, that money in this economy is non-interest-bearing fiat currency. Then let its nominal quantity be unexpectedly increased by a certain amount. At the instant immediately after this increase, but before any response to it, a state of disequilibrium characterised by an excess supply of money and an (on average) excess demand for everything else would obtain.

The equilibrium theorist and the buffer-stock exponent would agree upon what must happen to remove this disequilibrium: prices must rise as must output, and interest rates must fall, in some combination.[8] For the equilibrium theorist, however, the requisite changes would take place in *meta* time; because the very fact that it can be shown that the new quantity of money is incompatible with existing prices and quantities is sufficient reason to conclude that they cannot co-exist. For the buffer-stock advocate, the incompatibility in question is removed over actual time as the streams of expenditure which it sets in motion influence first interest rates and output, and then prices. For the new-classical, the real-balance effect which lies at the heart of our stability experiment guarantees that a discrepancy between the supply and demand for money will not persist for any interesting time interval; for the buffer-stock advocate, the same effect is made manifest in the movement over time of the macro-variables in which every macroeconomist is interested.

Though the buffer-stock approach is vulnerable to the usual charges of *ad hoc*ness in its reliance on unexplained wage/price stickiness, it does suggest a possible line of defence against this charge. If individual agents find it costly to vary money wages and prices, and to gather the information upon which to base such changes, then the availability of a buffer stock of money which softens for them the consequences of making errors about these matters will itself be a source of wage and price stickiness. The agent will trade off the cost of holding money against the costs of obtaining information and of changing prices. This argument would surely repay more careful attention than I have space to give it here.[9]

Be that as it may, the buffer-stock approach differs from orthodox 'Keynesian' theory too, even though the latter also relies upon price stickiness. For the Keynesian, interest-rate flexibility suffices to keep the supply and the demand for money in equilibrium.[10] In the Keynesian view, an increase in the supply of money such as we have just postulated will immediately drive down the rate of interest until the supply and demand for money are equal. As a consequence, the present value of the streams of returns expected to be produced by existing capital goods rises above the current supply price of newly produced capital goods. The flow demand for capital goods therefore increases, as does their output. Increased demand spreads throughout the goods markets as a result of incipient multiplier effects, and prices begin to rise. In turn, interest rates begin to increase too, and ultimately, if there are no more disturbances, the economy moves to a full equilibrium not too different from the eventual outcome of the new-classical version of this experiment. It does so, however, by way of a process during which the supply and demand for many items, but not for money, are either unequal or are kept in equality by quantity rather than price fluctuations.[11]

Because the buffer-stock approach relies on price stickiness as much as does orthodox Keynesian analysis, its account of the later stages of the transmission mechanism is essentially the same as the one just sketched out. Indeed the only, but far from trivial, difference between the two approaches concerns whether the initial impact on the rate of interest of an increase in the money supply is sufficient to bring the supply and demand for money into equilibrium immediately. In the Keynesian model it is, and in the buffer-stock approach it is not. This is a small enough difference, but it is an important difference for explaining empirical evidence. It is also a difference of some theoretical interest for it turns out to be a manifestation of the distinction between 'liquidity preference' and 'loanable funds' approaches to the analysis of the rate of interest, as I shall now argue.

It is usual to defend the postulate of price stickiness by noting that Walrasian markets do not in fact exist in the real world, so that it takes time for new information to be digested and acted upon by the endogenous agents who in fact set the prices at which trade takes place. Nevertheless it is also usual to argue that, in markets dominated by specialist traders whose major role is to gather information and translate it into price changes, prices do in fact behave very much as they would if they were determined by a continuous auction, in which supply and demand were always held equal. Prominent among these Hicksian 'flex price' markets are those for financial assets such as bonds. However, even granted that the rate of interest is a 'flex price', and granted that a sufficiently large change in it could keep the supply and demand for money in equilibrium, it does not follow that those who set the rate of interest are proximately concerned with the supply and demand for bonds, and not money.

To put it in the traditional language which I have already used, the theory of the interest rate that underlies the buffer-stock approach is a loanable-funds theory and not a liquidity-preference theory. Now of course, in an economy in full equilibrium, the interest rate, not to mention all other prices, takes a value at which savings and investment and the supply and demand for money are simultaneously equal. However, the notion of money as a buffer stock is at its most relevant when the economy is not in equilibrium, and there is no reason to suppose, as Harry Johnson (1951–2) long ago pointed out, the liquidity preference- and loanable-fund theories of interest are equivalent in such circumstances.[12] It is only in equilibrium models that questions about which prices convey what information and incentives, and to whom, are irrelevant. Leijonhufvud (e.g. 1981) in particular has continually reminded us that they are of the very essence when dealing with the social process whereby information is transmitted and individual activities co-ordinated in the presence of frictions which prevent a state of general equilibrium continuously obtaining.

Consider, in the light of these factors, the effects on the interest rate of an increase in the quantity of money. The buffer-stock approach has it that the efforts of agents to rid themselves of excess money holdings lead, among other effects, to a stepped-up flow demand for bonds in the economy. This in turn puts downward pressure on the rate of interest as bond dealers attempt to prevent their inventories of bonds being exhausted. Such a lower interest rate might make agents in general more willing to hold money, and might even induce bond dealers to increase their own inventories of money at the expense of bonds as a speculative measure. However, the proximate cause of this lower interest rate is an increase in the flow demand for bonds induced by an excess stock supply of money. It is hard to see how it could be sustained if it were large enough immediately to eliminate the very excess stock supply of money which had induced it in the first place.[13]

The matter at issue here is even more clear-cut in the limiting theoretical case in which the demand for money is independent of the rate of interest. Here the supply and demand for money can only be equilibrated by an increase in real income or prices. If it is granted that these variables change sluggishly, then after a change in the money supply there must persist a discrepancy between the supply and demand for money while the economy moves to a new full equilibrium; by assumption, no fall in the rate of interest can eliminate that discrepancy. In the 'vertical LM curve' case, then, the buffer-stock approach has much *a priori* appeal.

So long as money constitutes, on the margin, net wealth to the economy, many would agree that, in the presence of price stickiness, real-balance effects will have a direct and observable influence on expenditure on goods and services. In such circumstances it is not hard to argue that the case for the buffer-stock approach has a certain plausibility. However, where money is an 'inside' asset and is not net wealth, the real-balance effect is reduced to a matter of asset substitution working solely through the rate of interest. If we set aside the possibility of agents substituting directly from money into such real assets as consumer durables, the case in which monetary policy works solely through interest rates is one in which the capacity, or lack thereof, of the rate of interest to equilibrate the supply and demand for money becomes crucial to judging the relevance of the buffer-stock approach. If the interest rate can instantaneously equilibrate the supply and demand for money in such a case, then at the very least, the approach in question loses generality.

When Gurley and Shaw (1960) coined the term 'inside money', they applied it to the monetary liabilities of a privately owned banking system; they also argued that experiments of the kind I have been discussing, having to do with variations in the quantity of 'outside' fiat money, were virtually irrelevant for understanding the workings of any modern economy in which money is overwhelmingly bank money. Anyone who accepts this view, and who also regards the limiting 'vertical LM curve' case as more of an analytic curiosity than a serious empirical possibility, will regard the arguments that I have so far developed for the buffer-stock approach as being rather tenuous, but they would be wrong to do so. The extended and tortuous debate which followed the publication of Pesek and Saving's (1967) *Money, Wealth, and Economic Theory* established that Gurley and Shaw's version of the inside–outside distinction was quite misleading.

The debate in question established instead that the appropriate distinction is between interest-bearing and non-interest-bearing money: specifically, regardless of whose liability it is, any money which bears interest at a market rate is not net wealth on the margin, and any money which does not bear such interest is net wealth.[14] Thus it is changes in the quantity of competitive interest-bearing money whose influence is transmitted purely by interest-rate changes; but obviously an economy which uses such money is characterised by something approximating a vertical LM curve. The very economy in which the real-balance effect is reduced to a matter of asset substitution is therefore one in which changes in the rate of interest alone are unlikely to be able to eliminate a discrepancy between the supply and demand for money. On the other hand, the economy in which the demand for money is responsive to market interest rates, so that interest-rate changes might conceivably eliminate such a discrepancy, is an economy in which money is net wealth on the margin and in which real-balance effects fall directly on goods markets. In such an economy the role of the interest rate in the monetary transmission mechanism is less crucial to establishing the *a priori* plausibility of the case for the buffer-stock approach.[15]

The above arguments may or may not be convincing, but even those readers willing to entertain the idea that the interest-rate changes which come in the wake of a change in the money supply are not sufficient to equilibrate the supply and demand for money might still be inclined to underestimate the significance of the point. Certainly, it differentiates the buffer-stock approach from conventional Keynesian ideas in a somewhat less fundamental way than the notion of price stickiness distinguishes these two bodies of theory from new-classical analysis. Nevertheless, this theoretical difference is of considerable practical importance, because it leads to very different empirical predictions and to very different perceptions about what monetary policy can and cannot accomplish. That is to say, the case for the buffer-stock approach ultimately rests as much upon its empirical content as upon *a priori* reasoning.

## Empirical Questions

The key empirical difference between the conventional Keynesian and the buffer-stock approaches has to do with the existence, or otherwise, of a 'short-run' aggregate demand-for-money function. At the level of the individual agent, there is no problem. If some argument or other in the function determining the agent's long-run 'target' level of money holding changes, one needs only to suggest that the agent encounters increasing marginal costs in adjusting cash balances in order to derive a Marshallian 'short-run' demand function, or rather an array of such functions, each one defined with respect to a different period of time elapsing after the initial disturbance. However, one cannot treat the economy as a whole 'as if' it were just like one representative agent with regard to such an experiment: the individual agent can always change nominal money holdings by making market transactions, but the economy as a whole cannot usually do so.[16]

Suppose once more that the nominal stock of fiat money in an economy were to be exogenously increased. In that case, there would emerge initially excess money holdings for the typical agent and for the economy as a whole. The buffer-stock approach tells us that such an excess of money leads to positive real-balance effects in all markets. The typical agent undertakes expenditure flows designed to move along a path towards a new long-run target of real balances. Interest rates are pushed down, and output increases, but though the gap between them is narrowed, there still persists at this first stage in the transmission mechanism a discrepancy between the amount of money that agents in the economy wish to hold in the long run and the amount in circulation.

Suppose, however, that markets work in a Keynesian fashion, so that the rate of interest continues to fall so long as agents try to reduce their money holdings at any positive rate.[17] In this case, as White (1981) has argued, the rate of interest must move instantaneously to a value at which the *long-run and not the short-run* quantity of money demanded absorbs existing cash. This must happen because the costs which agents face in adjusting their cash holdings, and which underpin the short-run/long-run distinction at the level of the individual experiment, are never in fact encountered. When any incipient flow of cash into the bond market causes the rate of interest to move downwards, this latter movement is exogenous to the individual agent. Hence it does nothing to eliminate his incipient flow of expenditure on bonds. The latter continues until its source has been eliminated, and the source in question is the difference between his actual and long-run desired money holdings.

With interest-rate flexibility, then, the long-run/short-run distinction is empirically irrelevant, and a lagged dependent variable in the aggregate demand for money function is hard to justify in a Keynesian framework; but, as everyone knows, this variable is, as a matter of fact, much utilised and apparently badly needed.[18] Cycle phase average data, such as used by Friedman and Schwartz (1982), and data drawn from time periods long enough to be dominated by secular variations, have been used to estimate demand-for-money functions without resort to lagged dependent variables.

However, with quarterly data, and even annual data drawn from rather short time periods—fifteen to twenty years, say—it is usual to invoke adjustment costs and the Marshallian long-run/short-run distinction so as to achieve satisfactory econometric results. In recent years, though, such satisfactory results have proved harder and harder to obtain, even with the use of such an expedient: hence the growing concern among economists and policy-makers alike about instability in the demand-for-money function.

The buffer-stock approach claims to be able to account for the presence of a lagged dependent variable in empirical demand-for-money functions, and also yields suggestions about the causes of recently observed instability in the relationship. As I have shown elsewhere (Laidler 1982, Chapter 2), a demand-for-money function with a lagged dependent variable may be interpreted as a particular way of writing down the relationship between changes in the money supply and subsequent changes in prices, in which the entire transmission mechanism is approximated by a single 'black box' parameter which is equal to unity minus the coefficient of the lagged dependent variable. The fact that such an expression can be derived from the buffer-stock notion allows that this approach can, in principle at least, account for the empirical success of so-called short-run demand-for-money functions.

At the same time we have here an obvious starting-point for an explanation of why such short-run demand functions have been less successful in recent years. It is well known that the transmission mechanism of monetary policy is complex and subject to long and variable time-lags, and yet in the case of single equation 'demand for money' studies, the buffer-stock approach implies that the mechanism is embedded in one constant parameter. Would it be surprising if such a procedure proved satisfactory enough when dealing with periods of monetary tranquillity, but turned out to be inadequate when faced with the unstable money-supply behaviour of periods like the 1970s? If this conjecture is true, it might imply that the apparent fragility of the demand-for-money function in recent years does not stem from problems with that relationship, but is rather a statistical artefact generated by inadequate modelling of the transmission mechanism. Of course this is not to deny a role to institutional change in shifting the long-term demand-for-money function in the late 1970s; however, the question is not whether some of our problems arise from this source, but whether all of them do.[19]

Providing a possible partial solution to the puzzle of instability of the demand-for-money function is not the only way in which the buffer-stock approach tends to reinstate the importance of money for the behaviour of contemporary economies. It is often suggested that developments in financial markets have lately rendered money less interest-elastic in demand than it once was, and hence less controllable by the authorities. In the limiting, zero elasticity, case, so it is argued, the authorities cannot change the quantity of money at all by way of open-market operations: if changes in the price of bonds have no effect upon the public's demand for money, how can such changes cause the quantity of money in circulation to vary? If one takes the view that the economy is 'on' its demand-for-money function at each and every moment, it is hard to resist this argument.[20] However, the buffer-stock approach enables one to counter it in terms of what amounts to a dynamisation of Brunner and Meltzer's (e.g. 1976a) analysis of the money-supply process.

Brunner and Meltzer have long, and correctly, argued that, when the authorities raise the price which they offer for bonds, the public does not sell bonds to them because it wishes to hold more money. Rather the public sells bonds because it wishes to substitute higher-yielding assets, such as physical capital, for them in its portfolio. The quantity of money in circulation is thereby increased, not because anyone wishes to hold extra cash, but because to obtain it is a necessary intermediate step towards purchasing capital equipment and because, if all agents in the economy are simultaneously trying to do this, the cash in question can only be obtained by selling bonds to the authorities. Thus money which no one wishes to hold is nevertheless created by open-market operations. So long as the public's demand for bonds responds to interest-rate changes, in Brunner and Meltzer's terms so long as there is a non-zero interest elasticity of demand for credit, open-market operations can lead to the quantity of money in circulation changing even though the demand for money is totally interest-inelastic. This can happen only because the public's desire to substitute physical capital for bonds in its portfolio makes it willing, as an intermediate step, to accept money from the authorities over and above its long-run demand for that asset. It can only happen, that is to say, because money is a buffer stock.

## Concluding Comments

The conclusions to be drawn from this chapter are easy enough to summarise. It is natural to think of the money holdings of the individual agent fluctuating over time around their long-run desired level, but if prices in general are flexible then such fluctuations will not have any observable consequences at the level of the economy as a whole. Nor will they have such consequences if the interest rate always moves to keep the aggregate supply and demand for money in equilibrium.

In either case, if it is not impossible it is at least difficult to understand why lagged dependent variables are required in empirical work on the aggregate demand-for-money function; to explain why such functions began to display instability in the 1970s; and to see how open-market operations can be used to control the quantity of money in a world where so many assets which play the role of money bear interest at competitive rates. To these puzzles the buffer-stock approach offers a simple solution based on the straightforward suggestion that fluctuations in money holdings around their desired level characterise market experiments as well as individual experiments.

Quite apart from the qualitative aspects of the case for taking the buffer-stock approach seriously, upon which I have concentrated in this chapter, there exists, as I noted at the very outset, a large and growing body of successful quantitative work based upon it. There is space here only to mention some representative studies. As far as the demand-for-money function *per se* is concerned, the issues that I have raised in this paper have been investigated for the United States by, among others, Lewis (1978), Laidler (1980), Coats (1982) and Judd and Scadding (1982b), for the United Kingdom by Artis and Lewis (1976), and for Finland by Kanniainen and Tarkka (1983). The buffer-stock approach gets support from this work, particularly the more recent studies.

Single-equation experiments such as I have just cited are not altogether adequate for investigating the buffer-stock approach. It is, after all, a postulate about the transmission mechanism of monetary policy and this mechanism involves the whole economy, not just the demand-for-money function. In this context too, the approach has already generated a substantial body of literature. For the United Kingdom, one may point to the models of Jonson (1976b), Knight and Wymer (1975) and Coghlan (1981), not to mention the less formal analysis of Goodhart (1982b); for the Netherlands we have the work of Knoester (1979b), and for Australia the RBA 76/78 models of Jonson and his associates (e.g. 1976, 1980). To cite the above work does not imply that all of it is in every respect unquestionably satisfactory. No doubt careful scrutiny of any of the above-mentioned studies would lead to important questions requiring further work to resolve them.[21] Such a comment is always true, however, when new ideas are being developed and tested, and in any event, one can already see where further questions might in particular arise.

To begin with there is nothing unique in principle about discrepancies between the supply and demand for money when it comes to setting in motion streams of expenditure. Excess supplies of other financial assets too might be important because, as for example the analysis of Gray and Parkin (1973) shows, in a multi-asset world, money is simply the most liquid of assets held as a buffer stock and is not otherwise unique in this respect. Moreover, Purvis (1978) has explicitly analysed an economy with multiple financial assets, showing how the real-balance effect associated with discrepancies between the supply and demand for money is in fact a special case of a more general asset-disequilibrium effect (if I may be permitted the phrase). This work is of particular interest inasmuch as it uses a model in the Tobin (1969) tradition but argues that Tobin's practice of linking financial markets and goods markets solely through interest rates is misconceived. In addition to holding financial buffer stocks, economic agents also hold inventories of raw materials and finished goods. The interaction of the demand for inventories with the behaviour of stocks of financial assets is well worth investigating, both theoretically and empirically.

The importance of inventory fluctuations over the course of the business cycle suggests that such interaction would have to play a central role in any buffer-stock model of the cycle which was to prove a satisfactory alternative to the currently available new-classical explanations of Lucas (1975), Sargent (1976), and Barro (1978). Indeed it is hard to see how one can avoid according inventory fluctuations a central role in analyses of the buffer-stock approach. If, when there is an excess supply of money, expenditure in the economy exceeds the level it would otherwise attain by an additional flow driven by a real-balance effect, elementary national income accounting tells us that this expenditure will either not be satisfied at all or must be satisfied by running down inventories. It should also be noted that Howitt (1979) has argued that, in the presence of inventories, the distinction between models in which markets do or do not clear, is largely semantic. If that argument is accepted, the model whose future existence I am conjecturing here might turn out to be as much an extension of these explanations as an alternative to them.

In short, the theoretical basis of the buffer-stock approach to monetary analysis is well developed and simple, and it has already withstood a good deal of empirical testing. In his last survey paper on monetary economics, presented to a conference of the Money Study Group held at Oxford University, Harry Johnson urged us to develop ideas which are 'scientifically robust and sufficiently simple to be communicable to . . . students and policy-makers and the general public' (1974). The buffer-stock approach already has these characteristics, and as I claimed at the outset of this chapter, ought to be taken seriously, not least by those looking for a starting-point towards further progress in monetary economics.

## Notes

1 This does not mean that advocates of the buffer-stock approach regard the explanation of the evolution of monetary exchange as either uninteresting or impossible, but they do not regard it as central to the issues which particularly concern them. The reader is referred to Jones (1976) and Niehans (1978), Chapter 6, for analyses of this matter. It might be noted that, in his (1971) textbook, Chapter 2, Douglas Fisher made some play with the notion that a monetary system is a substitute for, rather than a complement to, the institution of a market. In stressing money's role as a means of exchange, the buffer-stock approach has much in common with Hicks's (e.g. 1982, Chapter 19) analysis of money as a 'running

asset'. This stands in contrast to Tobin's (e.g. 1969) stress on money as a store of value.

2 The inventory theoretic approach to the demand for money, as epitomised in the work of Baumol (1952) and Tobin (1956), has the individual's cash holdings fluctuating about an average value in a completely certain environment. Much of the basic analysis of the demand for money in a stochastic framework is surveyed by Orr (1970), where once again the concept of the 'demand for money' is explicitly an average over time or target quantity. The models to which I am referring here all deal with individual experiments, and their extension to the market experiment is far from a trivial business. Clower and Howitt (1978) deal with the market experiments that might arise from the Baumol–Tobin style of analysis, and in this sense represents a pioneering contribution to the buffer-stock approach upon which others might build.

3 The notion that money holding in a substitute for devoting resources to the generation of information is developed at some length in Laidler (1975), Chapter 1; it is also discussed by Brunner and Meltzer (1971). See too, Chapter 1 above.

4 This line of reasoning of course goes back to Patinkin (1965) and Archibald and Lipsey (1958). Its relationship to the buffer-stock approach is developed by Jonson (1976a) and Laidler (1982), Chapter 2. Note that Carr and Darby (1981) represents a recent attempt to incorporate ideas such as this into an empirical study of the aggregate demand-for-money function.

5 In the context of the macroeconomics of the open economy, the buffer-stock approach is a natural complement to the monetary approach to balance of payments and exchange-rate analysis. There is not space to take up these issues in this chapter; see, however, Jonson and Kierzkowski (1975) and note that this and several other important papers dealing with the buffer-stock approach, for example Jonson (1976b), and Knight and Wymer (1975), were written as contributions to the SSRC–Ford Foundation, London–Geneva Research Programme on International Monetary Economics supervised by Harry Johnson and Alexander Swoboda.

6 The papers of Akerlof (1973) and Tucker (1971) represent early attempts to come to grips with the analytic implications of this possibility in the context of macro general equilibrium models. I discussed related issues in Laidler (1982), Chapters 2 and 3, but when writing those chapters, I was unaware of the relevance of these earlier papers to my own work. Since I had read both papers at their time of publication, I owe their authors an apology for failing consciously to recall and acknowledge them before now.

7 The differences which I here analyse are between currently available versions of these two approaches. Peter Howitt (1979) has suggested that these distinctions become blurred once inventories of goods are introduced as objects of choice into a new-classical framework. (Also see Kawasaki et al. (1983).)

8 We are here dealing with the first-round impact of a change in the money supply. The particular combination in which the foregoing variables will change in a new-classical model will depend upon the extent to which the effects on the price level of the initially unexpected change in the money supply are misread by individual agents as reflecting changes in the relative prices of the particular goods and services that they sell. On this see Lucas (1972). I have dealt at length with the role of expectations in the transmission mechanism in Laidler (1982), Chapters 3 and 4. I neglect this issue here, not because it is unimportant but because it is not central to the matters I am dealing with and because space does not permit me to discuss it to any useful extent.

9 See Chapter 1 above, and note that Kawasaki et al. (1983) have shown, in the

context of the behaviour of the individual firm, how the possibility of holding inventories of goods may lead to price stickiness in the face of what the firm perceives as transitory demand shifts.

10 In particular this is a characteristic of the approach of Tobin and his many associates and followers. See, e.g., Tobin (1969). Note that Tsiang (1982), whose work is highly relevant to the buffer-stock approach, has criticised Tobin in particular for insisting on maintaining asset-market equilibrium at all points in his analysis of the transmission mechanism.

11 The sequence of events that I have just described is in effect what Chick (1973) aptly termed the 'pseudo dynamics of IS–LM'.

12 This line of reasoning has been a continuous and important theme in the work of Tsiang. See, for example, (1956) and (1982).

13 See Chapter 5 for a formalisation of this argument, which is at first sight similar to that of Artis and Lewis (1976) but is, in fact, crucially different from theirs. They made the *rate of change* of the rate of interest vary with the excess supply of money, while here I am arguing that it is the *level* of interest rate relative to some underlying long-run equilibrium value that depends on the excess supply of money. Artis and Lewis achieved promising empirical results with UK data, but subsequent work by Laidler (1980) suggests that their formulation does not fit US data. I am inclined to think that this lack of robustness on the part of the Artis and Lewis formulation reflects the fact that it misspecifies the relationship between excess money holdings and the interest rate.

14 Among the articles that helped establish this conclusion are Johnson (1969a), Marty (1969) and Patinkin (1969a).

15 It might be noted that in this chapter I am using the phrase 'real-balance effect' in the rather broader sense adopted by Patinkin (1967), In *Money, Interest and Prices* (1956) he used the term only to refer to the wealth effects of increases in the supply of fiat money. The question of whether the authorities can in fact vary the quantity of money in a 'vertical LM curve' economy is addressed below.

16 A fixed-exchange-rate, open economy can of course do just that. Even here though, the relevant costs have to do with balance-of-payments adjustments, and not those associated with individual portfolio adjustments.

17 The argument here is exactly parallel to that set out in Laidler (1982), Chapter 2, which shows that in the presence of price-level flexibility, a short-run demand-for-money function would not be observed. Lane (1983), pp. 112 *et seq.*, develops a more general version of this argument.

18 Note that I here say 'hard' and not 'impossible' to justify. If one tries hard enough one can probably reconcile any observation with the postulate that the demand and supply of money are maintained in constant equilibrium. Cf. Laidler (1982), pp. 51–2 and 96–101, for a more detailed discussion of this and related issues.

19 For a thorough discussion of these issues, particularly as they arise in the context of recent US experience, see Judd and Scadding (1982a).

20 This argument appears to have its roots in a certain passage of *The General Theory*: see Keynes (1936), p. 197. It was advanced as long ago as 1965 by Gramley and Chase, but has not been too popular, at least in an explicit form, in the North American literature since then. However, it frequently turns up in British Keynesian writings: see for example Hahn (1971), Kaldor (1980), and Hicks (1982), pp. 262–4. The counter-argument which I sketch out here has been developed at greater length by Howitt and Laidler (1979), Judd and Scadding (1982a) and Artis and Lewis (1981), among others.

21 Milbourne (1988) has now provided just such a survey. See also Chapter 1 above.

# 3

# On the Costs of Anticipated Inflation

## Introduction

The world-wide inflation of the 1970s has slowed down markedly in recent years, but even now, with price increases in the 4–6 per annum range, it is running at a rate which in the 1960s would have been regarded as intolerably high. Moreover the reduction in inflation rates that took place in the first few years of the 1980s was achieved only at the cost of unemployment levels unprecedented in the post-war period, and it is far from clear that there now exists the political will to achieve further significant reductions in inflation.

Because it is so difficult and painful to reduce inflation, there is a plausible case to be made for learning to live with it instead. It is widely argued that inflation is at its most socially destructive when it is not anticipated. However, unanticipated inflation is also relatively costless to cure. Depression and unemployment seem to be a necessary accompaniment to slowing down the inflation rate only when inflation expectations have become embedded in the price-setting and wage-bargaining processes; while, at the same time, the more fully adjusted the economy is to the presence of inflation, the less socially disruptive is its continuation. Neoclassical monetary theory would have it that, in the limit, when inflation is fully anticipated, the only costs it imposes are those associated with the community's attempts to economise on non-interest-bearing money balances. This limiting case is precisely the one in which the costs of reducing inflation in terms of unemployment—not to mention in terms of the other phenomena such as the disruption of the debtor–creditor relationships that would accompany an unanticipated reduction in the inflation rate—are maximised.

It is hardly surprising that many find the case for trying to live with inflation rather than attempting to cure it a strong one. In this chapter I shall examine one aspect of the case: namely, the neoclassical analysis of

41

the welfare costs of anticipated inflation. I shall argue that conventional theory does not properly represent the nature of those costs because it concentrates on the role of money as a store of value for the individual economic agent, to the exclusion of considering the effects of anticipated inflation on the roles of money as a means of exchange and a unit of account. My arguments strengthen the case against living with inflation, but they by no means make that case a clear-cut one. The most appealing feature of the application of Marshallian welfare analysis to inflation is that it appears to permit quantification of its costs, and I shall not here suggest means of quantifying the consequences of anticipated inflation which the following arguments suggest should also be taken into account when assessing its social costs.

This admission is hardly fatal. The costs involved in bringing down the inflation rate below its anticipated level, which one might want to compare with the costs of living with inflation, are not quantifiable either in terms analogous to the welfare measures that are normally adopted in dealing with anticipated inflation. The latter purport to measure utility foregone as a result of misallocating a stock of fully utilised resources. Debates about the costs of reducing inflation by way of monetary policy are not about whether such measures will result in labour—not to mention other resources—becoming unemployed, but rather how much unemployment will be caused, and for how long it is likely to last; and there is no way of which I know to measure the welfare costs of involuntary unemployment that would make those costs comparable to the consumer and producer surpluses usually dealt with by welfare economics.

Even though certain contemporary approaches to the theory of unemployment would have it that there is no such thing as involuntary unemployment, that unemployment involves resources being misallocated in the direction of search activity rather than being totally unused, there is no solution to the problem of measuring the welfare costs of unemployment along these lines. We can relabel 'unemployed' resources as 'misallocated', but the misallocation in question is not of the type that orthodox welfare analysis deals with, as anyone who reads, for example Alchian (1970) will readily discover. It is of the essence of orthodox analysis that agents act in response to incentives and achieve the expected outcome of their decisions. Misallocations arise because private incentives do not accurately reflect social constraints. Unemployment (interpreted as a shift of resources towards search activity) does not represent a misallocation of this type. It arises because individuals act on the basis of expectations which are not, in the event fulfilled. The *ex post* outcome of their actions differs from that which they expected *ex ante*, and we have no welfare economics of the consequences of such mistaken decisions.

The same type of argument applies to our ability to assess the importance of that other consequence of unanticipated changes in the inflation rate, the disruption of debtor–creditor relationships (in favour of creditors, be it noted, when the inflation rate is slowing down). Orthodox welfare economics has little to say about distributional effects which arise from privately appropriate responses to changed constraints, let alone about those which arise from erroneous decisions.

In short, we do not know how to quantify the costs associated with unanticipated variations in the inflation rate, and it is the burden of this chapter that we also know less than might have been thought about the nature of the costs involved in living with perfectly anticipated inflation. However, our inability to quantify such costs does not make them any the less real, or any the less worthy of discussion. The arguments that I present below suggest that the costs associated with anticipated inflation are more serious than conventional neoclassical analysis would have them. In the next section I set out a version of that conventional analysis as a preliminary to submitting it to what I hope will be judged constructive criticism.

## Neoclassical Analysis

The conventional analysis of the welfare costs of fully anticipated inflation is easily presented. Real-money balances $M/P$ are assumed to be produced at zero marginal social cost. In Figure 3.1 we draw the aggregate demand

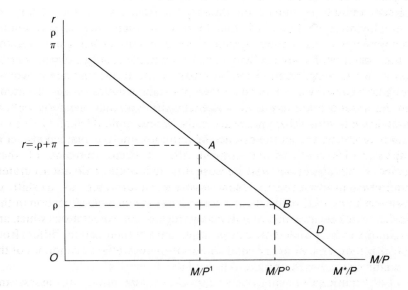

Figure 3.1 Welfare Costs of Anticipated Inflation

for them as a function of the nominal rate of interest $r$, the latter variable being the sum of the real rate of return on capital $\rho$ and the expected rate of inflation $\pi$. Initially, with a zero rate of inflation, and money balances bearing no explicit interest, $M/P^0$ real balances are held. If we now permit the fully anticipated rate of inflation to take the value $\pi$, $M/P^1$ of money balances are held instead. The conventional application of Marshallian consumer's surplus analysis to Figure 3.1 tells us that, as a consequence of inflation, the community loses economic welfare in the amount of:

$$AB\ M/P^0\ M/P^1$$

Now there are of course many awkward questions that can be raised about treating an area such as this under any demand curve, let alone under a demand curve for real balances, as a measure of economic welfare. Consumer's surplus only has a unique value given by the area under the *individual's* demand curve for a particular good on the quite stringent assumptions that the marginal utility of income to the individual is constant and independent of the quantity being consumed of the good under analysis. This problem is usually side-stepped in the welfare analysis of inflation by the (often implicit) assumption that the money is superneutral; variations in the inflation rate are treated as leaving the quantities of real output produced and consumed, and hence the marginal utility of other goods, unchanged.[1]

In a model with non-superneutral money, the consequences of varying the rate of nominal monetary expansion, and hence the inflation rate, would involve shifts of, as well as movements along, the demand-for-money function (unless we made the patently false assumption that the per head real income elasticity of demand for real balances was zero), not to mention changes in the real rate of interest. In such a case, welfare measurement would have to be undertaken with general equilibrium rather than partial equilibrium tools and we would have to face up to the thorny problems raised by the fact that, with non-superneutral money affecting output, some of the costs of inflation would already be reflected in variations in national income, while some would not be.

Quite apart from these issues, consumer's surplus analysis is concerned with the measurement of the economic welfare of an individual, not with that of some aggregate welfare concept. There are many who would question the propriety of discussing welfare in the aggregate without taking explicit account of distributional factors, while others would go so far as to question the meaning of any such aggregate measure, distributionally weighted or otherwise. Not everyone would agree with Robbins (1935) that such comparisons are beyond the scope of economics, but there can be no doubt that it would be hard to defend the proposition that there is some set of distributional weights that is so obviously superior to any other that a unique and widely acceptable aggregate welfare measure can be constructed.

Problems such as these are common to any application of Marshallian welfare economics and, though they are certainly relevant to the seriousness with which we take orthodox analysis of the welfare costs of inflation, the issues that I wish to raise in this paper concern other matters. They arise from taking a closer-than-usual look at the nature of money and the amenity flow that it provides.

The theoretical foundations for the welfare analysis of inflation sketched out above are to be found in Friedman's work on the demand for money, but Friedman was far more concerned with analysing the factors that influence the amount of money people will hold than in explaining why money is held. He referred to money as a 'temporary abode of purchasing power' and proceeded to analyse the factors determining the demand for it as if it were essentially the same as any durable good that provided a flow of services to its owner. He treated the theory of the demand for money as a special case of his permanent-income hypothesis of consumption, and in emphasising his theory's predictions about behaviour rather than paying attention to producing a set of precise and descriptively accurate assumptions to underpin it, he was simply putting into practice his own methodology of positive economics.[2]

Now there can be no doubt that, in treating money as if it were a consumer durable good, and in applying to the analysis of the demand for it the tools of Fisherine capital theory, Friedman and his associates laid the foundations of an enormous advance in our understanding of the interaction of money and economic activity. Friedman's theory of the demand for money is surely a prime example of the power of the 'as if' methodology applied to positive economics. But here we are dealing with an application of this analysis to a different set of questions from those that Friedman initially set out to address.[3] A simplifying assumption that is powerful and fruitful in one application of a theory may be dangerously misleading in another application. To modify one of Friedman's own examples, the pragmatism that rightly leads one to the view that the behaviour of an expert billiard player at the billiard table can usefully be predicted by analysing it 'as if' he were an expert mathematician can cause trouble if it leads one also to predict the same billiard player's performance in a mathematics examination on a similar basis.

The ease with which the costs of inflation dealt with above can be removed, according to the very analysis that enables us to identify them, suggests that some such problem might be present here. If the monetary authorities were to pay the holders of money balances the equilibrium nominal interest rate available on other assets, the opportunity cost of holding money would be zero and the economy would end up holding an optimal quantity of real balances $M^*/P$. That is to say, the introduction of such interest payments on money would not only undo the harm done by inflation, but also that done by the failure to pay a return, $\rho$, to money holders when the inflation rate is zero. If we take the foregoing analysis seriously as an account of the social damage done by anticipated inflation, any economy which has long undergone inflation at a more-or-less stable rate can avoid damage from letting inflation continue simply by paying interest on its money stock at the appropriate rate. Though we might find widespread agreement that such a step would help matters, it is hard to believe that there are many who would think that it would make inflation irrelevant.

Now some of the scepticism about the ease with which the above analysis suggests that costs of inflation can be removed arises from the fact that the model we have been considering implicitly starts from a situation in which everything except the rate of return on real balances is already fully adjusted to inflation. It deals with an economy in which taxes and transfers are completely and continuously indexed and in which the rates of return on all nominal assets other than money are already fully adjusted to inflation. For the latter condition to hold, a term structure of accurate inflationary expectations must be built into the term structure of interest rates, and must have been built into it for so long that no holder of a maturing or soon-to-mature long-term asset will receive *ex post* a real return that differs in any way from that which he expected to receive *ex ante* when he purchased the asset. To meet conditions such as these is a tall order, and it is clear why proposals for widespread indexation must be a necessary accompaniment to any proposal for living with inflation that rests on the proposition that the welfare loss associated with a less-than-optimal quantity of money is the only significant cost of living with inflation. Even so, there are other problems here to which I shall now turn in more detail.

## Criticisms

As we have seen, the analysis of the welfare costs of anticipated inflation is based on a theory which, in treating money as a 'temporary abode of purchasing power', emphasises its traditional store-of-value role. This theory views money as a durable good which yields an undefined amenity flow to its owner in a way that makes money exactly parallel to, shall we say, a refrigerator. There is no doubt that this approach has proved extremely fruitful in generating useful predictions about aggregate demand-for-money functions of the type used in short-run macroeconomic models. However, consider the archetypical isolated economic agent, Robinson Crusoe: he might obtain a flow of services from a refrigerator and hence demand one, but not from a 'temporary abode of purchasing power'. It would be absurd to postulate that he would demand real balances because they yielded him an amenity flow. Money's desirability as a store of value derives from its role as a means of exchange, and exchange requires more than one agent in the economy. Even the arrival of Man Friday would make no difference: two agents gain nothing from abandoning barter. It is only when indirect trade becomes a possibility that there is any gain to be had from adopting one particular item as a generally accepted means of exchange.

Money is inherently a social phenomenon, and yet the monetary theory on which our welfare analysis of inflation is based treats it as if money holding were a purely private affair. This theory takes it for granted that the economic welfare generated from any individual agent by his own money holdings is the only welfare produced by them, that the social product of the money stock is simply the sum of the private products accruing to the individual holders of its components. I would suggest, to the contrary, that there is something of the nature of a public good about money, and that we should be very wary of treating the sum of its private products as its social product. In order to develop further the conjecture that there are externalities in the consumption of money's services, let us first of all look at those theories of the demand for money that emphasise its means-of-exchange role, theories of the transactions demand for money.

The most popular transactions-demand model is the so-called Baumol–Tobin inventory approach. Appealing though it is at the level of the individual agent, I do not find this analysis very helpful at an aggregate level. Though the Baumol–Tobin analysis deals with money holding as a means of reducing transactions costs, the costs in question are those that arise in trading between money itself and interest-bearing assets, and not in trading among goods. In the aggregate this approach would have half the economy making continuous payments and receiving receipts at discrete intervals, and vice versa for the other half. To get the whole money stock continuously held, the continuous receivers would have to take cash to the bank to exchange for bonds at the same moment that the continuous payers took bonds to the bank in exchange for money. The economy could, in short, dispense with the bank, and having done that could achieve a further resource saving by adopting interest-earning bonds as its means of exchange.[4]

Baumol–Tobin 'money' has no social role to play, and those approaches to the analysis of the welfare economics of a money economy, such as Feige and Parkin (1971), that are based on this theory do not seem to be any better or worse founded than the neoclassical analysis under scrutiny in the preceding few pages. The work of Brunner and Meltzer (1971) seems to me to provide a more useful starting-point for analysing money's social role. They argue that the existence of a universally accepted means of exchange enables those involved in a market economy to realise the gains from trade at less resource cost than they would incur in its absence. Thus, by holding an inventory of money balances, individuals provide themselves with a buffer stock of a readily tradable commodity which enables them to carry out market activity on the basis of less information about the structure of prices than they would require in its absence. Such information is costly to generate, and money holding enables the individual to economise on its acquisition.

Now clearly when there is uncertainty about the behaviour of trading partners, about what goods are going to be available when and at what prices, there is going to be a stochastic element to the timing of any individual's pattern of payments and receipts. Patinkin (1965) makes such a stochastic element the basis of his theory of the demand for money by arguing that the inability to make a payment when it is called for imposes costs in terms of embarrassment on the individual. To this we may add that running out of cash unexpectedly is not only embarrassing but costly in other ways as well. It can lead to the unexpected cancellation of transactions plans which would have generated gains had they been followed through, and/or to costly sales of less liquid assets to replenish money holdings. Patinkin, however, does not add these riders because, in his analysis, trade among goods takes place, at equilibrium prices, before agents settle up in terms of money.

To approach the analysis of the demand for money along these lines makes it easy enough to see where externalities may arise from money holding. The random element that is present in any one individual's pattern of payments and receipts must arise from the decisions and actions of other agents. The more real balances other agents hold on average, the less likely it is that they will be unable to make a purchase which they would normally have undertaken, or that they will delay in handing over cash when presented with a bill; also, the less likely it is that they will unexpectedly present a bill of their own, or perhaps call in a debt, to replenish an unexpected shortfall in their own cash balances. Furthermore, an agent who runs out of cash can obtain it by selling some marketable asset, albeit at a cost in time and trouble if nothing else. The larger are other agents' money holdings, the easier, and hence less costly, is such an operation likely to be. Thus, any one agent, holding cash balances of a given size, is less likely to incur the costs of running out of cash, the larger are the cash balances of others, while those very costs of running out of cash will also be reduced. Any one agent's cash balances produce services not just for that agent then but for all other agents with whom his market activities bring him into contact.

Cash balances are not unique in this respect. An argument very like the foregoing one could be made about the demand for telephone receivers, or citizens band radios. However, this does not alter the fact that the social productivity of the money stock is higher than its private productivity, and it is of course changes in the social productivity of money that are important as far as the assessment of the welfare costs of inflation is

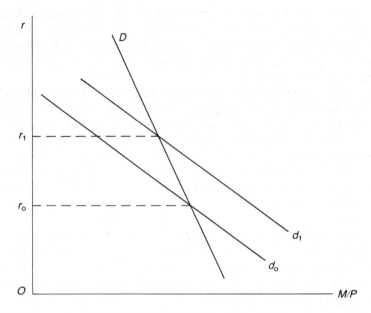

**Figure 3.2**    Demand-for-money Functions

concerned. The conventional neoclassical analysis of those costs, set out in
the previous section of this chapter, treats the economy's demand-for-
money function as if it could be generated by aggregating a series of
independent individual demand-for-money functions, but the arguments
put here suggest that these individual functions are in fact interdependent.

Figure 3.2 sets out what is involved. The curve $d_0$ shows the demand for
real balances of an individual agent as a function of the nominal rate of
interest. Such a curve is drawn from a given pattern of payments and
receipts, but as the nominal interest rate rises with inflation, the pattern of
payments and receipts changes as other agents attempt to economise on
cash, in such a way as to shift the curve $d_0$ outwards towards $d_1$. The curve
$D$ is a locus of the combined effects of such movements along shifts of the
curves $d_0$ and $d_1$. Aggregation over individuals of curves such as a $D$
produces the demand-for-money function for the economy as a whole
drawn in Figure 3.1. To some extent, trade credit practices which involve
penalties for late payments permit the external effects analysed here to be
internalised, since penalty charges can be raised with the rate of inflation.
This factor does not affect the qualitative nature of the argument advanced
here, though it may of course make a quantitative difference to its
importance. Be that as it may, the area under a curve such as $D$ does no
doubt have a welfare significance, but it is far from clear that the
significance is properly captured by treating the aggregate demand-for-

money function as if it were the result of aggregating curves such as $d$, though that is what conventional analysis does.

That same conventional analysis takes it for granted that the number of economic agents in the economy is exogenously given, but the term economic agent is vague to the point of ambiguity. Much of the literature on money in growth models, to which that on money and economic welfare is closely related, deals with the determination of output per head and analyses the determinants of the demand for money per head; in doing so it unquestioningly identifies the biological individual as the relevant economic agent. To identify the economic agent with the biological individual is dubious at the best of times, and to do so when dealing with monetary problems is totally misleading. It is firms and households whose activities are co-ordinated through markets in which money functions as a means of exchange. The activities of individuals within these institutions are co-ordinated on different bases. In a market economy individuals voluntarily join firms, households and other institutions, and it is over five decades since Coase (1937) pointed out that whether particular activities will be co-ordinated within an institution—specifically a firm in his case—on a command basis, or between institutions or institutions and individuals on a market basis, will depend upon the relative costs and benefits associated with these alternative means of organisation.

Now, clearly, one of the costs associated with co-ordinating activities through markets rather than within institutions is the cost of holding money. If inflation, even fully and correctly anticipated inflation, increases those costs, then it is to be expected that, on the margin, some activities which, from the social point of view, would be better co-ordinated through markets will instead be organised on some other basis, either within larger firms than might otherwise exist, or within cartel arrangements, or by resort to one form or another of government planning. Thus it is not only that, in the presence of inflation, existing agents will receive a smaller amenity flow from their cash balances and will have to spend more time and trouble planning their economic activities; it is also likely that there will be fewer agents participating in market activities. Thus we have another reason for believing that the relationship between the representative agent's demand-for-money function and the aggregate curve is complex. As the inflation rate increases and we move along the aggregate demand-for-money function, the number of economic agents (but not the number of biological individuals) is likely to decrease, and given that there are once-and-for-all costs involved in altering the institutional framework in this way, there can be no guarantee that such changes are reversible.

Conventional analysis takes no account of effects such as these when it measures the resource cost of inflation in terms of an area under the aggregate demand-for-money function, and they undermine the usual theoretical basis upon which such welfare analysis is justified. Although I have stressed only the economic aspects of the above arguments, they clearly have strong political and ideological overtones. In their light, it is not difficult to understand why it is that those who have most faith in the market mechanism as a desirable form of socio-economic organisation also seem to have the strongest objections to inflation. Though the argument I present here has to do with anticipated inflation, it is more usual to stress the capacity of unanticipated price-level changes for undermining market mechanisms. As I shall argue below, however, once we consider the role of relative prices in the allocative mechanism, and ask how inflation influences their operation, the distinction between anticipated and unanticipated inflation becomes unclear.[5]

The potential effects of anticipated inflation on the efficiency of the monetary system that we have been considering so far all arise from anticipated inflation making it more expensive for the individual agent to hold real balances. Our analysis has the monetary system becoming less productive overall as a result of inflation because the economy uses less money and not because anticipated inflation actually impairs its productivity. Thus the problems brought on by inflation that we have been discussing in the last few pages, though rather different from, and perhaps more serious than, those which conventional monetary theory tells us underlie the welfare costs of inflation, may nevertheless be avoided by the conventional remedy of paying interest at an appropriate rate on money balances. It is widely recognised that inflation which is less than perfectly anticipated undermines money's social productivity by making it a less efficient substitute for devoting resources to the generation of information upon which plans can be based. Even in a state of what might reasonably be referred to as perfectly anticipated inflation, however, there seems to be scope for such an effect, for there to occur shifts of, as well as movements along, what might be termed the marginal social product of real-balances schedule. The problem here is best seen by focusing on money's role as a unit of account.[6]

Money is the item universally acceptable in exchange for any commodity, and it is economic for all traders to state the price of the goods they have to sell, or wish to purchase, relative to money, the item for which they intend to exchange them. Thus money's unit-of-account function is closely related to its role as a means of exchange. Inflation makes money less productive because it makes the information about *relative* prices, contained in the array of *money* prices about which any agent may have information, less reliable and more difficult to interpret. To say this is to draw attention to the fact that the very notion of 'perfectly anticipated' inflation upon which conventional analysis is based, and which has underlain our discussion so far in this chapter, is rather more difficult to pin down than might have been thought, in a manner that is relevant to the real world.

It is customary to discuss 'the general price level' when talking about inflation, and the analysis with which we began this chapter implicitly treats that concept as if it were the price in terms of money of a single good; but of course it is not, it is an index number. By 'perfectly anticipated inflation' we must mean that the rate of change of that index number is correctly foreseen over every relevant time horizon and that this foresight is acted upon. In an economy in which there were no reasons for relative prices to change over time, a continuous upward change in the money price of each good at an equal rate would be consistent with a fully anticipated inflation, as would continuous changes at different rates in the money prices of individual goods, holding the rate of change of the price index constant, in an economy in which relative prices were changing.

The analysis we have carried out so far of the consequences of inflation would be adequate to deal with cases such as these. But what about the resource costs of changing prices, and of disseminating information about their having changed? If such informational costs did not exist then the monetary system as we understand it would not exist, as Brunner and Meltzer (1971) and Laidler (1975, Chapter 1) have argued. In their analysis money exists as a social device for overcoming such costs. Without them, there would be no money, and without money there could hardly be inflation. Thus it is difficult to defend ignoring such costs on the grounds of analytic simplicity when dealing with inflation, but that is what we have, in effect, been doing.

Part of the appropriate response to this problem is to note that economic agents do in fact have to devote real resources to changing prices and to spreading and collecting information about them; to the extent that there are more changes in money prices during inflation, the extra costs associated with making them are part of the overall cost of inflation. Costs of printing price-lists, or of changing price-tags, more often certainly are to be put down to inflation, but there is more at stake here than simply devoting more resources to printing and labelling. The costs of changing a price, and of spreading information about such a change, do not necessarily depend upon the size of the price change in question. Barro (1972) has shown that, where such costs are 'lump sum' in nature, the present-value-maximising firm will vary the price of its output in discrete steps in response to a continuous shift in the demand curve facing it. This argument implies that, during an inflation, firms will change their output prices discretely and also that input prices will rise in discrete steps. Moreover there exists no automatic mechanism to ensure that the timing of such price changes will be co-ordinated across firms and industries.

It is thus perfectly possible that the overall value of an economy's general price index can change at a continuous and perfectly foreseen rate while the pattern of relative prices underlying it fluctuates as different firms and industries change their output prices at different moments. Such inflation-induced fluctuation in the pattern of relative prices would both reduce the amount of information about relative prices to be generated from any particular sampling of money prices, and would also open up incentives for the allocation of resources to speculative activity that would not exist in the absence of inflation. Such speculative activity would tend to reduce fluctuations in relative prices, but at a real-resource cost which would not be incurred in the absence of inflation. Uncertainties about the time path of prices are recognised to lie at the root of much of the damage that so-called unanticipated inflation can do. The above arguments, in suggesting that they might be present even when the time path of the overall price index is fully anticipated, perhaps provide a basis for a closer integration than we have previously seen of the analysis of anticipated and unanticipated inflation.

These arguments lead to the conclusion that the social productivity of the monetary mechanism as a means of co-ordinating economic activity is reduced by inflation in yet another way overlooked by conventional analysis. Moreover, there are further incentives implicit in the mechanisms just discussed towards the organisation of economic activity by non-market mechanisms. Also, the costs in question here are not such as can be avoided by paying interest on money in an otherwise fully indexed economy. Indeed the resource costs of indexing taxes and transfers, and the scope for tax avoidance and such that would be opened up by changes in tax rates inevitably being made at discrete intervals, not to mention the difficulties of devising means whereby interest could effectively be paid on money, particularly on currency, are all examples of the types of costs we have just been discussing. In an inflationary economy it might be preferable to incur these costs than not to do so, but the absence of inflation would be a still more desirable state of affairs.

## Conclusions

It now remains to summarise the arguments presented in this chapter. Inflation is still deeply embedded in the economic system, and there can be few who see any prospect of finally ridding ourselves of it without generating significant unemployment for a substantial period of time. In the light of this, the alternative of living with inflation is certainly worth considering and is not without its advocates. No one suggests that living with inflation would be costless, but there is a large body of literature whose principal conclusion is that, once inflation has become fully anticipated, its only costs arise from the inefficiency in the monetary mechanism which, inherent in anticipated inflation, the incentives to economy in holding real balances lead to. This literature also suggests that these costs may be measured in terms of the appropriate area under the aggregate demand-for-real-balances function.

It has been the burden of this chapter to argue that this approach to assessing the costs of living with anticipated inflation misses many aspects of these costs, and that it does so because it overstretches the applicability of the assumption that the role of money in the economic system may be analysed as if money were simply a durable good yielding a flow of services to those who hold it. This assumption is powerful in generating predictions about what arguments belong in the demand-for-money function, and in organising analysis of the role of the quantity of money in short-run stabilisation policy, but is potentially misleading in the present application. Consideration of analysis which pays more explicit attention to the specific functions of money in the economic system points to at least three aspects of the potential costs of anticipated inflation that orthodox neoclassical analysis overlooks.

First, there is reason to believe that there are externalities in the consumption of money's services; that the social losses from individual agents' economising on cash balances in the face of inflation are greater than the sum of the private losses. Second, a market mechanism which uses money is by no means universal as a way of co-ordinating the economic activities of individuals. The more costly money is to use, the more aspects of economic activity are likely to be organised on some alternative, non-market basis. This tendency is also inherent in the final potential problem with inflation raised in this essay—namely the possibility that relative prices fluctuate as a result of inflation itself, even if the overall rate of inflation is completely stable and predictable. Such fluctuations would also tend to undermine the effectiveness of market mechanisms based on the use of money as a means of organising economic activity.

Now it should go without saying that the above arguments are tentative. I have presented no evidence which would enable anyone to judge their quantitative significance. However, although the ideas in question are not sufficiently developed here to be immediately susceptible to empirical tests of their importance, there is no reason why they cannot be so developed. They do, after all, potentially have implications about merger activity and its relationship to inflation, about the behaviour of relative prices during inflation, and so on. With further work we ought to be able both to derive such implications more precisely and to subject them to test. The only excuse for not doing so here can be that one can only accomplish so much in one essay. Nevertheless, if this essay convinces the reader that the ideas in it are worth further development, so that their empirical importance can better be assessed, and that, pending such further development, he should be wary of accepting orthodox neoclassical measures of the welfare costs of anticipated inflation as being well founded or in any way comprehensive, then it has fulfilled its purpose.

## Notes

1 The analysis sketched out here has its origins in the work of Bailey (1956), and represents an application to normative problems of Friedman's (1956) theory of the demand for money.

2 Cf. Friedman (1953a).

3 And of course Friedman took up these and related problems in his (1969) essay, *The Optimum Quantity of Money*.

4 But if we arbitrarily impose a requirement that transactions require money to mediate them, we may preserve the relevance of this model at the level of the economy as a whole. Even so, this extension becomes complex the moment we allow agents to choose the timing of their market transactions rather than simply imposing a consistent pattern on the economy, as the work of Clower and Howitt (1978) shows.

5 Leijonhufvud (1981) Chapter 9, originally circulated as a discussion paper in 1975, contains a particularly penetrating discussion of these issues.

6 The issues dealt with below are now usually referred to as 'menu cost' effects. For a survey of developments in this area which have taken place since this essay was written, see Konieczny (1987), Chapter 1.

# 4

## The New-Classical Contribution to Macroeconomics

### Introduction

Macroeconomics is prone to 'revolutions'—intellectual upheaval in which some new idea or ideas claiming to establish fresh and valid insights into the workings of the economic system sweep away a prevailing orthodoxy. The last fifty years have seen the 'Keynesian revolution' overwhelm 'classical economics' so-called, to be succeeded in turn by a 'monetarist revolution' which seemed to overthrow 'Keynesian' economics. In the last fifteen years or so 'monetarism' has in turn yielded to a 'new-classical revolution' which self-consciously, and much more thoroughly than monetarism, has sought to re-establish macroeconomics on foundations which bear a close resemblance to those of certain strands in pre-Keynesian economics.[1] In every case, the superiority of the 'new' approach has undoubtedly been oversold by its adherents, but, at the same time, insights and tools of lasting value have also been added to the corpus of economic knowledge.

This chapter is devoted to assessing new-classical ideas and to asking what of lasting importance this school of macroeconomics has contributed since the early 1970s. It deals in turn with the relationship between new-classical economics and monetarism, the relative explanatory power of these two bodies of doctrine over empirical evidence, and the claims of new-classical economics to embody a superior analytic method. It argues that, although the particular ways in which new-classical macroeconomics has applied its basic ideas (notably in its insistence that the interaction of the maximising behaviour of individuals be analysed in the context of

56

continuously clearing markets and that agents' expectations be represented by the predictions of the true model of the economy in which they operate) are unnecessarily restrictive, its stress on equilibrium behaviour conditioned by the state of individual agents' expectations as a basis for macro-modelling is nevertheless valuable and has been salutary for the discipline.

## Monetarism and New-Classical Macroeconomics

New-classical macroeconomics was initially a response to the inflation of the 1960s and '70s, and to monetarist analysis of that inflation. Indeed, in its earliest manifestations, it appeared to be nothing more than an attempt to restate monetarist analysis with greater rigour than its pioneers—notably Milton Friedman—had achieved.[2] In order to put matters in perspective it will be helpful to recall the nature of the intellectual problem which that inflation created for most macroeconomists. Quite simply the empirical evidence it generated proved to be utterly inconsistent with then-prevailing Keynesian views about how the economy worked, and about how policy could be used to improve its performance. Expansionary demand-side policies, predominantly fiscal, could, according to that orthodoxy, generate lasting reductions in unemployment at the cost of somewhat higher, but nevertheless stable, inflation. In the 1960s and early 1970s, a number of Keynesian experiments occurred. I use 'occurred' deliberately here: in some places, for example Britain, fiscal expansion was deliberately used in an attempt to generate real growth; but in the United States fiscal expansion had more to do with the politics of financing the Vietnam war than it did with any carefully calibrated economic policy experiment. Be that as it may, when the Keynesian experiments occurred, they failed.[3] Gains in output and employment, where they materialised at all, proved to be temporary, and inflation, instead of shifting once to a new higher level, rose continuously.

Monetarist macroeconomics (whose components were available before the event, be it noted) explained these facts by arguing first that Keynesian orthodoxy had underestimated the role of the quantity of money as an influence on aggregate demand in general and the behaviour of prices in particular; and second that the idea of a stable inflation–unemployment trade-off—the Phillips curve—was based on an implicit assumption that the private sector of the economy suffered from perpetual money illusion. To the pressure of aggregate demand as a proximate influence on the inflation rate, Friedman (1968)—not to mention Phelps (1967)—added the expected rate of inflation. Furthermore, because Friedman viewed inflation expectations as deriving from past experience, and as being formed in such a way that expectations would in fact come to catch up with experience eventually, he argued that any attempt to reduce the unemployment rate below that determined by the normal frictions inherent in the labour market would lead, in the long run, not only to higher, but also to rising, inflation.

From the point of view of policy prescriptions and empirical judgements about the reliability of particular functional relationships in the economy, monetarism presented a clear alternative to Keynesian orthodoxy but constituted no radical theoretical challenge to it. Keynesian models already contained a demand-for-money function, and if monetarism was correct in arguing that this relationship was more stable than had in the past been believed, such a modification could easily enough be accommodated.[4] If expected inflation belonged as an extra variable in the Phillips curve, and depended upon the past behaviour of inflation, that would alter one's view of what demand-management policy could accomplish, but it did not require any fundamental change in economists' vision of how the economy worked. There is no stronger evidence in favour of the latter judgement than the fact that the first explicit monetarist analytic models were recognisable extensions of the IS–LM model.[5] Moreover large-scale Keynesian econometric systems proved easily able to absorb monetarist ideas as well.

The difficulty here was that the new version of the Phillips curve was hardly more satisfactory than the old one from an analytic point of view. Though the proposition that money wages and prices tend, given expectations, to rise faster the higher the level of aggregate demand in the economy, might be a plausible enough empirical generalisation, it does not constitute an explanation of the phenomenon that relates it to the purposeful maximising-behaviour of individual economic agents. The monetarist 'expectations-augmented Phillips curve' was an empirical observation in need of an explanation, not a well-grounded structural relationship in its own right. In attempting to provide an explanation of it, new-classical economists, and in particular Robert E. Lucas Jr. (1972), set in motion the 'new-classical revolution', based upon two analytic devices, namely the aggregate supply curve and the rational-expectations hypothesis.[6] Though the rational-expectations idea has probably attracted more attention, it is its use of a particular version of the aggregate supply curve which constitutes the most fundamental innovation of new-classical economics. Keynesian macroeconomics (including its monetarist variation) can accommodate rational expectations, but it cannot be reconciled with the universal existence of the continuously clearing flexible-price competitive markets which are a *sine qua non* of the 'aggregate supply curve' explanation of the Phillips curve.

Sticky prices lie at the very heart of Keynesian macroeconomics, and it explains quantity fluctuations in goods and labour markets as equilibrating movements arising because prices do not immediately change when aggregate demand shifts. The postulate of price flexibility lies at the centre of new-classical economics. It has it that prices always move to equilibrate markets when demand shifts, but that individual agents, who are not fully informed about the behaviour of all money prices in the economy, mistake money price changes in the markets for the goods they sell for relative price changes. Hence they respond by changing the quantities of goods they supply. In the aggregate, an unperceived demand increase which raises the general price level therefore causes an expansion of output along an aggregate supply curve, and a fall of demand causes a contraction. Output and employment fluctuations such as we observe in the real world are, according to new-classical economics, voluntary responses to mis-perceived price signals. They occur because prices change. Keynesian economics (including its monetarist variant) explains quantity changes as occurring because prices do not change fast enough to keep markets cleared. In this vital matter the contrast between the two approaches could not be more stark.[7]

Now the clearing-markets hypothesis of new-classical economics is logically compatible with the idea that expectations are naïvely extrapolated from past experience, but the use of the two ideas in conjunction certainly strains credulity. If agents are in no way tied down by sticky prices, and make costly errors in quantity decisions because of faulty expectations about the behaviour of prices in markets other than those in which they are currently active as sellers, they have every incentive to make their expectations as accurate as possible, and to use all available information in order to do so. Maximising agents should be presumed to form expectations, as Sargent and Wallace (1973, p. 328) put it, so that they 'depend, in a proper way, on the same things that economic theory says actually determine that variable'. Hence, though the literature of the 1960s and early 1970s does contain examples of models which combine clearing markets with adaptive expectations, such hybrids soon vanished to be replaced by a substantial body of new-classical theory, based upon the twin hypotheses of clearing markets and rational expectations.[8]

## The Case for New-Classical Macroeconomics

Economists have no clearly agreed criteria for deciding among competing bodies of theory, but certain factors are widely accepted as being relevant. The ability to explain past events, or (even better) to forecast future ones, is highly valued, as is the closely related capacity to yield insights into the nature of policy options available, and into the likely outcome of whichever option is chosen. Also important are matters of logical coherence, and intellectual compatibility with other available and accepted doctrines. Proponents of new-classical macroeconomics have, at various times, claimed it to be superior to Keynesian and monetarist alternatives on all three criteria. There has been a considerable change of emphasis: in defending their work, new-classical economists now place much more stress on theory and much less stress on the alleged superior empirical content of their models than they did a decade ago.[9]

As will already be apparent, I quite agree that the western world's experience with inflation and unemployment of the 1970s constitutes a massive refutation of 'Keynesian economics' as the term was understood in the mid-1960s. Nor would I deny that the new-classical macroeconomics of the late 1970s, emphasising as it did the role of the quantity of money in generating inflation, and the crucial role played by expectations in the inflationary process, provided a superior explanation of that experience. If we were forced to make a choice between these two alternatives alone, we would have to accept the claims of Lucas and Sargent (1978) that their brand of macroeconomics is the only respectable one available. However, we are not forced to make this choice.[10]

Before the inflation of the 1970s was dreamed of, monetarists such as Friedman (e.g. 1959) and Brunner and Meltzer (e.g. 1963) had been attacking Keynesian orthodoxy for underestimating the importance of the quantity of money. Furthermore, Friedman and Phelps (surely no monetarist) had, as we have seen, criticised the idea of a permanent inflation–unemployment trade-off in the mid-1960s on the grounds that the behaviour of inflation expectations, themselves endogenous to the structure of the economy, would render any such trade-off temporary. As we have also noted, however, these ideas could be, and eventually were, easily incorporated into otherwise orthodox Keynesian models, but Keynesian models *so modified* do very well indeed in explaining the 1970s.[11] A system in which prices are sticky (though not rigid), in which quantities change to absorb demand-side shocks in the short run, and in which inflation expectations though mainly backward looking are endogenous, can account for the 1970s experience at least as well as any new-classical system based on price flexibility, clearing markets and rational expectations. To put it in terms of labels, the empirical experience of the 1970s does not force one to reject the 'monetarist' variation on the 'Keynesian' model and embrace 'new-classical macroeconomics'.

The methodological criteria proposed by new-classical economists in defence of their work have much in common with those sketched above, and implicitly or explicitly adopted by economists in general. If they did not, it would be hard to explain why their arguments have proved so widely persuasive. However, though claims to superior predictive power, and to deeper insights into the nature of economic policy processes, have certainly been made from time to time on behalf of new-classical macroeconomics, it has also, from the very outset, been presented as the product of a major advance in the application of analytical methods; and, with the passage of time, its proponents have come to place increasing emphasis on this last factor, claiming that their macroeconomics is more logically coherent and more closely related to micro-theory than anything which went before it. It is certainly true, as we shall now see, that these are the strongest arguments in favour of new-classical economics.

To begin with, and uncontroversially, new-classical economists tell us that an important purpose of macroeconomic models is to deduce predictions about the behaviour of an economy when subjected to various shocks. Equally uncontroversially, they argue that key components of such a model should be logically coherent and well-tested propositions about the behaviour of individual agents. That these propositions about individual agents should in turn be derived from analysis of rationally purposeful utility-maximising behaviour might be less universally accepted, but I do not wish to quarrel about this particular principle.[12] Reasons for controversy begin to arise only when we seek an institutional framework in terms of which it is possible to derive coherent predictions about the behaviour of the economy as a whole from knowledge of individual behaviour, and I shall argue in due course that the particular choice made at this point by the new-classicals is not the only respectable one available to us.

Be that as it may, new-classical economists propose that we model agents as operating in an environment of perfect competition, in which markets costlessly adjust to maintain the supply and demand for every good and service, not least labour, in constant equilibrium. Their competitive model differs from traditional treatments of perfectly competitive economies inasmuch as agents in it do not have full information about the structure of relative prices when they engage in trade. The demand-and-supply schedules which determine the equilibrium structure of market prices in a new-classical model are conditional, not upon full and accurate information about that same structure of market prices, but upon agents' perceptions (expectations is the more commonly used word) of that structure. Because agents are supposed to be purposeful rational maximisers, they form their expectations so that they differ from the actual values of the variables in question only to the extent of a serially uncorrelated random error. For agents to operate on the basis of any other kind of expectations would result in them encountering unnecessary losses, and hence in violating the purposeful utility maximisation assumption.

The 'rational' approach to modelling expectations formation has been translated by new-classical economists into the postulate that agents form expectations 'as if' they were fully informed about the structure of the economy in which they operate, and make mistakes only to the extent that the economy is subjected to random exogenous shocks, either in the form of 'policy surprise'—any systematic component of policy behaviour being, and being perceived to be, part of the economy's structure—or, in more recent literature, random fluctuations in technology, 'real shocks' as they are called. In such a framework, given currently (and only rather recently) available analytic techniques, it is possible to derive predictions about the aggregate behaviour of the economy directly from premises concerning individual behaviour. More to the point, these predictions in certain important ways mimic the behaviour of real-world economies, specifically in the matter of co-movements of money wages and prices and quantities of employment and output over the course of the business cycle, and indeed the very fact that new-classical macroeconomics involves the exploitation of these new analytic techniques is sometimes advanced as an argument in its favour.[13]

The really critical point, however, as far as the proponents of new-classical economics are concerned, is that the above-mentioned analytic techniques, in their current state of development, can be used to derive macro-predictions with empirical content from nothing but well-specified micro-premises only on the assumptions of representative agents operating in competitive markets cleared by flexible prices. A model which postulates some form of wage or price stickiness inevitably involves the use of some (allegedly) *ad hoc* element in forming the link between micro-postulates and macro-predictions. This is not because models of individual maximising behaviour that explain price stickiness do not exist, because they obviously do, but because our current analytic capacity does not permit us except in exceptionally simple examples (e.g. Howitt, 1981) to embed such behaviour in a model of the economy as a whole, to allow for the way in which such behaviour might influence expectations, and then explicitly to derive macro-predictions.

As a result, those who wish both to postulate phenomena such as price stickiness and to build models with empirical content, are led to introduce qualitative empirical 'laws' into them and to permit the data to find quantitative values for the parameters which characterise these 'laws'. One way of looking at the issues at stake here is in terms of alternative strategies for evading that perennial barrier to truly rigorous macroeconomics, the aggregation problem. The new-classical assumptions of representative agents plus perfect competition certainly permit clearly defined links to be established between individual and market experiments without recourse to empirical laws, but those links are only as defensible as the assumptions that permit them to be forged.

Even so, if we regard the presence of 'free parameters', as Lucas (1980) calls them, in a model to be a fatal drawback, then new-classical macroeconomics, with its assumptions of universal competition among representative agents, perfect price flexibility, and rational expectations, has no rivals. If it is objected that perhaps empirical evidence might nevertheless have a role to play in such a judgement, the answer offered by the proponents of new-classical economics, notably Lucas (1980), is that, since their basic model uses no 'free parameters', a model which fits the facts better, or at least as well, can always be constructed by adding one (or more) such parameter to a basic new-classical system. Economic models are not supposed to be descriptions of all elements of reality (whatever that might be); and to show that greater descriptive accuracy may be achieved by the addition of free parameters is said to be neither surprising nor compelling as an argument against new-classical economics. I shall now turn to an examination of this argument.

## Empirical Evidence and 'Free Parameters'

I remarked earlier that there is no completely agreed set of methodological criteria for judging economic models. As a matter of simple logic, it cannot be denied that, if rigorous connections between maximising premises and ultimate conclusions is regarded as the be-all and end-all of economic analysis, then new-classical macroeconomics is indeed the only game worth playing. The most that anyone who denies this viewpoint can do is explain why he thinks other criteria are relevant, show how they support his position, and hope that his reasoning will be taken seriously. Such is my purpose here.

My starting-point is that the ultimate aim of economic theory is to explain observations, in the sense of deducing statements which describe such observations from more general premises. Moreover, and quite crucially, such premises should also yield other statements whose truth is not contradicted by the facts. The more general the predictive power of a set of premises (and the more propositions about purposeful maximising behaviour, and the fewer theoretically unsupported generalisations relying upon 'free parameters' there are among them) the better. An economics which can deduce true predictions about all the phenomena that might interest us from nothing but premises about maximising behaviour is presumably the ideal towards which we are all striving. That we are unlikely to achieve this ideal is not the point, though. Rather it is that, even if we did stumble upon it, we could never know this. The most we can ever be sure of about our models is that they have not been contradicted by evidence gathered to date. In the very nature of things we can never know whether they are true in the sense that they never will be contradicted.

As a practical matter we must always be more concerned with criteria for choosing among less-than-ideal theories than with laying down unattainable and non-operational standards of theoretical perfection. For this rather humdrum task, primacy must be accorded to empirical evidence, because it is surely uncontroversial that a theory which makes systematically false predictions about some phenomenon is itself false, and in need of modification, no matter how closely it satisfies other criteria.[14] Even so, we must be careful when we advance this last proposition not also to demand that a theory's predictions be 'descriptively accurate'. A theory may abstract from all manner of phenomena, having nothing to say about them, and hence be 'descriptively inaccurate' (or incomplete), but that does not make it false. The question of falsity only arises when a theory yields definite predictions about some phenomenon which turn out to be untrue. Descriptive inaccuracy is an inherent quality of any abstract model; but falsity is not. To use a standard platitude of the elementary logic class as an illustration, the reason why the proposition 'all swans are white' is false is not that this statement fails to mention feathers, and into the bargain has nothing to say about ducks; rather it is that some black swans do exist.

My reason for denying the inherent superiority of new-classical macroeconomics is not, therefore, that there might be interesting facts from which it abstracts and about which it has nothing to say; rather it is that it makes false predictions about the very phenomena with which it purports to deal, and that if it is to be rescued, parameters every bit as 'free' as those utilised in the Keynesian (or monetarist) alternative seem to be required. The original task which new-classical economics set itself was to provide a foundation in qualitative microeconomic reasoning for Friedman's propositions about the temporary nature of the inflation–unemployment trade-off. The fact that it succeeded in doing so is, however, not an empirical argument in its favour. That statements describing a set of already known facts may be deduced from a model is evidence, not of its truth, but of the logical skills of the person who constructed it. An empirical test arises only when conclusions yielded by the same model about facts not used to discipline its construction and better still, initially unsuspected, are compared with those facts.

We may illustrate what is at stake here from an earlier episode in the development of macroeconomics. The fact that they were able to reconcile the apparent conflict between time series and cross-section evidence on the marginal propensity to consume did not constitute an empirical argument in favour of the theories of the consumption function developed by Friedman (1957) and Modigliani and Brumberg (1954). They knew about that evidence before they constructed their models and calibrated them to it. The important empirical content of the new theories of the consumption function, that which rendered them truly testable, lay in their ability to make predictions about other empirical regularities, concerning for example the demands for durables and non-durables, or the effects on consumption patterns of income variability, which had either not been observed, or were not understood to be related to the foundations of consumer theory, before the appearance of the models in question.

Though the danger inherent in basing the empirical case for new-classical economics on evidence which has already been used to discipline its construction has been recognised by its proponents, it nevertheless finds itself in trouble when its predictions about other facts are compared with evidence.[15] To begin with, new-classical economics gets rid of the free parameter linking money wage-and-price changes to 'excess demand' by postulating that the Phillips trade-off reflects, among other parameters of the system, the elasticity of the supply of labour with respect to real wages. In doing so it yields a testable prediction about the quantitative relationship between inflation and employment fluctuations. Empirical evidence shows that the relative amplitudes of those fluctuations do not square up with what we think we know from micro-studies about this supply elasticity. Aggregate employment fluctuations seem to be systematically much too large relative to inflation fluctuations to be treated as movements along a supply curve of labour when the labour force misperceives nominal wage changes as reflecting real wage changes, and hence to be accounted for along new-classical lines. Closely related, the nature of the interaction of employment and real wages over the business cycle is hard to reconcile with the new-classical postulate that the real wage is always equal to the marginal product of labour and that employment fluctuations involve movements along a downward-sloping marginal product schedule.[16]

In a new-classical world, quantities change because prices fluctuate. Output and employment should therefore vary at least simultaneously with (or perhaps lag behind) the price level; but it is a stylised fact of real-world business cycles that quantity changes seem to precede associated price-level changes. Moreover, if the price level is free to move to keep the supply and demand for money in equilibrium, the economy should always be on its long-run demand-for-money function; but empirical observations suggest that the economy is often and systematically 'off' this relationship for extensive periods of time.[17] In the early 1980s, predictions about all of these phenomena were put to the test in one real-world experiment which was surely just as damaging to the new-classical economics of the 1970s as the experience of the 1970s was to the Keynesian orthodoxy of the 1960s. Then, in a number of countries, sudden but nevertheless well-publicised monetary contractions were followed by unusually low real balances (relative to the values of the variables determining their demand), rapid and severe output and employment contractions, and only later by price and money-wage responses; according to new-classical economics they should have generated price changes on the spot, and, being well publicised, only a rather mild quantity response. This is not to say that the 1980s experience was any more the outcome of a conscious attempt to implement new-classical policies than was that of the 1970s the result of a conscious 'Keynesian' experiment. Nevertheless, before the event, new-classical economists did make confident predictions about the outcome of pre-announced monetary contraction. Thus in 1979 Lucas is recorded as having said: 'Ideally we should announce a monetary expansion policy of 4 per cent annually for the next seven years and stick to it. People would respond, and inflation would be cured with a minimal risk of a deep recession.'[18]

New-classical economists are, of course, aware of all these problems, and do have responses to them. To begin with, monetary contraction will only have its major effect on prices if it is expected that the authorities will persist with such a policy. The policy must be credible, that is to say, if it is to influence behaviour by way of its effects on expectations. In a new-classical model the less credible a policy is, the more will the price-level changes it generates be misread for relative price changes, and the larger will be the quantity responses. Perhaps policy was not credible in the early 1980s, despite the publicity. As to the arrival of quantity changes before price-level responses, this could have been either the result of our observations of the price level being unreliable, since they are based upon posted prices rather than those at which trade 'really' took place, or because the downturn in question did not stem from monetary contraction after all, but from some exogenous contractionary shift on the supply side of the economy. Why were economies apparently 'off' their demand-for-money functions? Perhaps these functions were estimated using data which only imperfectly measure the true variables upon which the demand for money depends. In this case, an apparent departure of the economy from its demand-for-money function might be an illusion created by measurement error.[19]

It may, of course, be that all of these propositions have some truth to them, but it is also the case that they offer to a new-classical economist a rich array of free parameters with which to rescue his model from empirical evidence. How fast, and by what mechanisms, does any policy become credible? How can we test propositions about measurement error when they result from our inability to observe the true variables? How are we to allocate responsibility for a particular cyclical turning-point between demand-side and unobservable supply-side factors without referring to the timing and amplitudes of price and quantity fluctuations? The point of all this is not to suggest that new-classical macroeconomics is unique in relying upon *ex post*, *ad hoc* postulates about the values of free parameters to reconcile it with empirical evidence. The criticisms that its adherents advanced of alternative approaches for using free parameters were not without merit. The point is rather that new-classical economics appears to be in the same trouble as these alternative approaches because it can avoid recourse to free parameters for just so long as it avoids confrontation with empirical evidence, and no longer. That can hardly be comfortable for proponents of an approach whose major claim to superiority lies in a claim that it avoids such problems.

Perhaps the new-classical economist would answer the foregoing argument with a 'so what?' After all, Lucas did tell us in (1980) that the addition of free parameters to a new-classical model would indeed improve its predictive performance. This answer will not quite do, however. A Keynesian (or monetarist) model, to the extent that it relies on expectations, must also face up to problems concerning the credibility of policy and hence is no improvement upon a new-classical system in this respect. However, it can dispense with conjectures about unobservable supply-side shocks, measurement error, and such, when confronted with the data. If we add the postulate of price stickiness to an ordinary full-information, Walrasian general-equilibrium framework, we may model the occurrence of quantity movements in advance of price changes in the face of demand-side shocks to the economy as an equilibrating mechanism, and we have no difficulties in generating persistence over time in fluctuations in real variables, including real balances. Nor do we have to puzzle over the relative magnitudes of price–quantity fluctuations. The empirical puzzles which require new-classical economics to add free parameters do not, that is to say, arise in the Keynesian framework it seeks to supplant, once a free parameter characterising price stickiness is allowed to do its work.[20]

The choice here is between two models, one of which (the new-classical model) happens to yield predictions about output fluctuations without resort to free parameters, and one of which (the monetarist version of the Keynesian alternative) does not; and it would be an easy one to make if other predictions yielded by the new-classical model were empirically supported, but, as we have seen, they are not. The choice between new-classical and Keynesian economics is thus a choice about which free parameters to use and at what stage in the analysis to deploy them when modifying a standard full-information, Walrasian model. It is not about whether to do without them or not.

## The Price-Stickiness Postulate

In the light of the preceding discussion, the monetarist variant of the traditional Keynesian model begins to look attractive. Moreover, as I shall now argue, its attractiveness is further enhanced by the fact that the free parameters it utilises are rather harmless, linking as they do rates of change of money wages and prices to the levels of 'excess' demand and supply in particular markets.

We must be careful here, because the phrase 'excess demand' has strong overtones of disequilibrium analysis to it, which would put the concept beyond the new-classical pale. The problem is really semantic, however. We too often refer to any non-flexible-price, Walrasian system as a disequilibrium one, hence implicitly defining 'equilibrium' as being synonymous with 'competitive equilibrium'. Here the phrase 'excess demand' denotes the difference between the level of output which markets currently generate, and that at which they would clear if all prices were completely flexible and all expectations completely fulfilled, and hence is compatible with the existence of a wide variety of non-Walrasian equilibria.[21]

Now Keynesian theory does not tie down the parameters linking the rate of price change to excess demand to any precise quantitative value, but they are nevertheless *not* left to take on whatever value might be needed to reconcile a model with any data it might encounter. These parameters are required at least to take a non-negative sign, thus ruling out a rather wide variety of logically possible observations whose real world occurrence would therefore refute the Keynesian model.

More important, the price-stickiness postulate amounts to a good deal more than an unfounded *ex post* and *ad hoc* rationalisation of otherwise inexplicable observations about the interactions of quantities and prices over time. It is, at the very least, a descriptively accurate, empirical generalisation whose truth is quite independent of any macroeconomic observations. In the real world, pricing in many branches of the labour market *is* characterised by contracts which set terms for money wages and endure for rather long time periods; similar long-term contracts, also negotiated in terms of money, *do* characterise many final-output markets as well; the contracts in question *are not* all negotiated at the same time, and they *do* overlap; it *does* follow from these facts that, in the aggregate, money-wage and price levels *will* display just the kind of stickiness with respect to demand changes that Keynesian macroeconomics postulates; and it also follows that quantities *will* indeed fluctuate, as Keynesian economics says they will, instead of prices. That *is* what the work of Fischer (1977), Phelps and Taylor (1977), and Okun (1981), among others, is all about.

Moreover, the microeconomics literature *does* enable us to explain wage-and-price stickiness in terms of maximising behaviour. Barro (1972) and Kawasaki *et al.* (1983), among others, invoke costs of changing prices as a reason for the phenomenon. There exists a literature, surveyed by Hall (1980), which explains wage stickiness as the outcome of contracts designed to share the risks inherent in demand fluctuations between firms and their employees. Mancur Olson (1984) has recently argued that the existence of rent-seeking coalitions in the market sector of the economy is likely to be associated with wage-and-price stickiness, for the simple reason that such coalitions find it easier to monitor the pricing behaviour of their members than to enforce agreements about quantities.

What then is the difficulty about accepting wage-and-price stickiness? The problem is that, though it is easy enough to explain the existence of sticky wages and prices at the level of the individual experiment, it has not, thus far, proved possible to explain why the stickiness in question should characterise *money* wages and prices as opposed to *relative* wages and prices. Thus Barro (1977b) purported to show that optimal contracts should be concerned with relative prices, and argued that models dealing with them cannot therefore be used to explain money-wage and money-price stickiness. Since contracts set in money terms do exist in the real world, the correct inference to draw here is that there must be something missing from the particular maximising models that deny their occurrence. Incredibly, new-classical economists seem to have concluded that the maximising models must be correct, that the facts about contracts cannot be what they patently are, and that they therefore must not be used as a basis for an empirical generalisation which, when inserted into a macroeconomic model, helps it to yield useful predictions about the world.[22]

Now, if the claim of new-classical economics to be able to deduce everything with which it deals from nothing other than fundamental premises about tastes and technology were true, the reluctance of its proponents to use an unexplained empirical generalisation about contracts being set in terms of money would be understandable. However, quite apart from its need for 'free' parameters already discussed, new-classical economics also requires us to accept important unsupported assertions about institutional arrangements. Consider: in every new-classical model agents trade, but the existence of trade presupposes a system of property rights and legal arrangements permitting their exchange; and new-classical models are frequently used to analyse policy problems of one sort or another, but the existence of policy presupposes both that a government of some description exists, and that this institution has a capacity for purposeful behaviour.

We might prefer it if we could explain the existence of these social institutions as the outcome of the maximising behaviour of the individuals who inhabit the economy. However, we do have to start somewhere, and our inability to explain social institutions as the consequences of individual tastes and technology should not prevent us from getting on with our economics.[23] Precisely; but what is monetary exchange, including the practice of contracting in money terms, if not a social institution on the same level as property rights, markets, and government? And why should our inability to explain it prevent us assuming it as a starting-point for certain pieces of economic analysis? If we do treat monetary exchange as such a starting-point, we can of course explain money-wage and price stickiness in terms of the analysis invoked above.

To sum up, the assumption of price stickiness used in conventional Keynesian macroeconomics does permit a degree of freedom in the determination of certain parameter values that is larger than ideal. Moreover, we do not, in the current state of knowledge, have a full understanding of the phenomenon. However, given the institution of monetary exchange, money-wage and price stickiness can be explained as the result of maximising behaviour; they do exist at the micro-level, and they do have certain implications for macroeconomic phenomena that appear to conform to the facts. Given the choice, therefore, between a macroeconomics which recognises the existence of price stickiness and one which refuses to do so, there does not seem to be very much harm done if we opt for the former, particularly since the alternative approach also seems to rely on a good share of free parameters and unexplained institutional assumptions to get results with non-falsified predictive comment.

## Expectations and Credibility

The notion that the world may, and indeed ought, to be modelled as if the activities of individual agents were co-ordinated in continuously clearing, flexible-price, competitive markets is one foundation of new-classical economics. The other is the rational-expectations hypothesis. The idea that expectations about the future behaviour of prices must be important determinants of current market behaviour is an old one, as is the closely related proposition that the economy can be said to be in full equilibrium only if such expectations are fulfilled.[24] In extending these notions by arguing, first, that we should think of expectations as being the output of an economic model, knowledge of whose structure is attributed to agents, and second, that for full equilibrium to rule, the model in question must be the 'true' one of the economy under analysis, new-classical economics has made a contribution of immense importance to our understanding of these matters. Economic theory has been permanently changed by these insights, and for the better.[25] That being said, I am not enthusiastic about the way in which new-classical economists have *applied* these insights. Two issues in particular are worth considering, the first having to do with the choice of the 'model' of the economy that one attributes to agents in analysing their behaviour, and the second having to do with interaction between policy authorities and the private sector, and specifically the way in which the question of 'credibility' is handled.

For analytic exercises designed to reveal the long-run equilibrium properties of economic models, it is of course quite appropriate to attribute to agents within the model knowledge of that same model. Any other basis for expectations formation would, under some condition or other, lead agents into systematic error, causing them to revise their method of forming expectations. Hence, it could not be a component of a full equilibrium structure. To say this, however, is not to say that this same procedure is appropriate as a foundation for applied work on any particular historical episode.[26] If it is true that expectations should 'depend, in a proper way, on the same things that economic theory says actually determine that variable', then surely, when trying to understand the behaviour of a particular economy at a particular time in its history, we should attribute to agents expectations based, not on what we now believe is the proper model of that economy, but rather on what the economic theory available and believed at that time and place said was a proper model.

We may illustrate this proposition with a concrete example. Among the seminal papers of new-classical economics are empirical studies, by Robert J. Barro (1977a, 1978), of the influence of money on unemployment, output and prices in the United States since the Second World War. It is the essential claim of these papers that only 'unanticipated' changes in the quantity of money affected employment and output (relative to trend) over this period. Agents inhabiting the economy at that time are treated by Barro as believing in the equilibrium-competitive model of new-classical economics, supplemented by a primitive version of the quantity theory of money, and as using this model for forming their expectations.[27] However, if, in the 1945–76 period agents really had held new-classical beliefs, there would have been no need for a new-classical revolution. As it is, we know very well that until the mid-1970s firm beliefs in a certain kind of Keynesian economics, whose centrepiece was a permanent inflation–unemployment trade-off, were the common property of American policy-makers and key private-sector agents alike. Indeed, the primary claim made by Lucas and Sargent (1978) to support the scientific importance of their work was that it had undermined just this Keynesian consensus. That being the case, logical consistency requires new-classical economics to model the economic history of the period in question by postulating that agents operating within the US economy used an erroneous Keynesian model to form their expectations. To do otherwise would be to wind up in a hopeless logical tangle.

The point illustrated here is of course quite general. New-classical economics argues, with great persuasiveness, that the nature of agents' information about the structure of the economy is itself an important component of that structure. If that information changes, then so does the economy's behaviour. If it is right so to argue, then the state of economic knowledge itself becomes a key ingredient of any economic model, and economic history cannot be studied without recourse to the history of economic thought. This latter insight is not new, of course. It is central to the kind of Austrian economics associated particularly with the later work of von Hayek, but he was led to this position from a starting-point very similar to the stance of contemporary new-classical economists.[28] The fact that the latter insist that agents, living at any time or place, should be thought of as believing that the economy they inhabit behaves 'as if' it was driven by the mechanisms highlighted by a theory first advocated by a particular group of American economists in the 1970s, certainly sets them apart from the later Austrians. The comparison here is hardly in favour of the new-classical economists, however.

A similar type of unhistoric *naïveté* is to be found in the way in which new-classical economics approaches the problem of 'policy credibility'. It is undoubtedly true that, in a new-classical world, a well-publicised change in, say, monetary policy, will only have its effects concentrated on prices if the publicity is believed. Just as the traditional Keynesian—though his ancestors here are Meade and Tinbergen, not Keynes—viewed the policy-maker's task as the maximisation of a social-utility function subject to a constraint given by the structure of the economy, so a new-classical economist regards the typical private-sector agent as maximising a private-utility function subject to a structure determined both by the activities of other private-sector agents and by the activities of policy-makers. Suppose that both policy-makers and private-sector agents are aware of this: how do they interact? The answer, we are told, will be found by the application of 'differential game theory' in which policy-makers and private-sector agents communicate and establish credibility with one another solely through observable behaviour.[29] Ultimately in such games an 'equilibrium' emerges in which each agent's maximising behaviour imposes a constraint on the other which leads to that behaviour being sustained. Analysis of this type is intellectually challenging, but a little scepticism about its empirical relevance is surely in order.

'Policy-makers' in the real world are not entities who exist outside of their society and economy. They are endogenous, self-interested, maxi-mising agents. Moreover, they interact with the private sector in many more ways than by giving and receiving market signals to establish their credibility. In particular, they achieve the positions that they do, and maintain them, as the result of political processes in which private-sector agents participate. A whole literature in the area of 'public choice' analysis is devoted to all of this, and I am not saying anything novel in drawing attention to these matters.[30] I am however suggesting that to rest one's analysis of macroeconomic policy making on 'differential game theory' is simply to ignore this critical dimension of the policy-making process. Perhaps political institutions have nothing to do with the way in which policy is made and changed; perhaps ideology has no influence here either; but I doubt it. Rather, I suspect that the new-classical approach to the analysis of policy-making, in ignoring these factors, threatens to lead us down a blind alley.

## Concluding Comments

The bulk of this paper has been critical of new-classical macroeconomics. This does not mean that such analysis has nothing of importance to say to us: quite the contrary. Though the 'new-classical revolution' has had exaggerated claims made on its behalf, and it is these exaggerated claims that I have been concerned to criticise in this paper, it is also the case, as noted at the very outset, that 'revolutions' in macroeconomics usually leave behind them contributions of lasting importance to be absorbed into the mainstream of the discipline. The new-classical revolution has certainly done this, as I shall now argue.

Consider first the new-classical insistence on equilibrium modelling. If it is desired to construct an economics with predictive content, then the postulate that agents formulate purposeful and consistent plans, and that they are able to execute those plans, is surely a useful starting-point; but at the level of the individual, the execution of such plans is precisely what we mean when we speak of equilibrium behaviour. If assumptions about the nature of plans do not permit us to say anything about actions, as they cannot if we entertain the possibility of 'disequilibrium' at the level of the individual agent, then an economics based on the analysis of the individual can have no predictive content. This idea is an old one, to be sure, having been a constant theme in Austrian economics from Menger (1871) onwards, but a glance at the macroeconomics literature of the 1960s will soon confirm that we had lost sight of it, and needed to be reminded of its importance. New-classical economics did just that.

The difficulty with new-classical economics lies not in the equilibrium postulate *per se*, but in its insistence that we model the economy as a whole as if the equilibrium strategies of individuals were formulated and executed in an institutional framework characterised by continuously clearing competitive markets. The fact that such a framework is the only one which, in the current state of analytic techniques, permits a seamless connection between the analysis of the microeconomic equilibrium of the individual and macro-behaviour, is no reason for insisting that macro-predictions obtained by other less pristine methods are unworthy of consideration. That, though, is what new-classical macroeconomics have, quite unjustifiably, been doing. However, we ought not to let dissatisfaction with a particular application of a methodological precept lead us to underestimate its general importance. Equilibrium modelling of individuals surely ought to be the basis of macroeconomic reasoning, and the fewer empirical generalisations about behaviour we need to make to get from such a basis to empirically robust predictions about the economy as a whole, the better.

Exactly parallel arguments to these may be advanced about the rational-expectations idea. This is hardly surprising, since there is a real sense in which this hypothesis is simply a particular consequence of the purposeful maximising postulate. The idea that the state of agents' knowledge, and the nature of their expectations about future events, form a key part of the economy's current structure, and help to determine the outcome of current maximising behaviour, is hardly new. It was, as has been pointed out, a prominent ingredient of Austrian economics; but, once more, a glance at the macroeconomic literature of the 1960s (replete as it is with exercises in which the consequences of alternative policy measures are derived from the same, allegedly structural, representation of the private sector of the economy) will show how badly we needed to be reminded of this insight.

As with the equilibrium idea, criticisms of the rational-expectations notion advanced above have been of the particular and very special ways in which it has been applied, rather than of the basic idea itself. It is at best logically dubious to analyse historical episodes 'as if' agents involved in them possessed a vision of the economy which has only been created in comparatively recent years. When the very purpose of the analysis in question is to expose flaws in the economics which was commonly believed during the episode under analysis, perhaps stronger epithets are called for. Nevertheless it is important to formulate hypotheses about the way in which the state of knowledge influences the structure of the economy at particular times and places, and to investigate the way in which that structure changes in the light of actual experience and of changes in economic doctrines. That is the key implication of the rational-expectations idea for empirical work.

Problems posed by the credibility of policy for the predictive content of, macroeconomics are also real. To argue, as I have, that new-classical economists do not seem to be following the most fruitful path in investigating such matters (which probably lie in an analysis of the way in which private- and public-sector agents interact through political processes) does not alter the fact that it has been the new-classicals' initial insights which have compelled macroeconomists in general to recognise the importance of these questions. They have stressed that a positive theory of government behaviour must be an important factor conditioning private-sector behaviour, and I have criticised them, not for advancing this view, but for failing even to attempt to incorporate currently available positive theories of government into their work.

It is worth pointing out explicitly that the problems with new-classical economics discussed in this chapter are, in a fundamental sense, different aspects of a single issue. At least since the first publication of Smith's *Wealth of Nations* (1776) economists have been arguing about the extent to which a society that organises its economic activity on the basis of voluntary exchange of private property rights can be expected to achieve a coherent solution to problems of resource utilisation and allocation (not to mention distribution). From their arguments has emerged an increasingly clear understanding that the analysis of the institutional framework within which, and the processes whereby, the decisions of agents are co-ordinated—not to mention the means by which the information upon which those decisions are based is disseminated—must lie at the heart of any attempt to come to grips with these issues.

New-classical economists insist that we assume agents to possess, as common knowledge, almost all systematic information about the structure of the economy relevant to their welfare before we model their decision-making. They also insist that, in analysing the interaction of agents, we must assume that their behaviour is co-ordinated by a price mechanism which never permits their plans to be incompatible for long enough to have observable consequences. In short, new-classical economics requires that we treat certain (and extreme) propositions about a market economy's capacity for solving problems of disseminating information and co-ordinating decisions, not as hypotheses to be questioned and investigated, but as axiomatic assumptions. To adhere to the 'first principles' of analysis upon which new-classical economics is based requires that we give up questioning the coherence of economic activity co-ordinated by markets and confine our activities to describing the nature of a coherence which is presumed to exist. If the popularity of Keynesian economics in the years following the Depression was, as Lucas is said to have told *Newsweek* (4 Feb. 1985, p. 60), 'based on political needs, not economic truth', then so, surely, as Howitt (1986) has remarked, does the current popularity of new-classical economics reflect its compatibility with the ideology of the new right.

And yet the pioneers of new-classical economics are no more ideologues than was Keynes. Disinterested seriousness about following the logic of an argument wherever it might lead is surely the hallmark of the writings of Lucas and Sargent, and let it be said explicitly that in this chapter I intend to accuse them of no worse an offence than permitting this very seriousness of purpose to lead them into carrying good ideas too far and sometimes in the wrong direction. If this characterisation of the 'new-classical revolution' is accepted, it has not, of course, in this respect been different from other periods of advance in economic knowledge. The Keynesian revolution and the monetarist revolution were both in their own ways equally open to criticism on such grounds in their respective days. More to the point, in rejecting the extremes to which new-classical economics has taken them, we should not lose sight of the fact that the ideas in question are, after all, good ones. When, as I hope it will, the main thrust of macroeconomics research returns to addressing problems of 'information and co-ordination', to borrow yet another phrase from Leijonhufvud (1981), it surely will do so with a much clearer understanding of the role of purposeful, maximising individual behaviour in the solution of these problems than could have been possible had the new-classical revolution never occurred.

## Notes

1 For an account of the nature of 'revolutions' in economics, illustrated with reference to Keynesianism and monetarism, see Johnson (1971). A number of commentators—e.g. Tobin (1981a), Howitt (1986)—treat new-classical economics as a 'Mark 2' version of monetarism. For a contrary view, see Laidler (1982,

Chapter 1), who argues that whereas, from the point of view of the analytical structure of the models it utilised, monetarism was a development of Keynesian theory, new-classical economics in important respects is a throwback to the Austrian economics of the 1920s and early 1930s. This theme also runs through much of this paper but, because the adjective 'neo-Austrian' seems to upset some people, I have not used it here.

2 Lucas has made this point on a number of occasions (e.g. 1980).

3 Note that, in this essay, I am using the adjective 'Keynesian' to refer to the economics of what Lucas (1980) referred to as the 'neo-classical synthesis'. I am not talking about the 'economics of Keynes', to borrow Leijonhufvud's (1968) phrase.

4 Harry Johnson as long ago as (1970) noted the effects of 'conditioned Keynesian reflexes' in preventing the idea of a stable demand-for-money function being incorporated into British Keynesian thought. American Keynesians, such as James Tobin (e.g. 1981) and Franco Modigliani (e.g. 1977) were much more open-minded in this respect.

5 Thus Milton Friedman's early 1970s 'monetary framework' (1974) was explicitly cast in IS–LM terms, while Brunner and Meltzer (e.g. 1976a) used an extended IS–LM model to expound their important insights about the role of credit markets in the process of money creation. So strong were the IS–LM roots of Brunner and Meltzer's work at that time that at least one commentator, Dornbusch (1976a), was misled into believing that their essential contribution could be grasped without any extension at all to the IS–LM framework. Dornbusch's misconception did at least have the productive consequence of provoking an exceptionally clear statement from Brunner and Meltzer (1976b) of where they saw their contribution as lying. This author too, in analysing inflation–unemployment dynamics in (1975, Chapter 7), used a vertical LM curve IS–LM model as a starting-point.

6 The aggregate-supply-curve interpretation of the Phillips curve was not a component of early monetarism though Friedman did accept it on at least one later occasion. In (1968) he said 'Phillips' analysis . . . contains a basic defect—the failure to distinguish between *nominal* wages and *real* wages' (Friedman's italics). In a pamphlet (1975, pp. 12–14) explicitly dealing with the role of rational expectations and such in monetarist analysis, while continuing to point up this nominal–real confusion, he characterised taking 'the *rate of change of prices* as the independent variable' as 'the truth', and taking 'the level of *employment* to be the independent variable' as 'error' (Friedman's italics). Friedman's acceptance of the aggregate-supply-curve interpretation of the Phillips curve, quite clear-cut in this 1975 pamphlet, was never thoroughgoing, however. Thus, the 'framework' of 1974 is used without apology as the theoretical starting-point for the analysis contained in Friedman and Schwartz (1982) and is quite incompatible with new-classical-style equilibrium macroeconomics.

7 I have discussed these issues in some detail in Laidler (1982), particularly in Chapters 1, 3 and 4. It is this fundamental theoretical difference which leads me to treat new-classical macroeconomics as a distinct body of analysis, rather than as a simple extension of 'monetarism'.

8 Thus the paper by Lucas and Rapping (1970), among others, contained in the famous Phelps volume of 1970, was based on just such a hybrid.

9 Compare, for example, Lucas and Sargent (1978) and their recorded comments in Klamer (1984) which led Klamer himself to argue that the new-classical revolution was a matter of method and rhetoric, rather than substance. Howitt (1986a) rightly criticises Klamer for this judgement.

10 As Lucas (1980) himself acknowledged. Not so Sargent: see Klamer (1984), pp. 66–7.

11 Which is not to say that no differences remained between Keynesians and

monetarists. For example, though there is little difference between this author's views on the way in which the economy works, and those expressed by, say, Modigliani (1977) or Lipsey (1981), I am much less optimistic than are they about the scope for stabilisation policy. In general, there is considerable continuity between the policy views of monetarists and new-classicals, and it is this continuity that persuades Tobin (1981) and Howitt (1986a) to take the work of the latter as an extension of that of the former. I regard theoretical differences as decisive in this matter of classification. See Laidler (1982), particularly Chapters 1 and 3.

12 The reader's attention is drawn to the use of the word 'purposeful' here. To adherents of revealed-preference analysis, for whom consistent behaviour is logically *equivalent* to utility maximisation, as opposed to being a *consequence* of it, the methodological case for new-classical macroeconomics, particularly as it relates to the rational-expectations idea will not perhaps be as strong as I here present it. It might be noted that, in stressing the individualistic maximising foundations of their model, as opposed to its empirical content, new-classicals are reverting to a weighting of methodological criteria used by the Austrians in the 1920s and 30s. See especially Robbins (1935).

13 Lucas (1980) comes close to arguing along such lines. I do not find this style of argument persuasive.

14 In his contributions to Klamer (1984), Sargent at one point appears to accept this view of the ultimate primacy of empirical evidence: see Klamer, p. 68. However, the general thrust of his work, and that of other new-classicals, seems to be to stress the importance of deriving results from what they take to be 'first principles'. For this indulgence in the 'Cartesian fallacy' they are, rightly in my view, taken to task by Brunner in his contribution to Klamer (see pp. 191–5). The reader who is familiar with Brunner's methodological views on these issues will recognise the common debt that we both owe to Karl Popper.

15 See, e.g., Sargent's comments in Klamer (1984), pp. 75–6.

16 On the matter of real wages and employment, see Geary and Kennan (1982).

17 See Laidler (1982), Chapter 2 and Lane (1983) for discussion of this matter.

18 See *Time* magazine, 27 Aug. 1979, p. 29. The basis of such prediction as this was the Sargent and Wallace (1976) analysis of the effects of rational expectations on the ability of the monetary authorities to influence real variables. Nowadays it is claimed that this paper was taken more seriously and literally by its readers than by its authors. (See Sargent in Klamer 1984, pp. 70–1). Certainly, the opening of the paper in question suggests that the analysis which it contains is to be treated as a counterexample to a prevailing Keynesian view of policy, rather than as a serious alternative, but its last two or three pages mount a strong case for treating it as just such an alternative.

19 A new-classical economist should treat the 'credibility' alibi with care. Before the event, Sargent and Wallace (1976, p. 181) developed what they characterised as a 'telling argument' against its empirical relevance. On the matter of the demand for money, see Goodfriend (1985) and Kohn and Manchester (1985).

20 Chapter 5, below, demonstrates that price stickiness is an *alternative* to new-classical assumptions in generating such results rather than a supplement to them, and does so in terms of a model in which agents are all 'in equilibrium' in the sense of being able to execute their *ex ante* plans, albeit not with the expected results *ex post*. Note that some new-classical economists—e.g. Barro (1977b)—have argued that even with sticky-wage-and-price contracts it is possible to model quantity fluctuations as taking place 'as if' they reflected appropriate market-clearing responses to variations in agents' perceptions of the marginal product and marginal disutility of labour. This is true enough, but it is hard to take seriously as an empirical proposition because it implies that agents have enough information to

take market-clearing decisions in the absence of price signals. For a discussion of this, see Laidler (1982), Chapter 3, pp. 90–2.

21 Recent work by Diamond (1984) and Howitt (1985) on search equilibria suggests that we ought not to take such uniqueness for granted once we get away from an economy presided over by a Walrasian auctioneer. The work to which I refer here provides a complementary analysis of potentially great importance to short-run sticky-price macroeconomic models.

22 Montgomery and Shaw (1985) have investigated the role of money-wage stickiness in an otherwise new-classical framework and have conceded it to be a pervasive phenomenon, but have argued that it has little explanatory power over quantity fluctuations. The basis for this last conclusion appears to be the assumption that, wage contracts notwithstanding, money prices are perfectly flexible, and hence it misses the point of Keynesian analysis which models quantity fluctuations as an alternative equilibrating mechanism to price fluctuations, and not as a response to them.

23 However, see Rowe (1989) for a pioneering attempt to come to grips with problems of this sort.

24 The argument was well developed by Hayek (1928), and according to Hansson (1983) a slightly later version of it, developed initially by Gunnar Myrdal, was seminal to much Swedish dynamic economics in the 1930s. See also McCloughry (1984).

25 I have developed this argument at greater length in Laidler (1984). The interaction of expectations and the structure of the economy is most fully developed by Lucas (1976) in what I suspect will turn out to be the most durably important paper of the new-classical revolution.

26 Thus I stand by the judgement offered by Laidler and Parkin (1975), p. 771, that 'The Rational Expectations hypothesis . . . is probably better suited to a characterisation of expectations formation in the very long run'. I do not wish to imply that my co-author would still subscribe to this view, though.

27 The argument here abstracts from more down-to-earth issues, such as whether the proposition that only 'unanticipated money' affects output is uniquely a prediction of new-classical macroeconomics (it isn't —see Chapter 5 below) or whether the data actually do support Barro's analysis (they don't appear to—see Mishkin, 1982).

28 Hayek paid increasing attention to the problems of knowledge as a determinant of economic behaviour and became less and less inclined to ascribe empirical content to what we would now call a full rational-expectations equilibrium, such as he described in (1928), from the mid-1930s onwards. The turning-point in his thought is perhaps to be found in Hayek (1937). On this matter see also McCloughry (1984).

29 Both Lucas and Sargent recommend differential game theory in their contributions to Klamer (1984): see pp. 55, 73. It is instructive to compare their discussion of this issue with Karl Brunner's contribution to the same volume, pp. 185–6. Brunner has, of course, long been acutely aware of the role of political processes in forming policies and conditioning the private sector's responses to them.

30 The contribution of Mancur Olson (1982, 1984) and of James Buchanan and his associates (see, e.g. Buchanan, Tulloch and Tollison, 1980) to this literature are well known. It is surely no accident that two prominent monetarists who have refused to join the 'new-classical revolution', Karl Brunner and Allan Meltzer, have also worked in the public choice area. It should also be noted that Harry Johnson drew similar conclusions to those developed here about the interaction of expectations, policy, and political processes as long ago as 1972: see (1972a).

# 5

## Some Macroeconomic Implications of Price Stickiness

### *Introduction*

Macroeconomic theory has two tasks: to explain important facts about the behaviour of real-world economies, and to provide a framework for analysing policy issues. It is expected to carry them out using an approach which is, as nearly as is feasible, logically compatible with microeconomic analysis. New-classical macroeconomics, largely the creation of Robert E. Lucas, Jr. (1972, 1973), is explicitly Walrasian in its foundations. Starting from the postulate of rational, maximising, individual agents operating in competitive markets, and without resort to any assumption of price stickiness, it explains certain facts about the occurrence of output fluctuations, and their co-movement with the general price level. Also, as Sargent and Wallace (1976) were the first to show, new-classical macroeconomics can, in certain simple situations, yield the implication that only unanticipated (and, therefore, if expectations are rational, random) monetary policy affects real economic variables. New-classical theory's explanatory power, over a wider range of facts than those mentioned above, leaves something to be desired. Specifically, not only does real output fluctuate, but its fluctuations persist over time; and real-money balances also vary in a persistent fashion around the values predicted by the long-run demand-for-money function. This behaviour, too, ought to be explained by a satisfactory macroeconomic model.

Now these facts can of course be explained by a *suitably extended* new-classical model. If we postulate rising marginal costs of changing output, persistence of output fluctuations arises as a consequence. If we assume that the arguments of the long-run demand-for-money function are measured with systematic error, we can also explain the stylised facts about the short-run demand-for-money function.[1] However, though as a general proposition the introduction of the information imperfections that are central to new-classical analysis into a basic Walrasian framework may be defended on grounds of *a priori* plausibility, no one has shown how the specific form such problems are postulated to take in that analysis relates to the maximising behaviour of individuals. New-classical analysis simply starts from the assumption that agents have certain information and not other knowledge. Its basis is, to this extent, *ad hoc*; and to add assumptions about adjustment costs and measurement error, as the range of facts to be explained is widened, simply compounds its arbitrary content.

In this chapter I shall show that introducing elements of price stickiness into a basic Walrasian model is enough to reconcile it with the above-mentioned facts. The price stickiness in question, as we shall see, must be persistent in order to produce these results. Though there is nothing new in the proposition that price stickiness enables us easily to generate persistent quantity fluctuations in a macro-model, the model's implications about the behaviour of money holdings do have more novelty, as we shall also see. Thus I shall argue that the price-stickiness assumption, because of its greater explanatory power, enables us to build a macroeconomic model which is, in a well-defined sense, less *ad hoc* than the new-classical alternative. I shall also show that a model based on price stickiness can yield a form of the Sargent–Wallace policy-ineffectiveness result. Those readers who find this latter proposition attractive need not therefore be deterred from considering the implications of price stickiness for fear of having to abandon it.

I shall not provide a rigorous justification in maximising behaviour for the existence of the type of price stickiness I shall postulate, any more than new-classical economists have explained why agents in their models know about some prices and not others, while simultaneously being equipped with both perfect knowledge concerning the variances of relative prices and the absolute price level, and the computational skills necessary costlessly to solve the signal-extraction problems that face them. However, to say that something has not been explained in terms of maximising behaviour is not the same thing as saying that it cannot be so explained. The analysis presented here does not purport to make a complete case for rehabilitating the price-stickiness assumption, but, in showing that it has more explanatory power than might previously have been believed, it does at least suggest that its microfoundations would be well worth investigating.

## Basic Analysis

The economy to be analysed is simple indeed. It is inhabited by firms and households which produce and consume non-durable goods. Exchange is mediated by money and, as an adjunct to their trading activity, agents hold money. As is common in macro-modelling, assets are classified as money and 'all others', so that the demand-for-money function completely characterises asset choice in this economy. Population and other resource endowments are given, and there is no economic growth. Time is divided into 'weeks', within which consumption, production, and money-holding decisions are formulated and executed. The technology used to produce output is such that where prices are free to vary, the supply of goods is a rising function of their relative price. The goods in question are heterogeneous, and output in the economy is measured as an appropriate index number. The supply of nominal money is exogenously given, and its quantity is determined at the beginning of each week. For individual agents, the general price level is exogenous, and so they vary their real balances by acquiring and disposing of nominal balances in exchange for goods as well as other assets. When they are not holding the quantity of real balances that they require, agents attempt to adjust them towards their long-run target level in part by varying their volume of planned expenditures, the target level in question being determined as a function of permanent income, which in this economy is a constant.[2] This assumption that the demand for money depends only upon permanent income is made purely for the sake of simplicity. No important results depend upon it, and I shall relax it later.

The foregoing assumptions will be maintained throughout the analysis of this section. The process by which prices are formed will vary, however. Suppose, first, that a fully-fledged Walrasian pricing mechanism is allowed to work, so that the economy operates 'as if' the prices of all goods were set by an 'auctioneer' at their market-clearing levels, and 'as if' every agent had full and costless knowledge of all those prices. With given tastes and technology, the level (and structure) of output will be constant period after period at its 'permanent' level; and, perhaps not quite so obviously, the general price level will move in strict proportion to the quantity of nominal money. This will be true even if only partial, as opposed to full, adjustment of money holdings towards their target level characterises the plans of individuals. The costs of portfolio adjustment that lead to slow adjustment on the part of individuals are not encountered when a completely, and to them costlessly, flexible price level changes real balances for them.[3]

As is well known, the basic new-classical model departs from the system I have just described in two ways. First, a stochastic element is introduced into the behaviour of relative prices and the absolute price level. Second, full information about the money prices of goods, other than those which they plan to sell, is withheld from agents when their production plans are made and executed. Hence, agents must form estimates of relative prices, and therefore of the general price level, when they make their plans about quantities, and they do so in the following way. First, agents use all the information available to them up until the end of the previous period to form a rational expectation of the general price level ruling in the current period. Since they know that the price level is determined by the interaction of the supply of nominal money and the demand for real balances, this expectation is based on rational forecasts of both magnitudes. They then modify this expectation in the light of information conveyed to them by the money price of their own output, thereby generating an estimate of what might helpfully be called the currently perceived price level. Finally, they use the resulting estimate in computing the relative price on which they base their production decisions. It is worth pointing out that this currently perceived price level might also be treated by agents as the relevant variable by which to deflate their nominal balances when they calculate their real money holdings; and, if this step is taken, the behaviour of the new-classical model is altered in ways which are hard to square with empirical evidence. It is more usual to deflate nominal balances by the actual price level, a procedure which would be appropriate if agents calculated their real balances using the price of the particular good they sold. Since it is desirable to present the new-classical model in as favourable a light as possible here, it is this latter, more conventional, assumption that is used.[4]

A log-linear version of the above simple new-classical system may be written as follows, where: $y^*$ is the permanent component of the logarithm of income; $y$ is its transitory component; $m$ is the logarithm of nominal money; $Em_s|I_{-1}$ is the nominal money supply that agents at the end of period $-1$ rationally expect to circulate during the current period, given information available up to the end of period $-1$; $p$ is the logarithm of general price level; $Ep|I_{-1}$ is a rational expectation of $p$ formed at the end of period $-1$; and $Ep|I$ is that expectation as modified by contemporaneously available information, or, as we have termed it, the currently perceived price level.

$$m_s = m_d = \delta_0 + \delta_1 y^* + p \tag{1}$$
$$y = v(p - Ep|I) \tag{2}$$
$$Ep|I_{-1} = Em_s|I_{-1} - (\delta_0 + \delta_1 y^*) = Em_s|I_{-1} - m_{s-1} + p_{-1} \tag{3}$$
$$Ep|I = (1 - \theta)p + \theta Ep|I_{-1} \tag{4}$$

Four clarifying comments about this model are in order here. First, $v$ is a structural parameter derived from the economy's aggregate production function. Second, equation (4) is Lucas's (1973) formulation, and the assumptions needed to derive it are described there in considerable detail. Third, the simplifying assumption that the demand for money is independent of the interest rate may be defended by postulating that money bears interest at a competitive market rate. Finally, with full current information, so that $\theta = 0$ this model reduces to the simple Walrasian constant output system discussed earlier.

Substituting (4) into (2) produces a more commonly-used form of the new-classical aggregate supply curve,

$$y = \mu(p - Ep|I_{-1}) \tag{2a}$$

where

$$\mu = \nu\theta$$

This model yields the following reduced forms to describe output and real balances:

$$y = \mu(m_s - Em_s|I_{-1}) \tag{5}$$

$$m_s - p = \delta_0 + \delta_1 y^* \tag{6}$$

Thus the new-classical model explains output fluctuations as being caused by unanticipated fluctuations in the money supply, without giving up the assumption of price flexibility and clearing markets; but it does not, in the absence of further extension, predict any persistence of fluctuations in output, nor does it predict systematic deviations of actual money holdings from their long-run desired level.[5]

Consider now an alternative version of the same basic model which introduces an element of price stickiness to *replace* the new-classical postulate that agents do not have contemporaneous access to information about the general price level, so that, in what follows, everyone is permitted to know that variable's value. Suppose that two kinds of sellers operate in the system, producing goods which are imperfect substitutes for one another: 'fix-price' firms who set their prices for the current period at the end of the previous period, basing them on expectations formed using information then available, and who stand ready to sell any amount of output at those prices; and 'flex-price' firms who may vary their prices as well as their output in response to demand pressures during the current period. The existence of fix-price firms, which are essentially the same as those postulated by McCallum (1980) in his discussion of the role of price stickiness in macroeconomics, can be justified by the possibility that, for some firms, the costs of price changes are high, relative to those of varying output.[6]

Before setting out a formal analysis of this model, an intuitive analysis of its properties (which do not, as will be shown in the next section of this chapter, depend upon the particular simple form of the demand-for-money function used here) will be helpful. Consider a week following one in which all price expectations were fulfilled and in which the economy was, therefore, in full equilibrium at permanent income; let expectations about this week's prices have been formed, and then let the nominal money supply be unexpectedly increased. With prices initially set at their expected levels, there will exist an excess supply of real balances, giving rise to a planned increase in agents' rate of flow of expenditure. This extra expenditure will be distributed between fix-price and flex-price producers. The former will, by assumption, supply any extra output demanded but the latter will raise the relative (and hence the money) prices of their output in order to reduce the demand facing them.

This price increase will have two effects. The overall increase in the demand for goods will be damped down as real balances are reduced; and its composition will be switched towards the output of fix-price producers. If there were no fix-price sellers, then the attempts of flex-price firms to raise their relative prices would be frustrated and, with each firm having full knowledge of the current price level, the latter variable would be forced up until the excess supply of money that caused the initial increase in demand for goods was completely eliminated. We would be back in a full Walrasian system just as we would be in the new-classical model if we allowed agents contemporaneous access to correct information about the general price level. So long as there are some fix-price sellers in the system, however, the process will stop short of this point. The price level will increase less than in proportion to the increase in the quantity of nominal money. An excess supply of real balances and its associated rate of flow of expenditure (and hence of output) will therefore persist and be observed.[7]

It will be apparent that the mechanisms just described represent an *alternative* way of escaping from the constant output prediction of the full Walrasian version of our basic system to those implied by new-classical limited-information assumptions. Even so, there is one noteworthy parallel between this sticky-price model and its new-classical counterpart: both are 'equilibrium' systems in the sense that all agents are able to execute all plans which they formulate; but both depart from full *Walrasian* equilibrium in permitting the *ex post* outcomes of those plans to differ from the *ex ante* intentions of agents. In the new-classical model, agents supply more output because they believe that their own relative price has risen but, after the event, discover their belief to have been false. In the sticky-price model, agents plan, *ex ante, as individuals*, to run down their cash balances by increasing expenditure but, *ex post, in the aggregate*, succeed in doing so only to the extent that the general price level rises. Unplanned fluctuations in 'buffer-stocks' of money absorb the differences between *ex ante* plans made by individual maximising agents and the *ex post* outcome of the market experiments thus set in motion.

Though the sticky-price model generates somewhat similar results about the capacity of monetary shocks to generate output fluctuations to those yielded by the new-classical framework, it yields different predictions about other factors. Just how different these predictions are depends upon which version of the two alternative forms of the expectations hypothesis embodied in equation (3) above we utilise. These two are equivalent in the new-classical model but not here.[8] In the new-classical model it was always true that

$$p = m_s - (\delta_0 + \delta_1 y^*) \tag{7}$$

Here it is not, but

$$Ep|I_{-1} = Em_s|I_{-1} - (\delta_0 + \delta_1 y^*) \tag{3a}$$

and

$$Ep|I_{-1} = Em_s|I_{-1} - m_{s-1} + p_{-1} \tag{3b}$$

are only equivalent expressions if equation (7) is true.

Our sticky-price model thus comes in two forms, depending upon which version of equation (3) we use. Equation (3b) ensures that prices are sticky not only *within* each period but between periods as well, and the economic interpretation of the differences here will be taken up again in due course. For the moment, note that the model's other equations are as follows:

$$m_d = \delta_0 + \delta_1 y^* + p \tag{1a}$$
$$y = \alpha(m_s - m_d) \tag{8a}$$
$$p = \beta y + Ep|I_{-1} \tag{9}$$

Equation (9) is, of course, algebraically equivalent to equation (2a) but is written as it is here to emphasise that the mechanisms linking output and price fluctuations in this system described above differ from those underlying the new-classical aggregate supply curve. Combined with equation (3a), this model yields the following reduced forms for output and real balances:

$$y = \frac{\alpha}{1 + \alpha\beta} (m_s - Em_s|I_{-1}) \tag{10a}$$

and

$$m_s - p = \delta_0 + \delta_1 y^* + \frac{1}{1 + \alpha\beta}(m_s - Em_s|I_{-1}) \tag{11a}$$

Combined with equation (3b) it implies instead:

$$y = \frac{\alpha}{1 + \alpha\beta}(m_s - Em_s|I_{-1}) + \frac{1}{1 + \alpha\beta}y_{-1} \tag{10b}$$

and

$$m_s - p = \frac{\alpha\beta}{1 + \alpha\beta}(\delta_0 + \delta_1 y^*) + \frac{1}{1 + \alpha\beta}(m_{s-1} - p_{-1})$$
$$+ \frac{1}{1 + \alpha\beta}(m_s - Em_s|I_{-1}) \tag{11b}$$

Though the interpretation of its parameters is rather different, equation (10a) is essentially indistinguishable from (5). This simple fact shows that empirical evidence to the effect that only 'unanticipated' money affects output does not enable us to distinguish between a new-classical flexible-price model and one incorporating price stickiness. Nevertheless, fix-price firms in this model base their prices on last period's information only. They are not permitted to vary them within the period if new data come to them. Thus full information about this period's money supply, made available during the period, would not cancel out the output effect as it would in a new-classical model. To this extent the implications of the new models do differ. Equation (11a) differs from (6) in having an 'unanticipated' money term on its right-hand side, and this latter difference might provide some further basis for distinguishing between the two versions of the basic model by referring to empirical evidence. However, this difference is, perhaps, a minor matter in the light of the properties of equations (10b) and (11b).

As is immediately apparent, these two equations are characterised by just the type of persistence effects which we would like any satisfactory macro-model to generate. Output's deviations from its permanent level are positively serially correlated in equation (10b), even though only unexpected money-supply variations have real effects. In this model, because the monetary authorities cannot vary the money supply more frequently than agents in the private sector can vary their prices, then, provided that $Em_s|I_{-1}$ is indeed a rational expectation of the money supply, standard policy-ineffectiveness results still hold. Equation (11b), the reduced form for real balances, contains a lagged dependent variable whose positive, and fractional, coefficient enables us to identify the parameters of the long-run demand-for-money function. Indeed, if 'unanticipated money' is a random variable and we write

$$\lambda - \frac{\alpha\beta}{1 + \alpha\beta}$$

then, (11b) may be written as a standard Goldfeld 'short-run demand-for-money function'

$$m_s - p = \lambda(\delta_0 + \delta_1 y^*) + (1 - \lambda)(m_{s-1} - p_{-1}) + (1 - \lambda)(m_s - Em_s|I_{-1})$$

Furthermore, Carr and Darby (1981) have suggested that 'anticipated money' belongs as an extra variable on the right-hand side of such an equation, and the model under analysis here provides an analytic foundation for this postulate.

It is easy to explain as a mechanical matter why equation (3b) produces these results. The equation in question introduces an element of persistence into our model's price stickiness and equation (3a) does not. With the latter, price stickiness is purely a within-period phenomenon.

Last week's prices have no effect on this week's outcome for anything. In the case of (3b), any departure of the model from full equilibrium last week will have consequences this week because of the use of the previous week's price level as a base from which to extrapolate expectations about this week's prices, expectations which fixed-price producers use to set their actual prices.[9] It should be noted that the *unconditional* expectations embedded in the model by using (3b) are nevertheless rational. Equation (11b) is a stochastic-difference equation which, in the long run, converges on the demand-for-money function for any systematic behaviour of the money supply that is captured in $Em_s|I_{-1}$. There is, that is to say, no room for systematic error in the long run in this model and hence no room for systematic monetary policy to have any lasting effects on real variables.

Even so, equation (3a) provides *conditional* expectations which are rational as well. It permits no systematic short-run errors to be made. In this respect it is undoubtedly a more immediately appealing formulation. Furthermore, the results that the model has generated about the behaviour of real balances arise in the context of a very simple form of the long-run demand-for-money function, and yet this model's main claim to novelty involves just those results. If the foregoing analysis is to be taken seriously, I must show both that the demand-for-money results are robust with respect to more elaborate formulations of the function and that there exist arguments for not dismissing short-run non-rationality of expectations out of hand. It is to a discussion of these issues that I now turn.

## Some Extensions

The model analysed in the previous section of this chapter was simple indeed, and there must naturally be some suspicion that the results it generated depend for their essential properties upon that simplicity. In particular, empirical evidence tells us that the demand for money is certainly related to the nominal rate of interest, and perhaps to transitory income as well as permanent income. Moreover, the nominal interest rate is usefully thought of as being the sum of a real interest rate and the expected inflation rate and, in turn, the former is thought of as exerting an influence on aggregate demand. A macro-model incorporating these properties is a good deal more elaborate than that analysed above but it does, as we shall now see, yield essentially the same predictions about the behaviour of output and real balances.

Defining new variables as follows: $r$ is the level (*not the log*) of the nominal interest rate; $\rho^*$ the 'normal' (in the Wicksellian sense) level of the real rate of interest; $\rho$ the difference between the current value of the real rate of interest and its 'normal' level; and otherwise using the same symbols as before, we may write

$$m_d1 = \delta_0 + \delta_1 y^* + \delta_2 y - \delta_3 r + p \tag{1b}$$

$$y = \alpha_1'(m_s - m_d) - \alpha_2 \rho \tag{8b}$$

$$\rho = -\gamma(m_s - m_d) \tag{12}$$

$$r = \rho^* + \rho + Ep_{+1}|I - p \tag{13}$$

$$p = \beta y + Ep|I_{-1} \tag{9}$$

$$Ep|I_{-1} = Em_s|I_{-1} - m_{s-1} + p_{-1} \tag{3b}$$

Here, note that if $\delta_2 = \delta_1$ we have a current-income form of the demand-for-money function. Apart from that, only equations (12) and (13) need any comment. Equation (12) argues that the rate of interest out of full equilibrium is determined by loanable-funds effects, under which an excess flow demand for bonds is created by an excess stock of money.[10] Equation (13) relates the nominal interest rate to the real rate using a Fisher effect. Note that here it is the *current* period's expectations of inflation that enter into things, rather than the previous period's as in equation (9), in order to capture the idea of relatively rapid adjustment of asset markets to information.

With some manipulation, this more complex model may be made to yield the following reduced form for output:

$$y = \frac{\alpha_1}{1 + \alpha_1(\delta_2 + \beta - \delta_3\beta) + \delta_3\gamma}[(m_s - Em_s|I_{-1}) - \delta_3(m_s - E|M_{s+1}|I)]$$

$$+ \frac{1 + \alpha_1\delta_2 + \delta_3\gamma}{1 + \alpha_1(\delta_2 + \beta - \delta_3\beta) + \delta_3\gamma} y_{-1} \tag{14}$$

where

$$\alpha_1 \equiv (\alpha_1' + \alpha_2\gamma) \tag{15}$$

The model's properties are, that is to say, in some respects much like those yielded by its simpler version. Unanticipated shocks to the money supply still cause real-output effects which persist, but expected monetary expansion between now and the next period also has real effects in the current period because of its effects on the current value of the real interest rate taken in combination with fix-price firms' inability to vary current prices. Thus the Sargent–Wallace policy-ineffectiveness result vanishes, as it often does in models in which expected inflation influences the demand for money.

As to the behaviour of real balances, if we substitute (3b) into (9), (12) into (8b), and then combine the two resulting expressions, we get

$$(1 + \alpha_1\beta)p = \alpha_1\beta(m_s - \delta_0 - \delta_1 y^* - \delta_2 y + \delta_3 r)$$

$$+ Em_s|I_{-1} - m_{s-1} + p_{-1} \tag{16}$$

Solving this expression for $p$, changing all signs, and adding $m_s$ to each side, yields:

$$m_s - p = \frac{\alpha_1\beta}{1 + \alpha_1\beta}(\delta_0 + \delta_1 y^* + \delta_2 y - \delta_3 r)$$

$$+ \frac{1}{1 + \alpha_1\beta}(m_{s-1} - p_{-1}) + \frac{1}{1 + \alpha_1\beta}(m_s - Em_s|I_{-1}) \quad (17)$$

This is, once more, an expression exactly akin to a Goldfeld 'short-run demand-for-money function' with an error term defined by 'unanticipated money'. This expression is, however, not a short-run demand-for-money function at all, but a quasi-reduced form of the complete model in which the parameters of the long-run demand-for-money function happen to be just identified.

Finally, it should be noted that, if we define

$$\alpha \equiv \frac{\alpha_1}{1 + \alpha_1\delta_2}$$

we may derive by further manipulation of (17):

$$m_s - p = \frac{\alpha\beta}{1 + \alpha\beta}(\delta_0 + \delta_1 y^* - \delta_3 r) + \frac{1}{1 + \alpha\beta}(m_{s-1} - p_{-1})$$

$$+ \frac{\alpha\beta}{1 + \alpha\beta}(m_s - Em_s|I_{-1}) \quad (17a)$$

Like equation (17) this expression is a quasi-reduced form of the complete model, and not a short-run demand-for-money function. Perhaps the possibility of deriving an expression which identifies the parameters linking the demand for money to the rate of interest and, crucially, permanent income in a system in which the demand for money depends upon transitory income too explains the difficulties that have been encountered over the years in using single-equation techniques to distinguish between permanent-income and current-income formulations of the demand-for-money function.

So far I have shown that the sticky-price model's predictions, notably those about the behaviour over time of real balances, which are after all novel and empirically interesting ones, do not depend upon the particularly simple formulation of the model employed in the previous section of this chapter. To this extent I have strengthened the case for taking the sticky-price postulate seriously. Nevertheless, my results depend not just on prices being sticky but on that stickiness persisting between periods; and this, in turn, involves expectations departing from a fully rational ideal in the short run. This property does not lead the model to predict any kind of permanent trade-off between output and inflation, such as characterised the Keynesian models of the 1960s, or even a systematic short-run one, such as is implicit in a model that uses error-learning or any other such mechanical-expectations generator. This sticky-price model is free of those characteristics of its predecessors which, rightly, trouble such commentators as McCallum (1986). Even so, the departure of the expectations embedded in the system from complete short-run rationality needs defending.

Such a defence might begin by noting that if they are to use the fully rational equation (3a), agents need to form the same money-supply expectations as they do to apply (3b), but they also need to know the parameters of the economy's aggregate demand-for-money function and to form expectations about its arguments. The extra degree of rationality in expectations obtained from equation (3a) would have to be bought at the expense of more investment on the part of agents in acquiring information. In a world where relevant information is costly, rather than being available free of charge, we cannot take it for granted that it will be acquired and used. It may not be worth agents' while to do so.

To require agents to estimate the parameters of the economy's demand-for-money function in a new-classical world is not onerous since there they are in any event presumed to be capable of solving the signal-extraction problem underlying the aggregate supply curve, equation (4). However, one of the advantages of a model built on price stickiness is that we do not have to credit agents with any more ability and knowledge than it takes to look up data on prices and the money supply, form an expectation about the latter, and base a price-level forecast on that expectation.[11] On the other hand, in the simple version of my model, the demand for real balances is simply $\delta_0+\delta_1 y^*$, and this defines the long-run average value of real balances in this system. If we took this version of the model as literally true, then it could be argued that even agents who started out using (3b) might be expected to learn how to use (3a) in due course.

It would be a different matter with a more complex demand-for-money function such as used in the model analysed earlier in this section. In that more 'realistic' system, fully rational expectations would be a good deal more costly to compute. Note, moreover, that, as Brunner and Meltzer (1971) long ago argued, money is a social institution which enables agents to economise on resources devoted to the generation of information. This idea turns up in 'buffer stock' models such as that analysed here, in the way in which fluctuations in money holdings absorb the consequences of errors in agents' *ex ante* plans.[12] A world in which fluctuations in money holdings enable agents to reduce the costs of misinformation is a world in which the incentives to reduce that misinformation to some technically feasible minimum, regardless of the resource costs of doing so, are reduced.

The foregoing argument, though perhaps plausible, will not quite do. Equation (3b) says that the expected rate of inflation used by fix-price firms to set their prices is equal to the expected rate of monetary expansion. Even if the firms in question remain ignorant of the economy's aggregate demand-for-money function, they can easily perceive that when the economy operates above (below) its long-run capacity in a particular period, then in the next period inflation exceeds (falls short of) the rate of monetary expansion. They could easily enough use such information to improve upon the expectations described in (3b). We can capture this idea by writing

$$Ep|I_{-1} = Em_s|I_{-1} - m_{s-1} + p_{-1} + \psi y_{-1} \tag{3c}$$

At first sight this seems to make no essential difference to the foregoing analysis. Modifying the simple version of our model in this way gives us, for output:

$$y = \frac{\alpha}{1 + \alpha\beta} (m_s - Em_s|I_{-1}) + \frac{1 - \alpha\psi}{1 + \alpha\beta} y_{-1} \tag{10c}$$

and for real balances:

$$m_s - p = \frac{\alpha\beta + \alpha\psi}{1 + \alpha\beta} (\delta_0 + \delta_1 y^*) + \frac{(1 - \alpha\psi)}{1 + \alpha\beta} (m_{s-1} - p_{-1})$$

$$+ \frac{1}{1 - \alpha\beta} (m_s - Em_s|I_{-1}) \tag{11c}$$

However, as the reader may readily verify, the 'first impression' that one gets from the above equations depends upon the condition

$$\psi < \frac{1}{\alpha} \tag{18}$$

holding. If we had equality here, which we would if agents correctly anticipated the amount of future price-level 'catch-up' that would follow a given departure of the economy from its long-run equilibrium output level, expectations would be rational, and persistence effects would be banished from the model. Is there any reason, then, to believe that maximising agents' estimates of $\psi$ will be systematically too small?

An argument which obviously owes much to Lucas's (1973) treatment of price-level expectations might be constructed as follows. Suppose, as it is empirically plausible to do, that by the time at which they must make their pricing decisions, individual firms have no information upon economy-wide output levels but only about their own sales and output. Suppose, further, that the latter variables are subjected to the effects of economy-wide and local shocks. Then, when the economy is hit with an aggregate demand shock, each firm, looking at its own sales and output, will attribute part of this departure from normal to local conditions and hence will underestimate the amount by which the economy as a whole is away from full equilibrium. In turn, each firm singly, and therefore all firms collectively, will underestimate the amount of price-level catch-up that is to come; but this is, of course, what we require if the economy is to behave 'as if' $\psi$ were systematically underestimated.

Now neither the foregoing arguments, nor any others, can make expectations that are not fully rational conform to the rational ideal. All they can do, and are intended to do, is suggest that in the presence of real-resource costs of forming expectations it might be economically rational (to use the phrase coined by Feige and Pearce, 1976) to stop short of this ideal. The basic analytic message of this and the preceding section of this chapter is that price stickiness which persists for more than one period yields empirically interesting predictions and that persistence of expectational error is one way of doing this and perhaps those who find anything less than completely rational expectations unpalatable might be encouraged to explore them.[13]

## Summary and Conclusions

It was the purpose of this chapter to show that a price-stickiness assumption was sufficient to enable us to explain not only why output fluctuates in response to monetary shocks and why such output fluctuations persist over time, but also why real balances vary, with positive serial correlation, around their long-run desired value. This has now been done and, though I claim no novelty for the first two predictions, it is surely of interest that the third of them can be shown to follow from the same assumption. It is also worthwhile to remind the reader of certain other desirable implications of the price-stickiness assumption which emerged in the course of the preceding analysis.

First, in the presence of price stickiness it is, as we noted, the expectation of the money supply formed at the end of period $-1$ that appears of necessity on the right-hand side of equations (10a), (10b) or (10c). This is of some interest because, as Boschen and Grossman (1982) have shown, if agents operating in an otherwise new-classical system have contemporaneous information about the value of the money supply, that is enough to prevent correctly measured fluctuations in this variable having effects on real variables. In the world as it is, such information is available at very low cost indeed but, as Boschen and Grossman also show, correctly measured and announced variations in the money supply do indeed seem to have real effects. Quite obviously, this observation, difficult to reconcile with new-classical macroeconomics, can easily be explained in a world in which some agents set prices on the basis of past information and are unable to change them even when provided with new data.

Second, in addition to the lagged dependent variable that appears on the right-hand side of equations (11b) or (11c), there is also a term in unanticipated money. As was pointed out above, Carr and Darby (1981) some time ago argued that such a term should indeed appear on the right-hand side of a 'short-run demand-for-money function' and justified this claim with an intuitive argument closely related to the analysis presented above. This analysis shows, however, that the equation in question is not a structural demand-for-money function at all but rather a reduced form or quasi-reduced form of a complete macro-model, and, to this extent, it considerably clarifies Carr and Darby's arguments. It also provides an explanation of why they and Laidler (1980) did indeed find a statistically significant role for unanticipated money to play in an equation very like (11b) or (11c) and essentially identical to (17).[14]

Closely related to the above point, it is well known that the last decade or so has seen considerable instability in the so-called 'short-run demand-for-money-functions' upon which the conduct of monetary policy in a number of countries has been based. Such functions are essentially similar to (11b), (11c) or (17) with the unanticipated money term on the right-hand side omitted. With a given monetary policy regime, one might expect 'unanticipated money' to be a serially uncorrelated variable with a zero mean, and in such circumstances its omission would create no problems. However, when the stance of policy is systematically changing, this variable might well be serially correlated and have a non-zero mean for as long as it takes the general public to learn about the change in question. To omit it at such times will lead to apparent shifts of the intercept of an equation such as (11b), (11c) or (17) downwards when policy is becoming systematically less inflationary, and vice versa. Thus, the analysis presented in this paper provides an important clue in the cases of the 'missing money' in the United States during the early 1970s, the unexpected velocity shift there in 1981–2, and the variations in M2 velocity in Britain in the 1970s recently analysed by Artis and Lewis (1984).[15]

The foregoing argument is, of course, a particular application of the so-called 'Lucas' Critique'—see Lucas (1976)—but the 'demand for money' is by no means the only aspect of the model analysed in this paper to which Lucas's argument is relevant. The parameter $\beta$, which measures the responsiveness of the price level to shifts in the level of aggregate demand and output, clearly has its value determined by the relative numbers of fix- and flex-price firms in the economy, among other factors. Parkin (1986a) has shown both that individual firms may choose their pricing strategy and that this choice will depend upon the economic environment, including perhaps that aspect of it which is influenced by monetary policy. An economy in which monetary policy is volatile is likely to contain a relatively large number of 'flex-price' firms, and vice versa, so that in an economy similar to that modelled here the slope of the short-run Phillips trade-off is likely to vary with the conduct of policy, as Lucas (1973) suggested, albeit for different reasons.

All in all, it would appear that a little price stickiness goes a long way in macroeconomics. It is important, therefore, to stress that in the preceding analysis this assumption is *not* simply an extra complication *added* to an otherwise new-classical model. Rather it *replaces* the new-classical assumption that agents lack sufficient information to enable them to distinguish between relative-price changes and price-level shifts. The agents in the sticky-price model I have presented have to be econometricians enough to form expectations about next period's money supply but, unlike their counterparts in the corresponding new-classical system, they are not required to estimate demand-for-money functions or solve signal extraction problems (though I have discussed the implications of them doing the latter with respect to information contained in output fluctuations). Moreover, because agents in the sticky-price world do not require the skills to solve the latter problems, there is no need to expect them to be particularly sophisticated econometricians when they forecast money.

In short, the sticky-price modification of the full Walrasian model is not only more fruitful in predictions than the relative-price/price-level confusion modification which lies at the heart of new-classical macroeconomics. It also has strong claims to be regarded as simpler into the bargain. Even though the postulate of price stickiness is, to a degree, *ad hoc*, it is not for that reason any less implausible than the postulates used to turn a full-information, flexible-price Walrasian framework into a new-classical model. These, too, lack compelling foundations in maximising behaviour. Thus, price stickiness should be taken seriously as a basis for macro-economic analysis, and its choice-theoretic foundations investigated.

## Notes

1 Goodfriend (1985) shows how measurement error can be used to explain systematic positive autocorrelation in the behaviour of real balances.

2 In the literature on the 'real-balance effect', such slow adjustment is derived from a simple intertemporal choice mechanism. See Archibald and Lipsey (1958), Patinkin (1965) and Jonson (1976a) for discussions of this. The empirical literature of the demand for money postulated portfolio-adjustment costs, usually quadratic, to obtain the same result. See, for example, Chow (1966) or Goldfeld (1973).

3 For demonstrations of this point, see Laidler (1982, Chapter 2) and Lane (1983).

4 See notes 8 and 9 below.

5 The properties of the model with the expected, instead of actual, price level included in the demand-for-money function were investigated. See notes 8 and 9 below.

6 It is precisely this type of firm that might set its prices by contracts, and indeed the mixture here between firms which hold their prices constant for the entire week and those which may vary them within the week is a minimal version of the overlapping contracts idea associated with Fischer (1977), Phelps and Taylor (1977), and Taylor (1979). The original distinction between 'fix'- and 'flex'-price markets is, of course, due to Sir John Hicks (1956).

Fix-price firms might well meet demand variations out of inventories, rather than current output. Such behaviour would introduce another source of persistence effects into the economy. That it is not discussed here reflects only the fact that it is not necessary to produce such effects, rather than any judgement that inventory fluctuations are unimportant in the real world. Similarly, Keynesian multiplier effects are ruled out of the analysis of the next few pages by the assumption that expenditure depends only on permanent income and excess-money holdings. If we let transitory income affect expenditure, these, perhaps empirically important but, in the current context, unnecessary, effects would be present.

7 This persistence of an excess supply of money is a manifestation of the 'buffer stock' effects discussed by Jonson (1976), and Laidler (1984). Note that if the demand for money depended on the interest rate, and if that variable always kept the supply and demand for money in equilibrium, the above arguments would not go through. Chapter 2 above argues that a loanable-funds approach to modelling short-run interest-rate behaviour enables us to avoid the problem.

8 But this proposition about the equivalence of equations (3a) and (3b) would not be true of the new-classical model if we used the expected, instead of the actual, price level in the demand-for-money function, or if we made the demand for money depend upon current instead of permanent income. See note 9 for further discussion.

9 But the use of (3b) instead of (3a) in the new-classical model also introduces a little persistence if we modify its demand-for-money function as well. Specifically, if we make the demand for money depend upon current income, we introduce positive autocorrelation into the behaviour of real income over time but not into the behaviour of real balances. To use the expected price level instead of its actual value in the demand-for-money function, and then to model expectations with (3b), induces autocorrelation into the reduced form for real balances, but it is of the wrong kind. The lagged dependent variable has a negative coefficient in this case. The relevant reduced form is

$$m_s - p = \frac{1}{1 - \theta}(\delta_0 + \delta_1 y^*) - \frac{\theta}{1 - \theta}(m_{s-1} - p_{-1}) - \frac{\theta}{1 - \theta}(m_s - Em_s|I_{-1})$$

To use (3a) in this form of the model takes out the term in lagged real balances here but still leaves a negative coefficient on unanticipated money. On this, see Laidler (1982, Chapter 3).

10 Such a mechanism is described in more detail in Chapter 2 above, and in Laidler and Bentley (1983).

11 Though neither the formulation used nor the purposes to which it is put are the same, the argument here is in the spirit of Akerlof and Yellen (1986).

12 See above, p. 84.

13 An obvious candidate here would be the overlapping-contract idea of Taylor (1979) and his associates. I hope that my own inability as yet to find a way of integrating this notion with the type of model analysed here will not deter others from trying.

14 Carr and Darby (1981) argue that unanticipated money should take a unit coefficient, and indeed it comes close to doing so in their work. It takes a fractional coefficient in equation (11b) simply because we allow prices to respond within the week to money unanticipated at its beginning. Carr and Darby implicitly assume a one-period lag before unanticipated money affects prices. It should be noted that though it happened to appear in print first, Laidler (1980) explicitly acknowledged Carr and Darby's then unpublished working paper as the source of some of the ideas it investigated.

15 Laidler (1985) briefly develops this idea but in a model with expectations modelled by error learning. Similar results emerge in that analysis to those presented here, and it is gratifying that although price stickiness is necessary to produce them, the particular type of stickiness generated by error learning is not.

# 6

# Monetarism, Microfoundations and the Theory of Monetary Policy

## Introduction

The originators of new economic ideas seldom see them work out as they intended. Once published, they become common property and evolve in the most unexpected ways. This proposition might, upon close inspection, turn out to be something of an over generalisation, but it is surely true of that bundle of ideas commonly known as 'monetarism'. Such commentators as Brunner and Meltzer (1987) and Leijonhufvud (1987) have noted, with alarm in the former case and amusement in the second, the way in which a doctrine whose slogan was 'money matters (and matters a great deal)' has during the 1980s seemingly inexorably evolved into one in which money is to all intents and purposes irrelevant. This evolution ought to cause considerable concern to those interested in practical matters of economic policy.

Not the least of the accomplishments of monetarism was to re-establish a public perception that monetary policy is important, and it made its case not by deploying any radically new tools of economic theory but by drawing attention to empirical evidence. Over the last two decades, I would be prepared to argue, nothing has happened in the real world to contradict this perception. However, within the community of academic monetary economists, attempts to provide 'sound' theoretical foundations for monetarism's empirical generalisations have led to the conclusion that the latter cannot be true. Whatever the textbooks of scientific method might advise to the contrary, economists have traditionally displayed a tendency to give priority to their theory when it comes into conflict with evidence, and that tendency seems to have been strongly at work in recent years. We thus find ourselves in a situation in which practitioners regard the conduct of monetary policy as important and the theory of monetary policy as interesting, while an increasing number of academics insist that the beliefs of practitioners about such matters are unsound.

In this chapter I shall examine the evolution of the ideas that have led to this impasse. I shall begin with a brief account of the theory of macroeconomic policy as it arose in the context of the so-called 'neoclassical synthesis', and show how monetarism modified that theory. I shall then show how the search for sound microeconomic foundations for monetarist propositions ended up undermining them. Finally I shall argue that the currently accepted microfoundations of monetary economics are fundamentally flawed, and suggest that the practitioner's notions about the importance of money, which are largely a legacy of the monetary economics that preceded the search for microfoundations, can after all find a basis in an alternative theoretical framework.

## Monetary Policy in the Economics of the Neoclassical Synthesis and Monetarism

The economics of the neoclassical synthesis, more usually and briefly, if inaccurately, called Keynesian economics, had as its centrepiece the Hicksian IS–LM diagram.[1] This well-known device is beautifully calculated simultaneously to portray a particular problem, an hypothesis about its causes, and a theory about its cures. The problem is 'unemployment equilibrium', the hypothesis is a failure of investment demand, and the theory of policy deals with the use of fiscal and monetary tools to influence income and employment.

Now the unemployment equilibrium portrayed in IS–LM analysis is, by modern standards, no equilibrium at all. It is, as Patinkin (1948) in particular made clear, more of a situation in which an economy might find itself from time to time, and from which it is thought unlikely to move towards a better ('full employment') state fast enough of its own accord. The explanation offered for the existence of unemployment by that model would hardly pass muster, either, by today's theoretical standards. The inadequate level of the marginal efficiency of capital underlying unemployment equilibrium arises outside of the IS–LM model, which, however efficient it might be for deducing the consequences of such a state of affairs, has nothing to say about its causes. Nevertheless, this framework formed the basis of a theory of macroeconomic policy which dominated the discipline for three decades, and whose influence now is still clearly to be seen in the structure of virtually every econometric forecasting model of which I am aware.[2]

The theory of policy to which I have referred amounts to a set of instructions: forecast investment demand (and perhaps exports too in the case of a significantly open economy); calculate the implied shortfall of actual from desired output; manipulate either monetary variables, and in particular the rate of interest, in order to induce a higher level of investment, and/or the twin fiscal variables government expenditure and taxes, to make good the shortfall directly. To the extent that time-lags in the effects of policy appear to present a problem, their consequences can be offset as they arise by further manipulation of policy variables.[3]

Though these instructions, and indeed the logic of the IS–LM model, leave room for monetary policy to be used as an instrument of stabilisation policy, the whole thrust of the policy doctrine which accompanied it was to emphasise fiscal policy. The 'liquidity trap' doctrine, and more generally the notion that the demand for money was highly interest-sensitive and perhaps unstable, suggested that the links between the LM and IS sides of the model, and by implication of the real world too, were weak and unreliable; and in any event it surely made sense to offset the consequences of one factor (investment demand) shifting the IS curve by directly manipulating other variables that could shift the same curve in the opposite direction. The role of monetary policy was thus reduced to the supporting one of perhaps supplementing, but at least not interfering with, the conduct and effects of fiscal policy.

Now all this leaves out of account a number of questions that immediately come to the mind of an economist trained in the 1980s. First of all, it might reasonably be asked, where does the behaviour of the price level come into all this? The IS–LM model can of course be deployed to analyse the inflationary effects of a level of aggregate demand in excess of 'full employment' output. Thus, the first edition of my *The Demand for Money* (Laidler 1969) used the behaviour of the model in both unemployment and full-employment modes to motivate its entire discussions, and Friedman (1974) used it as a device for expounding ideas about just these matters and showed that, at full employment, with output pinned down by supply-side factors, the model in question yielded many 'monetarist' implications.

However IS–LM is a clumsy device to use for analysing price-level fluctuations. The Phillips curve in its original form was quickly absorbed into mainstream (i.e. non-monetarist) macroeconomics because it provided a simple way of dealing with inflation as a policy problem. It treated the value of the inflation rate as a side-effect of the chosen target level of employment, a side-effect which nowhere fed back into the system, and one which could be mitigated by other policies designed to 'shift the Phillips curve'. Aggregate demand was, in the 'Keynesian' view, just one, albeit in the view of some (e.g. Samuelson and Solow 1960) important, influence on the inflation rate. Since monetary policy was in its turn also just one factor impinging upon aggregate demand, and an unimportant one at that, it had no special role to play *vis-à-vis* inflation in the economics of the 1960s.

The macroeconomics of the neoclassical synthesis thus downgraded monetary variables, and yet the first round of the monetarist challenge to that doctrine involved an attack on the effectiveness of *monetary policy* as a device for 'fine tuning' the economy, based on the proposition that its effects were subject to 'long and variable' time-lags. At first sight, this attack seems to have been misdirected, and yet Keynesians rose to its challenge and in due course came to defend monetary policy as a tool of stabilisation policy. The clue to understanding why this happened lies in the fact that this stage in the development of the theory of monetary policy took place in the United States. Stabilisation policy requires considerable institutional flexibility, in order that the time-lags involved in the recognition of a problem, and in the design and implementation of policy, are short. In the case of monetary policy, such flexibility is available to central banks which are unencumbered by constitutional or quasi-constitutional constraints. When it comes to fiscal policy, it is provided by parliamentary systems of government on the British model, but not by the American congressional system.

The tax-cuts implemented in the United States in 1964 were at the time hailed as a triumph of Keynesian policy, but they were proposed in 1962. To hold up a measure that took two years to implement as an example of active stabilisation policy is surely preposterous, for what this episode brings home is that, in the United States, such policy has to be carried on by monetary means or not at all. Fiscal tools are simply not available for this purpose. Though this point is seldom if ever made explicitly, it is of vital importance in understanding why the theory of monetary policy has developed as it has. The literature of macroeconomics since the Second World War is predominantly American, and a particular institutional peculiarity of the United States has come to colour a whole body of apparently 'general' literature to the point at which faith in the efficacy of monetary stabilisation policy has come to be regarded as the hallmark of 'Keynesianism', and a denial of that efficacy a characteristic 'anti-Keynesian' position.[4]

There was more to the rise of monetarism than the peculiar importance thrust upon monetary measures by the institutional framework of the American economy. As Harry Johnson (1971) long ago noted, it was also associated with the emergence of inflation as a serious policy problem. The modern quantity theory of money of Friedman and his associates was far from being a simple revival of the pre-*General Theory* doctrines that carried the same label, but it did have one all-important proposition in common with those earlier ideas: namely that variations in the quantity of money in circulation were an important independent cause of variations in the price level.[5] By the early 1970s, inflation was a world-wide problem, and this fact combined with the apparent success of monetarist hypotheses about the stability of the demand-for-money function to ensure that the

theory of monetary policy associated with monetarism attracted international attention in a way which earlier arguments about the unsuitability
of monetary measures for fine tuning had not. The suitability or otherwise
of monetary tools for counter-cyclical policy was a contentious issue mainly
in the United States, but a monetary explanation of inflation had a much
wider appeal.

It will be helpful to summarise just what the monetarist theory of
monetary policy amounted to. It asserted not only that inflation was an
important and undesirable phenomenon, but also that inflation was
predominantly the long-run effect of monetary expansion, and that
fluctuations in money growth had short-run effects on real income and
employment. Hence a monetary theory of inflation was supplemented with
a monetary explanation of cyclical fluctuations. The short-run effects of
monetary policy seemed to be subject to long and variable lags (between
six and eighteen months) and hence could not be exploited in the design of
stabilisation policy. However, since they were the main cause of cyclical
fluctuations in the first place, this presented no real problem. Eliminate
fluctuations in money growth and the cycle would be to an important
extent stabilised by that very act. Thus, if the rate of growth of the money
supply was set roughly equal to the secular rate of growth of output
by a rule (either self-imposed by the central bank, or imposed upon it
through political processes), long-run price stability would be assured, and
short-run real-income and employment stability would be enhanced
significantly.[6]

Now of course this theory of policy was never more than partially
implemented in the 1970s and 1980s, and as I shall argue in Chapter 7
below, widely held perceptions to the effect that it failed in practice are
largely (not entirely) misconceived. However, the actual policy experience
of the last two decades does not present the only challenge to monetarist
views about the appropriate conduct of monetary policy that has emerged
over that period. They have also come under a theoretical attack which has
done more to undermine their academic prestige than any empirical
evidence. The capacity of monetary fluctuations to have significant real
effects, not to mention the destructive nature of price-level variations in
general and inflation in particular, have been challenged; so too has the
basic proposition that variations in the quantity of nominal money will in
general have a significant influence on its value, not to mention the basic
preconception underlying all mainstream discussion of monetary policy
since the mid-nineteenth century that the behaviour of monetary variables
is a matter which government ought to concern itself with. Moreover, this
radical attack has emerged not from a self-conscious attempt to undermine
monetarism, but from analysis whose initial intention was to strengthen its
theoretical foundations.

## Microfoundations and the New Monetary Economics

I have already remarked that the IS–LM framework was well designed to enable economists to make deductions about the consequences of shifts in underlying behaviour relationships, notably investment demand, for real income and employment, and, when supplemented by the Phillips curve, about inflation too. It did not, in and of itself, have anything to say about those underlying behaviour relations. The latter issues were the concern of microeconomics, and the 1950s and 60s generated a rich literature on the maximising foundations of the consumption, demand-for-money, and investment functions.[7] The microfoundations of the Phillips curve too attracted attention, and the insights of Phelps (1967) and Friedman (1968) about the importance of expectations about the future-behaviour prices for the present behaviour of wages, and hence of prices, provided the basis of those characteristic monetarist propositions about the short- and long-run effects of monetary policy that I have already discussed above. However, this work had another less immediate but in the long run far more profound effect on the development of macroeconomics; and about that something should now be said.

If the expected future behaviour of prices affects their current behaviour, and if that behaviour is generated by the macroeconomic system, then beliefs about how the system works must themselves be fundamental components of the microeconomic framework underlying the behaviour of the aggregate economy. Moreover, the beliefs of agents, to be sustainable, had better be compatible with the structure of the economy to which they appertain. A critical implication of these insights, which arise from Lucas's (1972) seminal work on the macroeconomic consequences of 'rational expectations', was that the investigation of the nature of the markets in which agents interact replaced further elaboration of the microeconomics of particular behaviour relations at the very top of the research agenda of macroeconomic theory. Two characteristics of traditional IS–LM analysis, which had been taken over by monetarists and adapted to their own purposes by the time Lucas's work was published, have proved critical for the way in which such questions have been tackled. The first of these is that the system utilises a largely unquestioned assumption of nominal price stickiness from which the possibility of the occurrence of underemployment derives. The second is that the framework embodies the characteristic Walrasian vision of economic variables being simultaneously determined by the contemporaneous interaction of agents in what is essentially a single market.

If prices are sticky, the reason for that needs to be explained, and a model of the forces driving their behaviour derived, before a satisfactory theory of how expectations about price fluctuations are formed can be constructed. Microeconomics, though, provides no such theory that can easily be embedded in a general equilibrium framework.[8] On the other hand, the theory of competitive markets, based on the idea of complete price flexibility, does at least enable endogenous price expectations to be modelled systematically, and it had already been shown, by Lucas and Rapping (1970) among others, *before the advent of rational expectations*, that quantity fluctuations could be reconciled with price flexibility provided agents were permitted to make expectational errors. Hence the price-stickiness assumption became anathema; but once it was dropped IS–LM in effect reverted to being a particular and rather ordinary version of the Walrasian general equilibrium model.[9] In the process of acquiring market-theoretic microfoundations, macroeconomics thus lost its separate identity. Also, and crucially for the topic of this chapter, the scene was set for a wholesale revision of the theory of monetary policy which would downgrade the significance of money to a degree far greater than had Keynesian economics.

This is a claim that needs defending, because the change that Lucas and his associates seemed to have made to macroeconomics in the 1970s was to provide a better theoretical basis for monetarism, a doctrine for which money mattered above all things. Certainly in their analysis money caused real variables to fluctuate in the short run, and prices in the long run, just as it did in Friedman's work. However, short-run real effects depended upon monetary changes being *unanticipated*. Hence, *any* systematic rule for the behaviour of the money supply, and not just a constant growth-rate rule, would stabilise real variables. Only to the extent that anticipated inflation might lead to non-superneutrality and impose welfare losses on the economy did the choice of a time path for the money supply matter at all. Both of these implications of new-classical macroeconomics have led to trouble as far as the theory of monetary policy is concerned.[10]

Consider the question of short-run effects first of all. If agents really do form their expectations about the behaviour of the money supply in a manner that is commonly called 'rational', only random fluctuations in the money stock can possibly have real effects. Monetarism attributed a dominant role to monetary fluctuations in driving the business cycle, but it is hard indeed to think of the history of cycles as reflecting merely the consequences of a series of random shocks to the money supply. Indeed the plausibility of such an explanation is further undermined by the observation that data on the money supply are nowadays readily available on a weekly basis to anyone who cares to look them up in a newspaper. To be sure, these data are subject to reporting error, as Boschen and Grossman (1982) pointed out, but it does indeed stretch one's credulity to attach much responsibility for current business fluctuations to such a transitory phenomenon; and, in any event, Boschen and Grossman's empirical results showed that this implication of a literal interpretation of new-classical analysis was quite inconsistent with the data. In short, if one insists on maintaining price-flexibility and rational-expectations assumptions, it is difficult to accord money any significant influence over real income and employment, even if that does involve ignoring Boschen and Grossman's finding that announced, and therefore readily observable, fluctuations in the money supply do appear to cause output fluctuations.

Not only does acceptance of new-classical analysis undermine on *a priori* grounds the importance of money as a causative factor in short-run fluctuations. It also downgrades the importance of stabilising the cycle as a goal of macroeconomic policy. Even if the cycle were largely driven by random monetary impulses, only the initial response of output and employment to them can in any sense be regarded as sub-optimal. Subsequent fluctuations must reflect the economy's optimal response to the situation created by the initial shock. If the cycle is primarily the result of other impulses, such as the shocks to the production function postulated by Kydland and Prescott (1982), then even the initial fluctuation becomes a reflection of optimising behaviour. Now there is some value in these implications of new-classical analysis. We ought not to take it for granted, as we so often do, that smooth growth is optimal and that any departure from this pattern is undesirable and hence worthy of policy correction. The question does need re-examining. In the current context, however, the key point is that the answer given by new-classical analysis leaves no interesting role for money to play either as cause or as cure of the cycle. That analysis, if it is taken seriously, thus destroys an important component of the traditional theory of monetary policy.

The component in question is of course a comparatively recent addition to the area. It was only in the first two decades of this century that the possibility that monetary impulses might cause the cycle, and that monetary policy might and ought to be used to stabilise it, came to be seriously entertained by economists.[11] In earlier times, monetary policy was concerned with inflation and avoiding collapses of the monetary system rather than with stabilising real income and employment. In the context of inflation too, new-classical economics, or at least one offshoot of it, downgrades the significance of monetary policy. I remarked earlier that monetarism treats inflation as an important problem, premissing its concern on an analysis of non-superneutralities of money and their associated welfare costs. The latter were traditionally measured by an area, typically a triangle, under the demand-for-money function. They have long been a target of those who would downgrade the importance of money (and with justification, as I argue in Chapter 3 above). To such Keynesians as James Tobin (1977)—'It takes a heap of Harberger Triangles to fill an Okun Gap'—the relatively small size of the welfare costs of inflation thus assessed did not seem to justify the strength of monetarists' concerns about inflation; but the critique implicit in the so-called 'new monetary economics', to which the most visible contributors are Hall (1982) and Sargent and Wallace (e.g. 1982), goes much deeper.

Once again it is a matter of seeking microfoundations for a piece of macroanalysis, in this case the aggregate demand-for-money function. 1960s vintage monetarism typically treated real balances 'as if' a consumer-durable good, and included their 'services' in agents' utility functions. The new monetary economics asked what those services might consist of, and could find no answer arising within the structure of the general equilibrium model with which it was operating. The reason for this is obvious enough. To apply Walrasian market theory is to assume that the world operates 'as if' market clearing prices are costless to set, and as if the act of exchange is subject to no frictions. Hence a Walrasian model leaves no role for money to perform services as a means of exchange. Moreover, the implicit assumption of rational-expectations modelling, that agents can costlessly process and comprehend all information that is available to them, leaves no role for money to perform a useful service as a unit of account either. The only function for money that can arise in such a world is that of a store of value, and the 'services' that it yields to agents can only take the form of pecuniary return.

To treat money in this way of course immediately rules out of court the traditional analysis of the welfare costs of inflation. Indeed it goes much further, because any expected rate of return on money below that yielded by productive assets (including inventories of consumption goods if these are storable) will lead to its not being held at all. If money bears explicit interest at market rates, it becomes indistinguishable from other assets, but if it does not, and consists of some intrinsically valueless item, then expected inflation at any rate in excess of minus the real rate of interest immediately leads to money's disappearance from the economy, which nevertheless continues to function in its absence! This is not to say that an equilibrium in which money is held may not be preferable to one in which it isn't, because it might be, but it is to say that in the new monetary economics the welfare analysis of money is completely disconnected from price-level fluctuations *per se*. As Neil Wallace once put it, 'So far as we know, the claim that a stable price level is good is as naïve as the claim that a stable relative price between, say eggs and steel, is good. In fact it has been argued that the two are on the same footing' (Wallace 1982, p. 229).

The existence of a non-interest-bearing, intrinsically valueless store of value, which is what the new monetary economics means by fiat money, is certainly theoretically fragile, and the central question addressed by this body of analysis is how it can be that money's existence can be so pervasive a phenomenon in the real world. The answers that it offers are twofold. First it is argued that fiat money is a creation of the State, and would be unlikely to exist in the absence of legal requirements that it be held. The alternative to this 'legal restrictions' explanation of money's existence is that non-fiat money, in the form of well-defined claims over intrinsically valuable (i.e. utility-yielding) goods, is the only type of money that is generally viable in an unregulated market. In this view, then, it is the 'backing' of money that matters, both for its capacity to exist and also for the determination of its value. The price level no longer varies with the quantity of nominal money, then, but as a function of the expected future price level, whose behaviour in turn is dominated by the nature of monetary regulations and the quality of money's backing.[12]

This line of argument yields an immediate and quite distinctive implication for the theory of monetary policy: that private agents can safely be left to provide on their own account well-backed stores of value without the intervention of the government; and that legal restrictions which cause government fiat money to be held are likely to be welfare-reducing; in short, that monetary policy carried out by government is itself the problem, and not the solution to any problem arising elsewhere in the economy. There is a strong affinity between the new monetary economics and the arguments of nineteenth- and early twentieth-century advocates of 'free banking', as, for example, Cowen and Krozner (1987) have pointed out; but, as they also point out, the exclusive concentration of the more recent literature on money's store-of-value role adds an extra touch of radicalism to its message.

These developments in monetary theory have, until now at least, left practical policy discussions largely untouched. Monetary policy is still in most countries carried on on the basis of analysis derived directly from the neoclassical synthesis, though heavily coloured by monetarist ideas. By that I mean that monetary aggregates now play a much bigger role relative to interest rates in the design of policy than they did twenty years ago, that monetary measures in general are regarded as far more important relative to fiscal policy than they were then, and that active attempts to stabilise the economy by monetary means, though not (unfortunately in my view) entirely abandoned, are much more likely to be subordinated to longer-term price-stability goals. Policy is thus still based upon theory that almost any academic monetary economist would regard as at best old-fashioned, and at worst hopelessly obsolete and inadequate. However, the prospect of a monetary regime based upon the tenets of the new monetary theory is not an attractive alternative. It would attempt to take money out of the political arena and leave its behaviour to the market, and I do not believe that this would be either desirable or feasible, as I shall now attempt to explain.

## Money as a Public Good

Perhaps the most extraordinary development in monetary theory over the past fifty years is the way in which money's means-of-exchange and unit-of-account roles have vanished from what is widely regarded as the mainstream of monetary theory. The potential for such a disappearing trick was already inherent in IS–LM analysis, as such commentators as Clower (e.g. 1967) long ago noted, but it has been the new monetary theorists who have brought it to full fruition. As I have already pointed out, their adoption of the assumption of competitive clearing markets as an unquestioned starting-point for analysis leaves money no room to work as a means of exchange, and their similar treatment of the particularly extreme form of rational expectations that grants to all agents equal access to all available information in the economy, and free use of whatever analytic and computational skills are needed to process it, renders a unit-of-account function equally nugatory. In models based on such assumptions, 'money' can only appear as a store of value which yields purely private returns to the particular agents who hold it. It is not surprising that such models typically yield the policy implication that private competitive markets can be relied upon to provide the amounts of money that agents want to hold, and that government interference with their operation can only make matters worse rather than better.

Money is *not* just a store of value however. It *is* a medium of exchange and a unit of account, and in those roles the services it yields are inherently public. Competitive equilibrium analysis of the type that underlies the new monetary economics cannot comprehend these roles because the Walrasian market is an *alternative* social institution to money, not a complementary set of arrangements. To the best of my knowledge, no one has ever suggested that it is the task of economic theory to deduce the existence of a competitive Walrasian market from maximising assumptions. Rather we are satisfied to have theory tell us what public benefits, involving the transmission and processing of information and the elimination of transactions costs, such a market bestows upon all who participate in it. But the social benefits which any microeconomics text attributes to 'the market' include those which any macroeconomics text attributes to a system of monetary exchange. If a monetary economy solves the same problems as would a competitive market, it might often be safe to assume that it acts 'as if' it were in fact a market economy, and that is why conventional microeconomic analysis is a useful tool for analysing the real world. However, when it comes to analysing the processes of disseminating and processing information themselves, and those of co-ordinating activity, it is important to choose *between* assuming a monetary economy and a Walrasian market economy. It is a fundamental error to assume the existence of a clearing Walrasian market as the first step of an attempt to understand money.

The implications of the foregoing arguments for the theory of monetary policy are straightforward. That theory must start from the fact that money is a social institution whose services are inherently public if it is to be satisfactory; but if we start from this premiss, we must treat the design of monetary institutions as a political matter, because political processes exist, among other reasons, to help us internalise those externalities that voluntary private contractual arrangements cannot cope with.[13] We must, however, be careful what we deduce from this observation. In particular it does not inevitably imply that the monetary system must be provided by the public sector, or that indiscriminate public regulation of private-sector agencies within the monetary sector must be regarded as either inevitable or desirable. All it implies is that choices about the design of the monetary system and the way it is to operate are inherently political matters which cannot be settled in the market-place. The theory of public goods tells us that the demand for them must be articulated by a collective agency; it does not also say that they must be collectively supplied. A political decision to have unregulated private agents provide a monetary system may, then, be a viable option.

The public good that a monetary system provides, and the demand for which must be collectively articulated, arises immediately from money's unit-of-account and means-of-exchange roles. Economic computation *is* costly, as is the formulation of contracts, no matter what the latest in economic theory might assume to the contrary about these things. A common unit of account *does* make life easier for all concerned, and easier still if its value in terms of goods and services is stable and predictable (I deliberately avoid the word 'constant' here) over time. Moreover, stability of the value of the economy's means of exchange in terms of the unit of account also simplifies the planning of and execution of market transactions.[14] The maintenance of a stable and predictable time path for the purchasing power of money thus bestows benefits on all agents in the economy simultaneously, no one can be excluded from enjoying these benefits, and the marginal cost of extending them to extra members of the economy is zero.

Price-level stability is, therefore, a public good, in exactly the same way as a well-defined system of exchangeable property rights is a public good (or, for that matter, as a Walrasian market presided over by an auctioneer would be a public good, were such an institution ever to exist). The theory of monetary policy must then be concerned with the provision of an optimal time path for the purchasing power of money for a world in which making economic calculations and predictions is costly, and in which those costs vary with the nature of the time path in question. There is no need in the current context to offer a precise suggestion as to just what that time path should be. Suffice it to mention some of its characteristics.[15]

Computations involving a constant rate of change of prices are easier than those in which it varies, so there must be a presumption that variable inflation (or deflation) is sub-optimal. Moreover, the marginal costs of providing real balances in a non-commodity money system *are* zero (which does not mean that the fixed costs of establishing such a system are also trivial); but the support that this consideration gives to deflation at the real rate of interest as a policy goal must be weighed against 'menu cost' considerations. These imply that, when individual price changes are costly, a time path for the price level which reduces their frequency saves real resources. Moreover, the fact that some prices (e.g. money wages) are more costly to change than others has implications for the choice of just which price index to choose as a basis for policy. In practice then, the selection of the optimal price-level goal is very much a matter of complex 'second best' calculations, but ancient platitudes about not letting 'the best become the enemy of the good' apply with a vengeance in this case. The presumption that a low and stable rate of change of some representative price index is more desirable than high and variable inflation is strong. We should not, therefore, let difficulties of discovering a precise goal distract us from the importance of remaining in its vicinity.

Now we cannot take for granted the existence of a benevolent social planning agency dedicated to promoting the public welfare, so the theory of monetary policy has to concern itself with the design of these institutions intended to produce and maintain price stability. Here there is scope for considerable private-sector involvement in the provision of the public good under consideration, because old arguments in favour of 'free banking', notably those recently revived by Hayek (1976) and White (1984), have a great deal to be said for them. Elementary economic theory tells us that competitive institutions will provide their output up to the point at which their price equals marginal cost. In the case of banks, the relevant product is real balances, and the relevant marginal cost is approximately zero. This by itself does not guarantee stability of the purchasing power of any bank's liabilities. All it implies is that they will bear a nominal rate of return equal to the real rate of interest plus their expected rate of depreciation; but the imposition of any computation or transactions costs on either the emitters or the holders of the liability of any particular bank by a non-zero value for the latter component of their nominal return will lead to market mechanisms eliminating it and generating constant purchasing power for competitively issued bank money.[16]

If things were really that simple, then the private sector, completely unregulated, could be relied upon to provide a sound monetary system, but they are not. To begin with, the promise of stable purchasing power on the part of competitive bank liabilities must be credible, and that is best ensured by each bank standing ready to redeem its liabilities in something which is itself of stable purchasing power. In principle this could be a 'representative' bundle of goods stored by the bank, but considerations of costs and convenience suggest that it will be some claim to such goods, and that each bank will find it convenient to use the *same* claim as a first-line reserve. A competitive banking system thus requires what we usually call 'high-powered money' in order to settle clearing balances. Moreover, because of those economies of scale in reserve holding that have been well known since the work of Edgeworth (1888), there is a tendency to natural monopoly inherent in its provision. The existence of a central 'reserve agent' is not a product of regulation, but a natural consequence of the operation of a competitive banking system. When natural monopoly arises in the provision of a public good, one is bound to end up with either a public-sector enterprise, or a highly regulated private-sector one.

A central bank on the Bank of England model is one type of reserve agent. It is not necessarily the best model to follow, but the idea that central banks as we know them can be abolished without any other entity taking their place is not well founded. Nor is it the case that the existence of a central reserve agent marks the only departure from some atomistically competitive norm which economic theory suggests might characterise the institutions involved in the efficient private provision of money. Given the existence of a stable high-powered money, a competitive banking system will generate price-level stability only if the behaviour of the non-bank public makes it unprofitable for any individual bank to over-issue its own liabilities. If such liabilities are deposits, then an adverse clearing balance will immediately face the over-issuing bank and force it to mend its ways. If they are notes, then only if the public returns them for redemption to the issuing bank will such discipline be imposed. To spend a deposit automatically brings the clearing mechanism into play, but to spend a note does not. The public needs much more information about individual banks of issue than about deposit banks in order to discipline them. This well-known nineteenth-century argument may still be used today to justify restrictions on competitive note issue; and is it not efficient to place a monopoly note issue under the control of the reserve agent and use it as high-powered money?

Nor should we ignore the reserve agent's potential function as lender of last resort. Were bank liabilities a pure store of value, it could be argued that the rule of *caveat emptor* should be applied to those who had chosen to hold those emitted by badly run institutions. Only arguments about externalities in the provision and dissemination of information could be used to soften this stance. However, if private bank liabilities function as a means of exchange, then a social institution, namely the system of monetary exchange, is threatened by bank failures and there is a case to be made for public intervention. This does *not* mean that each and every badly run bank should always be bailed out, but it does mean that a public interest must always be weighed when a decision is taken about such an issue. To give the reserve agent a discretionary lender-of-last-resort function, then, is to create an arrangement to cope with a major externality. It is not to impose an unnecessary complication on the structure of an already ideally designed banking system.

Now the monetary system which I have just described turns out to look very much like the one we have. However, the existence of a central reserve agent, its lender-of-last-resort role, and perhaps its monopoly of note issue too, are, according to the arguments I have presented, responses to economic problems created by the very nature of money and monetary exchange. They are not the consequences of capricious intervention by an incompetent government which is the enemy of economic efficiency. Once one abandons the implausible notion that money is a store of value pure and simple, which dominates the modern literature on the microfoundations of money, and realises that this view of things stems from the fundamental unsuitability of Walrasian general equilibrium theory for the analysis of those microfoundations, it appears that government is after all an inherent part of an economically efficient solution to monetary problems.[17]

However, just because government is needed to cope with monetary problems it does not follow that its actions will always be disinterestedly chosen or competently executed. It is a well-known commonplace of the literature on microeconomic policy issues that considerations of externalities, public goods, and the ethics of the distribution of wealth all create problems which only a collective agency can cope with, and it is equally well known that a mere fraction of the government interventions that we see in real-world economic life can stand scrutiny as attempts to cope honestly with such problems. The traditional questions of the monetary policy literature about the use of rules or discretion in the conduct of policy, about the extent to which the reserve agent should regulate the behaviour of deposit banks, about how that agent should carry out its lender-of-last-resort role, about the appropriate choice of international monetary system for a world where the highest level of political authority is the nation state, are all real issues. They are not, as the new monetary economics would have it, artificial problems created for government by government.

## Concluding Comments

The intention of this chapter has been to argue that the traditional problems discussed in the monetary policy literature are after all worth arguing about. To the practitioner of monetary policy, or the interested layman, it might seem already clear that this is the case. The fact that in this instance I share the non-academic's judgement does not mean that it is pointless to put a little effort into restating the obvious. Though the policy framework at present in place in most countries does not seem to be too badly designed, and though the day-to-day conduct of monetary policy is not too bad either, at least by recent historical standards, there can be no guarantee that either the policy framework or the actual conduct of policy will continue basically unchanged into the future. Economic theory of the most abstract sort has, as Keynes (1936) noted long ago, a way of influencing practical policy in the long run. One body of analysis currently attracting a good deal of attention in the academic community, namely the new monetary economics, has profound implications for policy; but these arise, I have argued, from its being premissed upon a basic misconception concerning the role of money in the economy. The new monetary economics seems to me therefore to present something of a long-run threat to monetary stability in the real world, a threat to which it has been the aim of this chapter to offer a little opposition.

There are, of course many other threats to monetary stability. To say that collective agencies of some sort have an inherent role to play in the workings of the monetary system is not to guarantee that they will be well designed in detail or that they will play their part in a satisfactory way; nor indeed is it to say that there is any unanimity among monetary economists on just what a 'well-designed' monetary authority would look like, or what 'satisfactory' conduct on its part would be. To define the frame of reference for debates about monetary policy as I have attempted to do in this essay is not also to specify their outcome. I shall discuss these other issues below (cf. Chapter 7). That I do not take them up here simply reflects the fact that one can deal with only so much material in one chapter; it does not imply that I regard these issues as unworthy of discussion.

## Notes

1 Hicks (1937) is the *locus classicus* of this diagram.

2 The Liverpool model of the UK probably goes further beyond an orthodox IS–LM structure than any other forecasting model. Nevertheless, the demand side of this model does have a familiar look to it! See Minford (1980) for a readily available account of this system.

3 Lerner (1951) provides a good example of this strand of thinking about the problem of time-lags. It was not until the work of Phillips (e.g. 1954) that the serious nature of this problem for stabilisation policy came to be widely appreciated.

4 One can do no better than cite the presidential addresses to the American Economic Association of Milton Friedman (1968) and Franco Modigliani (1977) to illustrate this assertion.

5 But the emphasis on the importance of money relative to that of other factors is stronger in Friedman's work than in the typical pre-*General Theory* account of the quantity theory.

6 The *locus classicus* for this position is, of course, Friedman (1959).

7 On the consumption function see Modigliani and Brumberg (1954) or Friedman (1957), on investment see Jorgenson (1967), and for a survey of the literature on the demand for money see Laidler (1969, Part II).

8 Microeconomics does of course provide a rich array of partial-equilibrium treatments based on models of oligopoly behaviour. See, e.g., Kawasaki, McMillan and Zimmerman (1983).

9 This much, of course, was already apparent to anyone who had read the sections of Patinkin (1956) that dealt with price flexibility.

10 On the significance of unanticipated monetary changes for real variables see Sargent and Wallace (1976). For a survey of the salient results on superneutrality, see Laidler and Parkin (1975, Part 2).

11 The two best-known advocates of a monetary theory of the cycle during this period were probably Irving Fisher (e.g. 1911) and Ralph Hawtrey (e.g. 1913).

12 And as I noted in Laidler (1987), this prediction hinges upon the demand for money being highly elastic with respect to the opportunity cost of holding it. In this sense, the 'backing' theory of money bears an uncanny resemblance to the Keynesian theory of the speculative demand for money.

13 See Weldon (1973) for a pioneering discussion of the public-good aspects of money, and Vaubel (1986) for a recent and extensive discussion of the pros and cons of treating money as a public good, and its implications for the desirability of competitive monetary regimes. Vaubel is reluctant to treat money as a public good, lest he abandon the case for competitive money in the process.

14 This is not a view that everyone would share. Cowen and Krozner (1987) is an excellent source of information on the literature, both old and new, that makes the case for separating money's unit-of-account and means-of-exchange functions.

15 I am well aware that a full discussion of the aims of monetary policy should deal with the desirability (or otherwise) of using it as a tool for stabilising real variables. I discuss this matter at some length in Chapter 7, below, and neglect it here for lack of space rather than from a lack of things to say on the topic. Suffice it here to say that I would prefer to direct fiscal policy to stabilisation goals.

16 A much-neglected, but excellent, commentary on the links between competition and efficiency in the provision of monetary services is Johnson (1968).

17 Note that this conclusion runs contrary to that of Bagehot (1873), who regarded a competitive monetary system with decentralised reserves as 'natural' and the system he actually described and defended as being the product of fortuitous government intervention in financial markets.

# 7

# What Do We Really Know About Monetary Policy?

## Introduction

To be successful, economic ideas must satisfy two audiences. They must convince academic economists of their *a priori* theoretical reasonableness, and of their empirical content as well. They must also persuade those concerned with the formulation of economic policy of their relevance and usefulness. Since the latter group contains many individuals who have little or no academic training in economics, a successful economic idea must be simple and easily grasped by the intelligent layman. In the light of these formidable requirements, it is hardly surprising that successful economic ideas are few and far between. Moreover, to be successful is not necessarily to be correct. It is one thing to convince academic economists of the logical coherence of an idea, and of its explanatory power over past events, and to persuade policy-makers of its usefulness; it is quite another to have policies based on it work out as expected.

This chapter is concerned with one particular economic idea that was, beyond any shadow of a doubt, successful by the above-mentioned criteria, but whose correctness has been opened up to question by recent experience with its policy application. The idea to which I refer is Milton Friedman's proposition that the aggregate demand for money is a stable function of but a few arguments, and the policy application in question is the last ten years' experience with those monetary policies more or less related to it.[1] In this chapter, I shall set out the idea in question, ask how well it has held up in the face of sustained contact with reality, and draw some tentative conclusions about the future conduct of policy.

113

## The Demand for Money and Monetarism

The theoretical ingredients of Friedman's propositions about the nature of the demand for money are to be found in his celebrated (1956) paper 'The Quantity Theory of Money—a Restatement'. There he argues, first of all, that the aggregate economy can be modelled 'as if' made up of individuals, any one of whose behaviour may be treated as 'representative' of the economy as a whole. Second, he argues that any such typical individual will desire to keep on hand a certain stock of money. Third, he argues that the size of this desired stock will depend upon just a few easily observed economic variables. Specifically, it will vary with the individual's permanent income and the costs of holding assets in the form of money rather than other assets, which can be represented by the level of nominal interest rates; and in proportion to the general price level.[2] Finally, and crucially, he argues that in the real world, the quantitative nature of the dependence of the demand for money upon these few variables is stable over time; that there are no other factors systematically affecting the demand for money; and that random variations in the demand for money are very small relative to those variations attributable to fluctuations in the above-mentioned variables.

The theoretical coherence of these ideas of Friedman's was never contentious. Economists were reasoning in terms of the behaviour of 'representative agents' long before Alfred Marshall (1890) made them self-conscious about doing so. Furthermore, in formulating monetary theory as a particular aspect of the theory of asset choice, Friedman was developing an already well-established line of inquiry whose roots can readily be traced to the Marshallian tradition in monetary economics. This, however, does not mean that his ideas were uncontroversial. The pre-Keynesian quantity theory, which Friedman invoked in the title of his article, had indeed treated the quantity of money as an economic variable of strategic importance, particularly for the determination of the general price level, but the Keynesian revolution had shifted the focus of macroeconomics, and by the 1950s economic orthodoxy attached little significance to this variable.[3] To argue as Friedman did that money mattered was, in the 1950s, a radical step in and of itself. Moreover, neither Keynesian monetary economics, nor the earlier quantity theory tradition, had ever suggested that the demand-for-money function could be treated as stable over time. The second radical element in Friedman's work lay in his controversial *empirical* assertion that it could be so treated.

Until the 1930s, the very idea of any economic relationship being empirically stable was regarded as highly unlikely. However, the success of Keynesian economics, based as it was on the idea of an empirically stable consumption function, combined with the development of econometrics as a sub-branch of the discipline, meant that by the 1950s there could be no objection on grounds of principle, as there would have been in the 1930s, to Friedman's contentions about the demand for money. Their truth or falsity was open to econometric testing, and by the end of the 1960s, the empirical issue seemed to have been settled in Friedman's favour. Test after test for a wide variety of times and places appeared to confirm the stability of the demand-for-money function, and hence to establish the importance of the quantity of money.[4]

By the end of the 1960s, then, Friedman's fundamental ideas about the demand for money had become academically successful, but in the course of the academic debate it had also developed in a particular direction. During the course of the debate, notions about the importance of money as a determinant of the behaviour of the general price level that came directly from the quantity theory tradition became more prominent than they had been in Friedman's original (1956) essay (though this idea had been central to the other essays of the volume to which it formed an introduction). The relationship between the demand for money and interest rates was played down, so that real income and prices (or their product-money income) were presented as the critical variables determining the demand for money. Moreover, Friedman argued that, as a first but frequently empirically relevant approximation, real income was determined by factors on the supply side of the economy. Thus, the general price level was left as the principal variable in the demand-for-money function that could change in order to maintain equilibrium when the supply of money varied.[5]

By about 1970 an academically successful proposition about the demand for money had thus been transformed into the notion that price-level fluctuations were to be attributed to variations in the money stock too great to be absorbed by real-income growth. In this form it had acquired the simplicity required to make it successful in the policy arena too; and this at the very time when inflation was becoming the central problem for macroeconomic policy. The early 1970s saw a number of attempts to cure what was widely thought to be 'cost-push' inflation, by a combination of wage and price controls and expansionary demand-side policies designed to reduce the social conflicts that were believed to underlie that cost-push inflation. When they failed, 'monetarist' notions, derived from Friedman's work, were already available to underpin the design of alternative policies based, as everyone knows, on the implementation of target rates of growth for the money supply. In short, Friedman's monetary economics had become a thorough success, in the sense described at the outset of this chapter, in a little less than two decades.

As I remarked earlier, to be successful is not necessarily to be right, and many would argue that the ideas under discussion here have not fared too well over the last decade. On the policy front, a world-wide economic slow-down more or less coincided with the implementation of monetary-policy regimes based on money-growth targets, and critics of such policy regimes were quick and persistent in attributing this slow-down to them. On a more fundamental level, the stability of the demand-for-money function, which provided the scientific basis for the policy regimes in question, has proved to be a good deal less robust than many would have believed possible fifteen years ago. As a result, the close linkage between the behaviour of money and prices upon which 'monetarist' policies rely has been opened to question; and closely related, widespread doubts about the ability of the authorities to control the money supply accurately enough to exploit such a linkage have also arisen. Policy-makers, who were never too comfortable in the first place with the degree of pre-commitment implicit in the adoption of money-growth rates, have offered this instability and its apparent implications as reasons to play down money-growth targets, or to abandon them outright. This reason has appeared to be a good one to many academic commentators, because previously stable empirical demand-for-money functions in many countries *have* been shifting around. This is a well-established result, coming from a wide variety of studies: it is not just a claim advanced by those who were uncomfortable with the new ideas about money from the outset, however pleased they may be to see their discomfort apparently vindicated.

All in all, the stable demand-for-money function has given many signs of suffering the same fate as another successful post-war economic idea, the stable inflation–unemployment trade-off. Like the Phillips curve, the demand-for-money function began to disappear the moment it was made the basis of real-world economic policy. If this interpretation of the evidence is the whole story, then the only answer that we could give to the question 'What do we really know about monetary policy?' would have to begin with some such phrase as 'precious little'. My own preferred answer, however, begins 'Not as much as we thought we did ten years ago, but still quite a lot that is useful,' and I shall devote the balance of this chapter to explaining why.

## *Demand-for-Money Instability*

I noted earlier that, somewhere in the process of becoming thoroughly successful, the idea of a stable demand-for-money function became simplified and transformed into a proposition about the relationship between money and inflation. Though the transformation may well have been necessary for the idea to make an important impact in policy debate, the simplification was nevertheless an oversimplification. This fact lies at the root of much popular disenchantment with 'monetarism'.

In economic analysis, the purpose of a demand function is to enable us to predict the consequences of supply-curve shifts. If the demand for money depends only on the price level, the highly appealing result that reducing the rate of growth of money will reduce the rate of growth of prices is immediately implied. If the demand function takes the form originally proposed by Friedman, the likely implied effect of a slow-down in the rate of monetary expansion is some combination of rising interest rates, falling real-income growth, and falling inflation. Just what combination however, and with what timing, cannot be deduced from consideration of the demand-for-money function alone. It must be derived from an analysis of a complete model of the economy in which all the factors determining the interaction of these four variables (at least) are specified.[6]

Perhaps some of the advocates of a monetary attack upon inflation were overoptimistic about its capacity to work without significantly affecting interest rates, real income, and employment, because of their beliefs about the nature of these other interactions. Beyond doubt any such overoptimism was undermined by events. Even so, the fact remains that the behaviour of interest rates, real income, and prices in the last ten years has been quite compatible with the existence of a stable demand-for-money function of the type originally proposed by Friedman. Furthermore, it is now possible to argue that the lasting effects of the monetary slow-down have indeed been concentrated on the inflation rate. Its influence on interest rates has proved temporary, though long lasting enough to be a matter for serious concern, and recently there has been a considerable resurgence of economic growth. Even though unemployment rates have remained uncomfortably high, and from the point of view of monetarist economics, inexplicably so, this evidence suggests that even the simplified version of Friedman's idea has some long-run validity. The monetary cure for inflation did work after all, though at a greater cost than many of its advocates expected. Moreover, it was much more effective than the earlier medicine of demand expansion combined with price controls. That treatment actually made the disease a good deal worse.

Popular reasons for disenchantment with 'monetarism' do not, that is to say, stand up very well to scrutiny. The experience of the last few years has taught us a few things about the conduct of monetary policy, which I shall discuss in due course, but it has not demonstrated that money does not matter. On the contrary, manipulation of the quantity of money has been shown to be a powerful, perhaps a dangerously powerful, policy tool. However, these popular reasons for disenchantment are not the only or indeed the main ones we must discuss. The fragility of empirical demand-for-money functions, even quite complex ones, provides a much more serious challenge to the ideas which I am discussing in this chapter.

Empirical tests of demand-for-money functions carried out in the 1960s seemed to establish a quite remarkable stability in the relationship, not only over time in specific economies, but across economies as well. By the late 1970s, however, beginning with Steven Goldfeld's (1976) paper on the United States function, things were seen to be going wrong. As with the success of the relationship, so its breakdown was not confined to one country. In country after country in the late 1970s, it appeared that the demand function for whatever particular aggregate had been chosen as the basis of monetary policy had begun to shift around. Goodhart's law—that any monetary aggregate chosen for policy manipulation will immediately become unreliable for that purpose—began to give every indication of becoming a successful economic idea in its own right. There have, I believe, been three sets of reasons for this problem.[7]

First, there is a simple matter of myopia. The original studies that seemed to establish the stability of the demand for money were carried out with long time-series of data. Though the goodness of fit of the relationships in question was high it was by no means perfect. All studies produced occasional runs of data that did not lie on the predicted functions. The latter were right on average, but not year by year. If the demand-for-money function had been used as a basis of policy in the past (which of course it was not) policy would have been in considerable trouble in those badly predicted years. Such errors do not matter with the hindsight that the econometrician brings to them, but they do to the policy-maker who lives through them. To put it simply, in going from the econometrics of the demand for money to its policy application, too many people forgot about the error term. They should not have been surprised when it reminded them of its existence.

There is, though, a second matter to discuss. A significant number of recently observed shifts in the demand function have been of a once-and-for-all type. The culprit here seems to have been institutional change in the financial sector which has changed the economic significance of the aggregates treated as dependent variables in studies of the demand for money, and used as policy tools. This change, as Jonson and Rankin (1986) have argued, in turn seems to have three interconnected causes. In part it is a spontaneous development in the private sector of the economy, in part it is the response of the private sector to particular regulatory environments, and in part it is a result of policy-induced changes in those environments. Whatever its cause, that institutional change could affect the demand for money is an intuitively obvious idea, and yet early studies of the relationship seemed to demonstrate its stability independently of any consideration of this factor. In this respect, it is now clear that they were misleading.

To begin with, the data that they used were constructed, with benefit of much hindsight, after the period to be studied. Those who constructed the data took into account the effects of evolving institutions in deciding which financial assets should be included (and when) in a consistent-over-time series for money.[8] Thus the early studies to which I have referred *did* after all make allowance for institutional changes. They did so, however, in the construction of the data they utilised, and not by including variables measuring such developments in regression equations. In interpreting the results of these studies, economists overlooked the role played by institutional change in generating them. It was predictable (but not predicted), then, that in policy experiments based on measures of money selected *ex ante* rather than *ex post*, the ongoing fact of such change should make its presence known.

Recent studies have shown that not all of the effects of institutional change on the demand for money were in fact incorporated in the process of data construction. Such change is a continuing process, and because studies of the demand for money carried out for lengthy time periods are dominated by trends in both money and income data, those of its effects on the demand for money, not already incorporated in the relevant data, tend to be attributed to the income variable by regression equation. Bordo and Jonung (1981, 1987) have made an extensive study of this matter using data from five countries, and have been able to show, in each case, that the demand for money is indeed a stable function of a few arguments. According to Bordo and Jonung however, among those arguments are variables measuring institutional developments. Moreover, quantitative measures of the parameter linking the demand for money to income are erroneous if these factors are ignored.

Now we must be careful how we interpret this evidence. It does appear to show that, once institutional change is allowed for, it is still possible to maintain the idea of a stable aggregate demand-for-money function. But this does not mean that earlier views about the relationship between the demand for money and monetary policy need no alteration. Institutional change is hard to predict. Sometimes it is spontaneous, but sometimes it occurs as a response to policy measures as well. The fact that, once we allow for it, we can derive a stable demand-for-money function, does not therefore imply that this function can be used as a reliable basis for the design and conduct of future policy. The route from the postulate of a stable demand-for-money function to the derivation of principles for the conduct of monetary policy is a good deal less direct and easily navigated than most of us thought ten or fifteen years ago. I shall take up the implications of all this for policy issues in more detail below, but, before doing so, I must discuss a third source of demand-for-money instability.

The theory of the demand for money tells us about the relationship between the quantity of money demanded and the factors determining it; but the quantity of money *demanded* is not itself a directly observable magnitude. The quantity of money *in circulation* is observable, however; conventional empirical studies of the demand for money have assumed that all money in circulation is willingly held, and hence have used the supply of money to measure the demand for it. Now, to obtain satisfactory results with empirical demand-for-money functions, it is necessary to postulate the existence of time-lags in the relationships, and much recently observed instability in demand-for-money relationships has occurred in the parameters measuring those time-lags. One possible resolution of this problem, which I find appealing, is cast in terms of the so-called 'buffer stock' approach to analysing the demand for money.[9]

This 'buffer stock' approach notes that agents hold money as an inventory of readily available purchasing power, and that they permit the size of that inventory to vary as it acts as a buffer between fluctuations in the value of their receipts and outlays. The 'quantity of money demanded' on this interpretation is the average or target value that agents attempt to maintain over time for their money holdings. It is not an amount which they ensure they have on hand at each and every moment. In this view, fluctutations in the quantity of money in circulation will, in the first instance, simply be absorbed into temporary buffer stocks of money, and will only slowly affect expenditure as agents attempt over time to move their cash holdings back towards their long-run average target value. Moreover, though the individual can get rid of money by spending it, the economy as a whole cannot do so if the money supply is indeed under the control of the monetary authorities. Hence, when the money supply fluctuates, the economy will be 'off' its demand-for-money function until the arguments of that relationship, interest rates, income and prices, move to re-equilibrate the supply of and demand for money.

All this, however, means that, in studies which treat the quantity of money in circulation as an accurate measure of the demand for money, fluctuations in the supply of money induced by policy will erroneously be interpreted as fluctuations in the quantity of money demanded. Moreover, if the lag effects picked up by such conventional studies are in fact the result of interest rates, real income, and prices responding to the efforts of agents to restore their cash holdings to some target level in the wake of supply-induced disturbances, these lag effects too might be expected to show instability when the quantity of money in circulation is itself fluctuating by a significant amount. In fact the monetary contradictions of recent years have been far from smooth processes. Money growth has varied a great deal around a downward trend. According to the buffer-stock approach, this very fact ought to have been responsible for the appearance of instability in conventionally measured demand-for-money functions.

As in the case of institutional change, we must be careful with the interpretation of this argument. If it is true, it does imply that the demand-for-money function is not as unstable as the results of conventional studies would suggest. However, it also implies that the relationships, between the supply of money and the variables upon which the demand for money depends, are more complicated than straightforward supply-and-demand analysis would lead one to believe. Since it is precisely these relationships that must lie at the heart of any monetary policy experiment, the 'buffer stock' interpretation of the apparent instability of the demand-for-money function does require us to modify our views about what is and what is not a feasible set of tasks for monetary policy to undertake. I will now turn to a discussion of these policy issues.

## Monetary Policy

Though the nineteenth-century quantity theory treated money as of critical importance for the determination of the general price level, and though its adherents attached great importance to price-level stability, they did not advocate that the quantity of money be actively manipulated by some policy authority with the aim of achieving such stability. In part this was because nineteenth-century economists had a healthy scepticism about the willingness of anyone in authority to act in the public, as opposed to his own private, interest; but it was also due to their belief that the velocity of circulation was an unpredictably unstable parameter. They preferred a policy regime in which the price level was stabilised by other means and the quantity of money enabled to fluctuate in order to meet the public's, as they saw it, volatile demand for money (though nineteenth-century economists would not have used this phrase): hence the widespread support for the gold standard among them.

The First World War effectively destroyed the gold standard, though its final demise was not to come until 1931. Even so, proposals to place control of the quantity of money at the centre of things were rather rare in the 1920s and early 1930s. The literature of this period typically discussed the means whereby the rate of interest could be manipulated in order to maintain a stable price level by ensuring that (to put it in modern language) the full-employment level of investment was kept equal to the full-employment level of saving.[10] A by-product of the successful implementation of such a policy would be a time path for the behaviour of the money supply compatible with the economy's demand for money. In this sense, money mattered to the contributors of this literature, but not as a policy instrument. The importance of money was further downgraded as a result of the intellectual revolution which followed the (1936) publication of Keynes's *General Theory*, which replaced the price level by the level of employment as the central concern of macroeconomic policy. Keynesian analysis, to the extent that it accorded any importance at all to monetary policy, always treated it as subsidiary to fiscal policy as an income-stabilisation device.

When the revival of interest in the quantity of money began in the 1950s, it was, as we have seen, accompanied by the radically new idea that the demand for money was a stable function of just a few arguments. This new idea implied that the velocity of circulation, though not constant, was reliable enough to provide a basis for a monetary policy which did indeed involve controlling the money supply with a view to achieving price-level targets. Along with the new theoretical idea, went a new policy idea also developed by Friedman (1960): namely that price-level (and indeed general macroeconomic) stability could be greatly enhanced by putting the quantity of money on a predetermined growth path from which it would not be allowed to deviate. This policy idea, the 'money-supply growth rule', provides a useful focus for any discussion of the policy implications of the evidence about the demand for money generated over the last ten years.

The first thing to be clear about here is that policies of setting medium-target growth-rate ranges for the money supply, the actual form in which the new ideas about money discussed in this chapter found their way into the policy arena, were somewhat removed from Friedman's proposals completely to replace discretionary policies by such a rule. Such policies were, by their very nature, open to change in the future, and because they involved *target ranges* for money growth, instead of a *well-defined path*, they left considerable room for short-term manipulation of the money supply into the bargain.

That 'monetarist' ideas should be translated into policy actions in this way had a great deal to do with the state of the economy at the time at which those ideas became fashionable. When Friedman proposed a money-supply growth rule permanently binding upon central bankers, the economy (or at least the US economy about which he was writing) was to all intents and purposes inflation free. His proposal was thus one for ensuring continued stability in an already stable economy. By the time his ideas became popular, the economy was in an altogether different condition. In the mid-1970s inflation was both high and rising in the US and elsewhere. The policy problem was not to maintain, but to restore stability; and an immediate move to a rate of monetary expansion compatible with long-run price stability would have had devastating effects on real income and employment. That rate of expansion had to be approached gradually from above, and for this purpose medium-term growth targets, open to revision in due course, seemed to be required. Nevertheless, now that inflation is on the verge of acceptable ranges in a number of countries, it is not inappropriate to ask what the implications of the evidence generated over the last decade might be for the pursuit of a monetary growth-rate rule.

As we have seen, even what was at least supposed to be a gradualist policy seems to have had serious effects on interest rates and real income, and the straightforward hypothesis of a stable demand-for-money function has been badly battered. Though I shall not end up defending a simple growth-rate rule in this chapter, I shall argue that the evidence referred to above is less damaging to such a proposal than is often imagined; and I shall argue that medium-term growth-rate targeting is still both feasible and desirable. Though such a policy regime stops far short of a rule, it is still a good deal closer to it than to any monetary policy regimes that were thought desirable before the 1950s.

My basic reasons for taking this position are to be found in my interpretation of the evidence on the outcome of monetary policy over the last ten years and on the instability of the demand-for-money function in particular. I readily agree that much of the real slow-down that we have seen, particularly in the early 1980s, should be attributed to monetary policy; but surely this argues for avoiding the kind of monetary policy that produced the problem. Two properties characterise money growth vetween the mid-1970s and 1983. Its rate was on average below the growth rate of nominal income, and it was also very volatile. If we are to avoid further real contractions induced by monetary factors (and I would not wish to rule out the possibility of contractions traceable to other sources) it would seem that a falling and volatile money-growth rate is to be shunned. To set money-growth targets within rather narrow ranges, and with a positive trend roughly equal to the economy's underlying long-run real-growth rate, would accomplish this.

But what about instability in the demand for money? If the money supply behaves itself, cannot demand fluctuations nevertheless have disruptive effects? In principle they certainly can. I have argued above that some of the apparent instability we have observed in the demand-for-money function has been attributable to the kind of random fluctuations that are present in any real-world economy. I have also argued that some of it has been due to instability in the behaviour of the money supply. Such sources of instability in the demand function as these are very damaging indeed to the case for using monetary policy as an active tool of short-run stabilisation policy, such as advanced by Modigliani (1977). This approach to monetary policy lies at the very heart of the American 'Keynesian' tradition, and is quite alien to that tradition as it has evolved elsewhere, which stresses the stabilising powers of fiscal policy. The difference here arises from the fact that American political institutions are incapable of delivering the rapid changes in fiscal policy that are required to make it a credible stabilisation device, so that advocates of fine tuning there are forced to rely on monetary policy. If short-run instability in the demand-for-money function undermines the American 'Keynesian' view of monetary policy, however, it does little harm to the case for gearing that policy to the pursuit of medium-term objectives. Random errors do tend to cancel out over time, and if money growth is not volatile, then money-supply fluctuations cannot disturb the relationship between the quantity of money and the variables affecting the demand for it.

If random errors and supply-of-money shocks were the only causes of recent instability in empirical estimates of the demand-for-money function, it would still be possible to make the case for basing policy on a simple money growth-rate rule. However, they are not. There is still the matter of institutional change to consider. New financial assets do get created, old ones do change their significance in the structure of the economy, and such changes are difficult enough to recognise as they happen, let alone to predict. A money-growth rule that was supposed to be binding ever afterwards on the authorities would have to embody a particular definition of money in its formulation. If it didn't, the authorities could evade the discipline of the rule by changing that definition as it suited their purpose. But, in the presence of institutional change, someone somewhere has to have the freedom to make such changes, otherwise the effects of the rule on the time path of the economy will deviate from its framers' original intentions as the institutional background changes. If they are to maintain a stable monetary environment by controlling the 'money supply', the relevant authorities must, as Jonson and Rankin (1986) argue, have discretionary power. Binding rules are not technically feasible, but medium-term targets, which permit a little discretion in the short run, and more in the long run as they are updated and revised, are.

This implication of recent experience has caused a number of commentators to go one step further, and to argue for gearing monetary policy to the pursuit of a stable target range for the growth rate of *money income* rather than the money supply *per se*.[11] On an abstract and purely technical level, these two proposals amount to very much the same thing. After all, the purpose of choosing a particular target for money growth is to attain a more distant, but a nevertheless ultimately more important, goal for the behaviour of the price level; and hence, if real income is supply-side determined, of money income. Jonson and Rankin's (1986) discussion of the use of a 'check-list' of variables in the conduct of monetary policy shows this procedure to be more closely related to 'targeting' than may appear at first sight. They argue that, at times of rapid institutional change, the growth rate of any monetary aggregate is an unreliable indicator of the stance of policy, and that information about the likely future behaviour of money income is available in current data on such variables as interest rates, the exchange rate, inflation rate, and so on. They then argue that such information can be used in the design of policy intended to stabilise money-income growth without the need to specify targets for the behaviour of any specific intermediate variable.

There can be no strong arguments against these procedures on grounds of theoretical principle. However, in practice I still prefer policy targets to be set in terms of the quantity of money rather than money income or as a function of some 'check-list'. The time-lags between policy actions and their effects on money income are long and badly understood, as are the relationships between income growth and any 'check-list'. Also money income is susceptible to shocks from sources other than monetary policy. A policy geared either directly to money-income growth, or indirectly through a check-list, is therefore more difficult for outsiders to monitor and criticise on a continuing basis than one based on money growth. Given that policy-makers must be given discretion over monetary policy, and given the many pressures to act irresponsibly to which they are inevitably subjected by political processes, the more easily monitored and criticised they are, the better. This argument does not, of course, preclude the authorities from using a 'check-list' of variables in choosing where, within their target range, money growth should actually be; nor does it preclude the deployment of data on the behaviour of other variables in the defence of a change in policy towards money growth, should that be deemed desirable. Its intent is to ensure that policy goals are stated clearly in advance, and that any change in policy be quickly visible and subject to public debate. The simplicity of using money-growth targets as the centre-piece of policy has much to recommend it in this respect.

Now not everyone reads the evidence in this way. Some commentators, while agreeing that institutional changes make it impossible to take discretion away from monetary policy-makers by imposing a monetary growth rule upon them, note that there are alternative ways of tying them down which do not suffer from this defect. In particular, requiring the monetary authorities to stand ready to convert money at a fixed price into some stable-valued item—some non-inflationary foreign currency for example, or some commodity, of which gold is of course the archetype— would take away their discretionary powers. It would also effectively tie down the behaviour of the price level and permit the money supply to fluctuate in whatever way is necessary to satisfy the demand for it. Therefore, they propose that we return to a regime very like that which ruled in the international economy before the First World War. Though well enough conceived in principle, I believe that there are important practical objections to these proposals.

To begin with, to remove the authorities' freedom of action, an exchange rate would have to be really fixed. An adjustable peg system would simply open up the possibility of discretionary policy by another route. Bearing this in mind, and even setting aside the problem of finding some currency or commodity stable enough to make a desirable standard, we must not forget that real shocks as well as monetary shocks impinge on the world economy. Adherence to a fixed exchange rate requires an economy which suffers an adverse terms-of-trade shift to adjust by forcing down domestic money wages. The alternative, under a money-growth target regime, is to allow the depreciation of a flexible exchange rate not offset by money-wage increases to bear the brunt of adjustment. Of course the ultimate real consequences of either adjustment must be the same, and of course, in a fully rational world, one form of adjustment would be as easy as the other. However, we should design monetary-policy institutions with the real world in mind, and an exchange-rate depreciation, which indirectly affects everyone at once, is more likely to be absorbed by an economy without disruptions than the alternative of a series of piecemeal and uncoordinated money-wage reductions.[12]

Second, for a fixed-exchange-rate regime to be viable for the world economy as a whole, or for a substantial segment of it, macroeconomic policies in general, and monetary policies in particular, would have to be co-ordinated among participating countries. I have nothing against the international co-ordination of policies, quite the contrary; but policy authorities with sufficient self-discipline to co-ordinate their policies with those of other countries so as to maintain their exchange rate fixed on some stable-valued currency or commodity, could surely also be trusted with the more modest task of setting and sticking to sensible domestic money-growth targets. To put the same point in another way, the first task is to induce discipline in domestic policies. If this is accomplished, stability of exchange rates will take care of itself. If it is not, then a fixed-exchange-rate regime will prove impossible to implement and sustain. It is not, therefore, a viable alternative to money-growth targeting as a basis for policy.

This is not, though, to argue that the international monetary system imposes no discipline on the conduct of domestic policy. The theoretical ideas of Russel Boyer about 'currency substitution' under flexible exchange rates, first written up in 1973 (but not published until 1978) have been amply borne out by recent experience. As Melvin (1985) has shown, using European data, a country whose domestic monetary policy is volatile will make agents engaged in international trade unwilling to hold its currency, and hence will find its international transactions complicated by a weak and fluctuating exchange rate. International monetary mechanisms, that is, encourage the pursuit of stable domestic monetary policy even in the absence of fixed exchange rates.

The question of whether the domestic money supply is indeed controllable does, of course, still arise, and there is not space to discuss it in detail here. Suffice it to make the following observations. First, the experience of the 1970s and early 1980s does show that attempts to control the money supply, by first monitoring income and prices, and then directly manipulating interest rates in the hope that the economy's efforts to stay 'on' its demand for money function will keep the money supply on track, are misconceived. As Howitt and Laidler (1979) argued, such a policy package ignores the links between interest rates and the behaviour of credit markets, and the strategic role of bank credit creation in the generation of money, independently of the demand for money *per se*.

Second, and more generally, it is impossible to lay down mechanical formulae whereby the money supply can be controlled without referring to the institutional framework. However, if this is variable, the discretion which must be accorded the authorities in setting money-growth targets will also have to extend to their choice of monetary control techniques. My own preference would be for some type of monetary base control applied to a rather broad aggregate, but precise operating procedures for its successful implementation must inevitably depend upon the structure of any particular financial system. Given the degree of discretion for the authorities implied here, and given the many pressures to which they are subject, the need for constant monitoring of their actions, already referred to above, is all the more pressing. The case for money, as opposed to money income, targeting is thus further strengthened by questions about the controllability of the money supply.

## Conclusions

What then do we really know about monetary policy? As a matter of logic, we know that, if the time path of real income is, in the long run, driven by supply-side factors, the interaction of the supply and demand for money determines the behaviour of the general price level. We know, also as a matter of logic, that, if the demand for money is indeed a stable function of but a few arguments, then keeping the money supply on a stable growth path will stabilise the behaviour of the price level. Shocks induced by the money supply itself would clearly be ruled out in this case, and steady money growth will act as a useful built-in stabiliser against the effects of other shocks. The trouble, as we have seen, is that logic does not tell the whole story in this particular case. There are a few awkward facts to be considered too. Though the evidence does seem to be bearing out the prediction that money affects mainly prices in the long run, experience has been less kind to the postulate of a stable demand-for-money function.

The existence of random fluctuations in the demand for money is not in and of itself an insuperable difficulty. They do imply that steady money growth will not deliver perfect price stability on a quarter-by-quarter or even a year-by-year basis, no matter how carefully its rate is calibrated to the rate of growth of real output. However, their influence will tend to cancel itself out over time. As to fluctuations in the relationship between the quantity of money and other variables, which are the results of variations in the quantity of money itself, these can obviously be no problem in the context of steady money growth, troublesome though they may be for the interpretation of historical data generated when policy was unstable.

Institutional change, however, does present real difficulties. It has long been a complaint of the critics of 'monetarism' that, in modern economies, with their complex financial systems, it is far from clear just what is and what is not 'money' for purposes of designing policy. It used to seem possible to answer such criticism by conceding its logical validity while denying its empirical importance. It no longer is, and this fact has important implications for monetary policy, as I have argued. Its conduct either must be placed in the context of a set of constraints involving fixed exchange rates and some form of commodity convertibility, or must permit a good deal of discretion to the relevant national monetary authorities both in their choice of which aggregate to control, and in the means whereby that control is achieved. Since I do not believe that the former alternative is viable, we seem to be left with the second.

How then should the monetary authorities use their discretion? I have suggested that they should do so in such a way as to keep whatever shifting definition of money may be appropriate to a given time and place on a time path that is consistent with the pursuit of long-run price stability. Such a policy would appropriately be implemented in terms of a public commitment to target ranges for 'money' growth, revised at regular intervals. I make this second suggestion not because of the potentially stabilising effects of money growth targeting on agents' expectations. These effects have surely been shown to be of minor importance in the last few years. Rather I advocate medium-term money growth targeting because it seems to me to provide the best way to expose the authorities to monitoring and criticism.

Real economic variables do get subjected to troublesome shocks. There is, and will remain, a political demand for 'effective' short-run stabilisation policy. Though monetary policy clearly can have powerful real effects in the short run, so that there is always a temptation to use it for such stabilisation, I have argued in this chapter that the timing of these effects is too uncertain for it successfully to be used in this way. A key problem, then, is to prevent the monetary authorities responding to demands for stabilisation measures and, in attempting to meet them, rendering the economy less, rather than more stable. If binding rules are not viable, then continuous public monitoring presents an alternative way of attempting to constrain the authorities to behave responsibly. Providing for it, therefore, is no light matter. A policy regime that forces them to state their intentions for money growth *ex ante*, and hence permits their performance to be continuously observed and criticised in the light of these intentions, will make it more difficult for them to succumb to the temptation to aim at more ambitious goals.

Another defence against the misuse of monetary policy, complementary to this one, would involve the availability of alternative means for stabilising the real economy. Here one's mind naturally turns to fiscal measures. I would be willing to argue that these are useful tools of short-run stabilisation, *provided they are used against the background of a monetary policy regime that is unequivocally devoted to the pursuit of price-level stability*. Moreover, in parliamentary systems, such tools can be deployed and implemented quite rapidly. In the United States it is another matter, and it is surely no accident that so much of the opposition to abandoning the idea of using monetary policy for short-run stabilisation arises in a country whose institutions render fiscal weapons unsuitable for this purpose.

There is not space here to enter into a detailed discussion of fiscal policy.

Suffice it to say that there are, as I have said, good reasons why there should be a political demand for short-run stabilisation policy; and my purpose in this chapter is *not* to argue that this demand should not be met, but only that it should not be met by monetary means. As should by now be apparent, I say this because my one-sentence answer to the question 'How much do we really know about monetary policy?' boils down to 'Enough to prevent it doing harm, but not enough to use it to do good'. I hope for all our sakes that this answer does not prove to be too complicated to be politically successful.

## Notes

1 Of course Friedman's propositions about the demand for money form the basis from his case for a monetary policy 'rule' as set out in *A Programme for Monetary Stability* (1960). This matter is discussed below.

2 The reader who is familiar with Friedman's essay will recognise that I am simplifying its content a little here. I am not mentioning its analysis of the subtle interrelationship of income and wealth, and I am ignoring the role of an array of interest rates on various assets both real and nominal, as well as expected inflation, as separate measures of the opportunity cost of holding money. Instead I refer only to nominal rates in general. In the present context, I hope it will be agreed that these simplifications are harmless.

3 The relationship between Friedman's work, the quantity/theory tradition and Keynesian monetary economics, is contentious. Relevant contributions to the discussion of this issue include Patinkin (1969, 1986), Parkin (1986b) and sections of Friedman (1974).

4 Lionel Robbins's (1935) *Nature and Significance of Economic Science* expressed great scepticism about the stability over time of empirical relationships in economics, a scepticism which was widespread (though not universal) among his contemporaries. The first (1969) edition of my own *Demand for Money* gives, I hope, a reasonable account of how the evidence on the demand for money appeared at that time.

5 This is not the place to write a history of the development of Friedman's monetary thought. Nevertheless, the interested reader will find the role of interest rates played down in (1959), the emphasis shifted from the demand for money *per se* to money/money-income relationships in Friedman and Meiselman (1963), and the suggestion that holding real income constant is often a useful first approximation, in Friedman (1974). It should be pointed out explicitly that the revival of interest in money was not solely the result of Friedman's efforts. In this context, the work of Karl Brunner and Allan Meltzer, e.g. (1963), is also particularly worthy of notice.

6 The reader's attention is drawn to the use of the word 'likely' in this discussion. I have described here a response in which each argument in the demand function moves in the direction that it would have to take if it alone was to restore equilibrium to the supply and demand for money. Of course a richer array of possible responses than this is logically conceivable. For a further discussion see Chapter 1 of the (1985) edition of my *Demand for Money*.

7 The law is named after its originator, Professor Charles Goodhart. It represents a special case of Robert E. Lucas's (1976) general scepticism about

assuming the stability of empirical relationships in the face of changes in the conduct of policy. For recent discussions on the stability of the demand for money function, see Judd and Scadding (1982a) and Laidler (1985).

8 The relevant source to consult for details of the construction of US money statistics is, of course, Friedman and Schwartz (1970).

9 A number of Australian economists and economists who have worked in Australia, notably at the University of Adelaide, have made important contributions to this strand of monetary analysis. See Artis and Lewis (1976), Lewis (1978), Jonson (1976a, 1976b) and Jonson et al. (1976) for examples. I have attempted to survey its salient features in Chapter 2, above.

10 American quantity theorists working in the tradition of Irving Fisher (1911) are something of an exception here. It is in comparison with this type of policy analysis that Friedman's work has its strongest claim to continuity with the quantity theory tradition.

11 Among the proponents of stabilising money-income growth as opposed to money-supply growth are Sam Brittan (1982) and Robert Gordon (1983). For a penetrating survey of the theoretical issues involved here see McCallum (1985).

12 These issues are discussed in more detail in Chapters 8 and 9, below.

# 8

# International Monetary Economics in Theory and Practice

## *Introduction*

In the history of monetary economics, questions of practical economic policy have been the single most important impetus to research, even apparently purely theoretical research. The economic well-being that the monetary system has so much to do with promoting is a legitimate matter of political concern, and in the modern world the institutions whereby that concern is expressed and dealt with are overwhelmingly national in character. International institutions do exist, but their main role is to disseminate information and provide forums for discussion, not to exercise political power. Political power resides at the level of the national state, and it should therefore not be surprising that a body of analysis designed to deal with policy issues views the world principally from the vantage point of the policy-makers of the nation state. Though some contributors to interational monetary economics, e.g. Robert Mundell (1971) and John Floyd (1985), have concerned themselves with the functioning of the world economy as an entity in its own right, the bulk of the literature that I shall survey here is written from the former viewpoint.

Policy prescriptions must, of course, be based in part on political judgements but, if policy prescriptions are to be viable, they need a sound analytic foundation. My principal aim in this chapter is not so much to derive detailed policy prescriptions for the monetary aspects of Canada's international economic relations, as to set out the economic considerations that must be taken into account in arriving at such prescriptions. I shall certainly have much to say about policy and about the choice of exchange-rate regimes in particular. I shall therefore find it impossible to avoid making political judgements. However, in what follows, I shall stress what economic theory and historical experience suggest is and is not economically viable rather than get involved in a detailed discussion of the implementation of specific policy measures.

My analysis will be limited in one other important respect. I shall discuss international monetary matters principally as they impinge upon so-called market economies. In practice, that means economies with more or less freely convertible currencies whose international economic relations involve to a significant extent the decentralised activities of individuals and privately owned firms. What follows is thus mainly relevant to the international economic relations of advanced Western economies and perhaps relevant to the international economic relations of the rapidly developing market economies of South-east Asia. There can be no doubt that the relationships of these economies to the Eastern bloc and to the many less developed countries—by no means all socialist—that have adopted a largely non-market approach to organising their economic activity have a monetary aspect. However, given the lack of market institutions underlying these relationships, the analysis that follows has less to say, at least in a direct fashion, about them. Though I shall not entirely ignore these matters here, I shall pay relatively little attention to them. This is not because they are unimportant, but rather because they are sufficiently important to warrant a study in their own right.

The essay is in two parts. First, theoretical issues are discussed: the monetary approach, fixed exchange rates among national monies, domestic policy under fixed exchange rates, domestic policy under flexible exchange rates among national monies, and the international monetary system under flexible exchange rates. Then, in the second part, three topics are analysed: the Bretton Woods system, the recent experience with floating rates, and international monetary reform.

## The Monetary Approach

Practical matters cannot be discussed in a vacuum. Much of this chapter will be concerned with sketching a theoretical framework in terms of which questions about the international monetary system can be posed and evidence on its operation organised. In particular, the chapter will deal with insights yielded by the theoretical and empirical literature of the past decade or so; this literature has been devoted largely to debating the virtues and vices of the so-called monetary approach to analysing balance-of-payments and exchange-rate issues.[1]

The phrase 'monetary approach' has more than one interpretation in the literature. In some contexts, the phrase refers to a very special set of hypotheses about how the real world operates: the demand-for-money function is stable; purchasing-power parity is continuous in the sense that, adjusted for changes in exchange rates, the price levels of individual countries move in lock-step with one another; the international mobility of capital is perfect; and so on. Although each postulate may be a useful approximation to reality in a particular time and place, we shall see that none is generally true. Hence 'monetary approach' is used here more loosely to refer to a method of analysing balance-of-payments and exchange-rate issues which stresses the interaction of the supply of and demand for money.

In this sense, the monetary approach is not a new body of analysis yielding results different from those of other bodies of theory that stress, for example, the role of relative prices in determining trade flows. Rather, the monetary approach provides an alternative and usually simpler way of achieving the same results as would a correct application of these other bodies of theory. What is crucial is that the monetary approach ensures that the monetary elements of balance-of-payments and exchange-rate behaviour cannot be overlooked. The monetary approach is particularly helpful in getting to grips with the consequences for the balance of payments and exchange rates of domestic monetary policies; since much of the instability that has characterised the international monetary system over the past two decades had its origin in unstable domestic monetary policies, the monetary approach is an analytically powerful and simple tool for interpreting recent history.

The analytic power and simplicity of the monetary approach are not achieved costlessly. Though its results are often theoretically clear-cut, they must be applied to real-world situations with care. The approach stresses long-run phenomena, such as the relationships among monetary policies, exchange rates, and price levels. It pays less attention to short-run issues, such as fluctuations in output and employment. Since the duration of these short-run fluctuations is best measured in years, that the monetary approach treats these fluctuations as temporary does not mean that they are unimportant. On the other hand, the long run in economic life is not just a series of short runs. Rather, 'long run' refers to underlying trends that, though always present, are sometimes obscured by shorter-run fluctuations. It is one of the great strengths of the monetary approach that it forces us to pay attention to such trends, because coherent and sustainable economic policy cannot be designed without reference to them.

It is helpful to begin our discussion of the monetary approach on a rather abstract level. Such abstraction will not reveal the whole truth about the world we live in but will help us see clearly certain important properties of that world which are otherwise easy—but dangerous—to overlook. First, let us consider an idealised world in which trade and capital flows among nations are completely unregulated and in which there is a supranational monetary system which provides just one money, equally acceptable in all countries.[2] With the important difference that there is no 'rest of the world' to which it is open, such a world somewhat resembles the contemporary Canadian economy, with the provinces cast in the role of component countries and the Bank of Canada presiding over the monetary system. Such a world economy has never existed, nor is it ever likely to, and assertions about its properties cannot be directly tested. Indeed, even within Canada, trade and capital flows are not totally unregulated. Nevertheless, as will become apparent as this essay develops, the assertions we are about to discuss do not entirely lack a basis in real-world experience.

It is a well-known proposition that, at any given time, the aggregate of economic agents in an economy seek to maintain their money holdings at a target level which depends on their real income (probably averaged over a period of years, including future years so that expectations are involved here), the level and structure of nominal interest rates on assets other than money, and the general price level. In theory, the aggregate demand for money is strictly proportional to the general price level. As an empirical matter, the stability of the aggregate demand-for-money function—whether at the level of the national or the world economy—is far from perfect. The demand-for-money function shifts over time in response to institutional changes in a manner as difficult to predict *ex ante* as it is easy to rationalise *ex post*; it is also subject to random variations, particularly from quarter to quarter and even from year to year. However, the relationship is so robust on average over two or three years that it must not be ignored in the conduct of monetary policy. Although the relationship cannot be used as a basis for fine-tuning the economy, it must be taken careful account of in the interpretation of economic history, not least recent history.[3]

The monetary approach starts by assuming that such a demand-for-money function exists, not only for each national economy but also for the world economy as a whole. Furthermore, if real income and real rates of return can be treated as depending, at least on average over time, on such factors as the size and productivity of the world labour force and stock of capital, and if prices are flexible, the money supply in this world economy must determine its price level. The assumption of free trade ensures that differences in the price level among countries are sustainable only to the extent that the prices of non-tradable goods and services vary among countries. The distinction between non-tradables and tradables here depends upon the physical possibility of the good being traded internationally at a reasonable transactions cost, and not upon whether it actually does cross a national boundary. The assumption of capital mobility ensures that a similar statement can be made about interest rates. Only if the net balance on combined trade and capital accounts of each country with the sum of the others is equal to zero can a balance-of-payments equilibrium be said to exist in this world.[4]

Any country with a balance-of-payments surplus will find itself with a net inflow of money from the rest of the world. That inflow's interaction with the domestic demand-for-money function will put downward pressure on domestic interest rates and upward pressure on domestic output and prices. These tendencies will weaken the balance of payments until their source is eliminated, but that source is the balance-of-payments surplus with which we started. Clearly this argument also works in reverse, and leads directly to the following insights: in such a world, the role of the balance of payments is to allocate the world money supply among the national economies making up the world economy, and any balance-of-payments surplus or deficit is a temporary phenomenon reflecting a discrepancy between the quantity of money available in a particular economy and the quantity demanded.

## Fixed Exchange Rates among National Monies

All this is very simple, but the international economy of which Canada forms a part is more complex. How do the complications of the real world affect the relevance of this simple analysis? There has never existed an international economy based on free trade in goods and capital that has used one money. However, under the Bretton Woods system (the international monetary system of more-or-less fixed exchange rates that was set up after the Second World War and which collapsed in the 1970s), there did exist a rather liberal international economic order in which national currencies, emitted by domestic banking systems, were exchangeable against one another at more-or-less fixed rates. Such a world differs in a number of conspicuous ways from a world which uses a single currency.

To begin with, along with the national currency go a series of domestic institutions which apparently make it possible for the supply of any particular national currency to be changed by means other than balance-of-payments flows. The central bank and the commercial banking system are able to buy and sell domestic debt instruments, whether emitted by the government or by the private sector, in exchange for the domestic money that forms the liabilities of the central and commercial banks. There might exist a specifically international money in such a system, but instead of circulating domestically in each country, this money plays a specialised role, being held more or less exclusively by the banking system in the form of international reserves for use in settling payments imbalances. The amount of such reserve holdings on the asset side of the banking system's balance sheet is matched by liabilities held by the general public in the form of domestic money.[5] Balance-of-payments flows still affect the domestic money supply, but indirectly through the purchases and sales of foreign-exchange reserves by the banking system rather than by direct entry into domestic circulation.

The above-mentioned differences, important as they are from the viewpoint of the individual country, must not be allowed to obscure the all-important similarity between this world and one of a single money when this world is viewed from the perspective of the international economy: a series of national currencies linked by fixed exchange rates still constitute a meaningful aggregate which may be described as the world money supply; it is still meaningful to talk of a world demand-for-money function as an aggregate relationship in its own right which, interacting with that world money supply, determines a price level common to all parts of the world economy; and it is also meaningful to talk of a world interest rate to the extent that capital movements are free. For the individual country, the interesting question is whether and how far it can insulate itself from such world-wide influences, when it has a national currency and domestic monetary institutions.[6]

When discussing the relationship between the world and domestic price levels under a fixed exchange rate, it is vital to distinguish between two very different issues. First, might the domestic price level in a particular country systematically diverge in the long run from that ruling in the rest of the world under fixed rates (or a world money)? Second, to what extent can the authorities of a particular country, desiring an inflation rate different from that ruling in the world at large, achieve that different rate in the long run when national monies do indeed exist? The distinction between tradable and non-tradable goods is important here. In Scandinavian terms, the distinction is between the open and sheltered sectors of the economy— the open sector producing goods sold on a world-wide market in competition both at home and abroad with the output of other countries, and the sheltered sector, as a result of the technical nature of its products, having sole access to a closed domestic market.[7]

In any country, the domestic price level is a suitably weighted average of prices ruling in both the open and sheltered sectors, but it is only prices in the open sector that may be said to be determined directly on a world-wide basis. However, the open sector competes with the sheltered sector in domestic markets for inputs, notably labour, and, so the argument goes, the domestic wage rate is largely determined by the world price for tradable output adjusted for the productivity of the domestic labour force. With the price that the sheltered sector must pay for labour thus fixed, and given the productivty of labour there, the price of non-tradable output is also determined.

If the relative sizes of the two sectors, or productivity differences between them, vary among countries, so will price levels; moreover, if rates of productivity growth differ between sectors among countries, so will inflation rates among countries. In a world of fixed exchange rates, therefore, there is no reason to expect that every country will have the same price level or the same inflation rate, any more than there is reason to believe that the cost of living should be the same in every part of Canada or that its rate of change should everywhere be the same—though domestic labour mobility tends to dampen any tendency for regional price-level disparities to open up continuously within a single country. The point of all this is that the existence of overwhelming evidence to the effect that national price levels and inflation rates do diverge systematically from one another under fixed exchange rates does not mean that domestic authorities have any more long-run control over their own country's inflation rate than they would have under a single world money. In either case, their control would be indirect at best and would arise from the possibility of affecting domestic productivity trends.

## Domestic Policy under Fixed Exchange Rates

Suppose that an attempt were made to slow down, by monetary means, the inflation rate in a particular fixed-exchange-rate economy. The authorities would begin to sell bonds to the public to reduce the domestic rate of monetary expansion; in doing so, they would put upward pressure on domestic interest rates. If capital were mobile internationally, this interest-rate pressure would attract an inflow of capital; to maintain the exchange rate, the authorities would buy foreign-exchange reserves with newly issued money. If domestic bonds and foreign bonds were perfect substitutes, that would be the end of the story: there would occur a substitution of foreign-exchange reserves for domestic bonds among the banking system's assets, with no change in the money supply and no consequences for domestic prices and their rate of change.

With less than perfect capital mobility, the authorities' actions would initially reduce the monetary growth rate, which would put downward pressure on domestic aggregate demand. The tradables sector would be induced to switch output from domestic to export markets, while the sheltered, non-tradables sector would shrink, releasing resources to the tradables sector. The balance of payments would improve, reserves would flow in, and upward pressure would be put upon the rate of growth of the money supply. To be sure, the authorities might offset this pressure for a while by so-called sterilisation operations, selling domestic bonds at a greater rate than initially, but such operations could not go on for ever unless the authorities were willing to accumulate reserves without limit.[8] Therefore, any attempt to use monetary policy to drive domestic prices away from the time path inherent in the interactions of world prices and domestic-productivity trends is eventually futile under a fixed exchange rate. Monetary policy can affect the balance of payments and alter the ratio between domestic bonds and foreign-exchange reserves in the portfolio of the banking system, but in the long run that is all that monetary policy can do.

The phrase 'long run' is important here, because there always exists the possibility under fixed exchange rates that because of some temporary shock, the domestic price level will take a value incompatible with prices ruling abroad at the current exchange rate. In such a case, monetary policy can, and indeed must, be deployed to correct such a disequilibrium. However, it was shown by Laidler (1975, Chapter 9) that, where contractionary monetary policy is required, it might be appropriate to accompany it with a devaluation to mitigate its short-run effects on real income and employment. This conclusion of course presupposes that the fixed-exchange-rate regime in operation permits such an adjustment.

Though many exercises carried out by proponents of the monetary approach to balance-of-payments and exchange-rate analysis concentrate exclusively on the consequences of monetary shocks, it does not follow that if, in the long run, monetary policy affects only the balance of payments, the balance of payments is affected only by monetary policy. For example, an increase in the productivity of labour in the tradable-goods sector will undoubtedly lead to a balance-of-payments surplus for a while.[9] The resulting increase in the domestic money supply will partly go to satisfy an increased demand for real money stemming from the rise in domestic income inherent in such a productivity increase; but the increase in the domestic money supply is also likely to be associated with an increase in the domestic price level as money wages, and hence prices, rise in the non-tradables sector. To give another example, an increase in the world demand for the particular products of the domestic export sector will improve the terms of trade and lead to a temporary balance-of-payments surplus. In this case too, an increase in the domestic wage level and price level is likely to accompany the resulting increase in the money supply, but some of the increase in the money supply will again be absorbed by an increase in the demand for real balances associated with an increase in the economy's real income. Of course, foreign demand can fall or increase; if demand falls, the processes just described work in reverse. If permissible, an exchange depreciation (appreciation) might be used to offset the contractionary (expansionary) effects on real income and employment that would be likely to accompany adjustment under a rigid fixed parity.

The proposition that monetary policy influences only the balance of payments under a fixed-exchange-rate regime is, as we have seen, strictly and generally true only of the ultimate effects of monetary policy. However, when capital is perfectly and instantaneously mobile internationally, any attempt by the domestic authorities to change the money supply is immediately offset by repercussions on the capital account of the balance of payments. If it is possible for domestic interest rates to vary for a while relative to those ruling in the rest of the world, expansionary monetary policy might increase domestic aggregate demand for some time, with higher output and a rising domestic price level (relative to its sustainable long-run path) being the temporary consequences; contractionary policy would have the opposite effects. How long such temporary effects might be sustainable is not a matter about which one can generalise. The more sensitive are trade flows to relative price variations, and the more mobile is capital in response to interest-rate differentials, the shorter and less significant these effects can be. As a practical matter, the scope for capital mobility to undermine even the temporary effectiveness of monetary policy seems greater than that of trade flows. In any event, in the absence of changes in the world economy, the policy that produces such temporary effects must always be given up eventually if a fixed exchange rate is to be maintained. It might even have to be put into reverse for a while, if that policy's effects on the banking system's holdings of international reserves take them outside some desired limits. Here again the possibility of parity changes might arise as part of the adjustment mechanism.

There is also fiscal policy, of course: and one of the principal messages of the well-known 1960s-vintage Mundell–Fleming model of macroeconomic policy in an open economy is that, under a fixed rate, monetary policy is powerless whereas fiscal policy is particularly effective.[10] That model has it that, with a fixed exchange rate and a high (in the limit, perfect) degree of capital mobility, expansionary fiscal policy cannot be crowded out by rising interest rates. Furthermore, that prices are largely determined on world markets means that the main effect of fiscal policy must be on domestic income and employment. Unfortunately, viewed from the vantage point of analysis developed in the 1970s, including the monetary approach, there are a few important qualifications to this optimistic result.

To begin with, and obviously, this result can hold only in an economy in which resources are initially less than fully utilised. If they are fully utilised, increased demand for output will tend to put upward pressure on domestic money wages and prices and hence have an adverse effect on the trade balance. In effect, the resource constraint on the economy's capacity to supply output will ensure that extra government expenditure or private expenditure induced by tax-cuts crowds out production elsewhere, including that of export and import substitutes. Moreover, the resource constraint is not one that is suddenly encountered at a specific level of output. Rather, the constraint becomes more and more binding as output expands toward capacity, and a degree of crowding out will, therefore, be encountered even in less than full employment situations. A higher level of real output will be associated with higher imports and hence with a deterioration of the trade account. Given a high degree of capital mobility, this deterioration could certainly be covered by capital inflow; but such an increase in net indebtedness abroad implies a need to run a trade-account surplus at some time in the future, both to service an increased foreign debt and to repay it eventually. To the extent that the public understand this need and take account of this reduction in their future incomes when planning current expenditure, private-sector expenditure will fall, and a form of crowding out will come into play.

The possibility that an increasing foreign debt might engender doubts in world capital markets about a country's ability to maintain its exchange rate in the long run is a possibility not normally assumed to arise in theoretical analyses of fixed-exchange-rate regimes. However, this possibility can be important in the real world under regimes which permit parity changes. If domestic fiscal expansion does lead foreign lenders to begin to entertain such doubts, their behaviour will in effect falsify the assumption of a high degree of capital mobility upon which the Mundell–Fleming results depend, for lenders will demand an interest premium (perhaps rising over time) for continuing to hold or increase their holdings of domestic debt. A crowding-out mechanism would come into play, but in this instance it would be more important in the context of a sustained expansionary fiscal policy than in that of short-term, counter-cyclical measures.

The effectiveness of monetary and fiscal policy as demand-management tools is limited under fixed exchange rates, and so is that of wage and price controls as long-term anti-inflation devices. As Johnson (1972c) argued, at least for relatively small open economies, to try to control the long-run inflation rate by way of price controls under a fixed exchange rate is to attempt to use domestic tools to influence a variable whose behaviour is primarily determined by world markets; and such an attempt is unlikely to succeed for very long. Indeed, any short-run success that such a policy might have would strengthen the longer-run forces it was seeking to offset. If money wages and prices in an open economy are kept by controls from rising as fast as they otherwise would, the balance of payments will improve and domestic monetary expansion will speed up, thus increasing demand-generated inflationary pressures, which will continue to build up as long as controls exert any influence. Inevitably, under such circumstances, controls will break down. Of course, if they were combined with exchange controls and a rigorously enforced system of import quotes, so that the economy was put on to something akin to a command footing, they might then have more effect, provided that there existed strong political support in favour of such a policy regime, but it is hard to believe that such support would be forthcoming under normal peacetime circumstances.[11] However, if the problem faced by the domestic economy is a short-run burst of *domestic* inflation incompatible with trends in the world economy, temporary wage and price controls might—at least in principle—ease the return to equilibrium, provided controls are co-ordinated with other policies.

As far as the effect of fixed exchange rates on domestic policy is concerned, the foregoing analysis, which is based upon Johnson's 'The Monetary Approach to the Balance of Payments' (Johnson, 1972b), confirms long-held beliefs. Under such a regime and given a rather liberal international order as far as trade in goods and, in particular, capital is concerned, the operations of the balance-of-payments mechanism put severe limits on the conduct of domestic policy. Although goods markets seem to adjust sufficiently slowly for the constraints they impose to be long-run in nature, it is a different matter with capital markets. With a highly integrated world capital market such as now exists, a fixed-exchange-rate economy has no choice but to accept the world interest rate. Therefore, monetary policy under a fixed exchange rate is primarily a device for influencing the balance of payments and hence for maintaining the exchange rate, not a tool which can systematically be used for domestic stabilisation purposes. Although fiscal policy can be used for domestic stabilisation, it is more likely to be effective over short periods than to be capable of producing important effects sustainable in the long run; and wage and price controls have no chance of influencing inflation in any lasting fashion.

In the past, such conclusions as these have been widely believed to provide the basis of the case for flexible exchange rates. These conclusions certainly seem to imply that a fixed-rate regime puts a balance-of-payments constraint upon the conduct of domestic policy that would not exist under flexible exchange rates. In large measure, this conclusion is misleading. The basic constraint on domestic economic policy arises from national economies having finite productive resources and forming part of a larger world economy. Under fixed exchange rates, this constraint manifests itself in the behaviour of the balance of payments and is particularly visible. As we shall now see, it does not go away under flexible exchange rates: it simply manifests itself in different, less immediately recognisable ways.

## Domestic Policies under Flexible Exchange Rates among National Monies

Provided national monies are convertible into one another at fixed rates of exchange, their aggregation is straightforward and unambiguous, and the notion of a world money supply has a clear meaning. To someone analysing the world economy, the most significant difference between fixed and flexible exchange rates is that with flexible rates the idea of a world money supply is no longer clear-cut. The world economy continues to exist, but it is no longer the natural place in which to study the interaction of the supply and demand for money. As we shall see, to say that the notion of a world money supply is not clear-cut under flexible rates does not mean that it is totally without meaning or relevance, or that such a regime raises no issues for the behaviour of the world economy *per se*. Nevertheless, it is convenient to begin our discussion of flexible exchange rates at the level of the nation state. Here the obvious questions, much discussed in recent years, concern the extent to which the adoption of flexible rates both protects the economy from shocks originating abroad and removes constraints from the conduct of domestic policy.

Under flexible exchange rates, the domestic banking system has no obligation to exchange domestic for foreign money at a fixed price. Therefore, even in the long run, the domestic money supply is completely under the control of the authorities, and those factors that under a fixed exchange rate lead to balance-of-payments flows lead under a flexible rate to exchange-rate changes. Given that there exists a stable demand-for-money function at the level of the national economy, and given that, on average in the long run, the time path of real-income and real-interest rates is determined by supply-side factors, including those characterising the world economy, control of the quantity of money also gives the domestic authorities control of the long-run average value of the domestic inflation rate, which no longer depends upon the interaction of the world-price-level and productivity trends in various sectors of the domestic economy. Instead of being a constant whose maintenance forces the domestic money supply to conform to the behaviour of other variables, the exchange rate is free to move to reconcile the behaviour of domestic prices with that of prices in the rest of the world.

Under flexible rates, monetary policy is not the only factor affecting the exchange rate, any more than under fixed rates it is the only factor affecting the balance of payments. Just as an increase in productivity in the traded-goods sector or an increase in world demand for the goods that sector produces will, under fixed exchange rates, usually lead to an increase in the domestic price level relative to that in the rest of the world, so, under a flexible rate, will such changes usually lead to an appreciation of the currency.[12] In either case, the cause in question must lead to the price of labour in the domestic economy rising relative to that of the rest of the world. Under a flexible rate and with a given quantity of nominal money, the domestic price level will also tend to fall as a result of the influence of an increase in real income on the demand for money, but not by enough to offset the tendency of the currency to appreciate. The non-tradables sector and those parts of the tradables sector not directly affected by the shock under consideration will therefore contract, just as they will under a fixed rate when a higher domestic wage and price level puts pressure upon them.

Flexible exchange rates do nothing to shelter an economy from the consequences of underlying shifts in the conditions of supply and demand for the goods and services it produces and consumes. Such shifts usually require *relative-price* changes to accommodate them, and though these shifts will manifest themselves in different *money-price* behaviour under different regimes, they will still occur. There is nothing that can be done by domestic monetary policy to offset such real changes under any exchange-rate regime. The most that can be claimed here for a flexible exchange rate is that, relative to a fixed rate, a flexible rate might under certain circumstances ease the transition to the new equilibrium required by some exogenous real shock. In particular, where that shock requires a fall in domestic real wages relative to those in the rest of the world, it may be easier for this transition to occur by way of a currency depreciation, with domestic money wages remaining constant or even rising a little, than by way of a fall in domestic money wages with the exchange rate held constant.[13]

Even this conclusion cannot be taken for granted. Because a currency depreciation permits a real-wage cut to be imposed simultaneously on everyone, the conclusion will be true for an economy in which the need for a fall in real wages is perceived but is held up under a fixed exchange rate by the reluctance of any sector of the labour force to be the first to accept a money-wage cut. However, in an economy in which there is what Hicks (1974) called real-wage resistance, so that the dynamics of money-wage behaviour are heavily conditioned by the interaction of wage and price levels, a currency depreciation might be but the first twist of a so-called vicious circle of price and money-wage inflation accompanied by continuous depreciation and domestic monetary expansion. There is nothing inherent in the structure of an economy operating a flexible exchange rate that ensures that an inflationary bias will be imparted to price-level behaviour. However, if that economy has a labour force whose resistance to real-wage cuts is accompanied by the political power to influence the monetary authorities, such a bias becomes a real possibility.[14]

It has long been known that the adoption of a flexible exchange rate permits the domestic economy to choose its own long-run inflation rate, and this fact was at one time seen to constitute a major advantage for such a regime. Expansionary domestic policies which might have led to a high long-run level of employment also, according to the logic of the Phillips curve, led to inflation; and the adverse consequences of inflation for the balance of payments under a fixed-rate regime seemed to impose a serious and unnecessary constraint on the achievement of domestic goals of high employment. This argument is now recognised as quite false. The Phillips curve exists as an apparently stable relationship only as long as economic agents' expectations of inflation remain rather stable over time; in an open economy, an important factor guaranteeing the stability of expectations might be a fixed exchange against a non-inflationary world money. Thus the removal of the fixed exchange rate that constrains economic policy from exploiting the Phillips trade-off, also removes the trade-off, which was in fact never a stable long-run relationship. Expectations about inflation become geared to domestic inflationary experience—or perhaps to the pronouncements and actions of domestic policy-makers—and though the flexible-rate economy is able to choose its own inflation rate, it can realise no permanent gain in terms of income and employment from higher inflation.[15]

Even so, the long-run inflation rate is a variable of political importance,

and in the absence of any systematic inflation–unemployment trade-off
there would be widespread agreement that price-level stability, or at least a
low inflation rate, is a desirable goal in its own right. In a fixed-exchange-
rate world and in the absence of severe restriction of trade and capital
movements, such a goal is attainable for the individual country if, and only
if, the international money that lies at the base of the system is more or less
inflation-free in the long run. Although the case for flexible exchange rates
in the 1950s and 1960s was as often as not put in terms of the ability they
conferred on the domestic authorities to choose a higher inflation rate than
that ruling in the rest of the world, and thereby realise output gains, the
case in the 1970s and 1980s may be cast in terms of flexible rates permitting
those same authorities to choose a lower and perhaps more stable inflation
rate than that ruling elsewhere.

The argument here is correct as far as it goes. A flexible-exchange-rate
country may choose its own long-run inflation rate and may change that
rate independently of the world inflation rate; if the world inflation rate
should change, there is no reason why a flexible-exchange-rate economy
should import that change. It does not follow, however, that it is an easy
business for a country to change its inflation rate relative to that of the rest
of the world, or that a country is insulated from all side-effects when the
world inflation rate changes. The very same wage and price stickiness that
lends a degree of short-run independence to domestic monetary policy
under a fixed exchange rate, and that might confer a short-run advantage
on flexible exchange rates in the face of real shocks, ensures that the
insulating powers of flexible rates against monetary shocks are far from
complete. The general issue to which we are referring here is exemplified
by the problem of exchange-rate overshooting analysed in literature by
Niehans (1975) and Dornbusch (1976b). The overshooting argument is a
special case of a more general argument about the insulating properties of
flexible exchange rates which has been made by Turnovsky (1979). To the
extent that a monetary change elsewhere in the world has a short-run real
impact on interest rates or output abroad, it will also have consequences
for real domestic variables even under a flexible-exchange-rate regime.
Just what these effects will be will depend upon the degree of domestic
wage and price flexibility, and, as Burton (1980) in particular has stressed,
the state of domestic agents' information about the nature of shocks
impinging upon the world economy.

As I have remarked, overshooting follows from the assumption of wage–
price stickiness, and arises in the following way. When a country reduces
its rate of monetary growth, the ultimate effect is a slow-down in its
inflation rate, a fall in its nominal interest rates, and a steady appreciation
of its currency. However, if wages and prices are sticky, the initial effect of
such a change in policy is mainly an increase in nominal interest rates.
Agents operating in capital markets are presumed to understand these

effects and to take account of them in planning their activities. The first-round effect of these activities therefore must be a capital inflow, which will continue to drive up the current value of the currency until the expected return on holding assets denominated in domestic currency is brought into equality with that ruling elsewhere in the world. Since domestic nominal interest rates are now higher, since domestic money wages and prices move only sluggishly toward their long-run values, and—crucially—since this sluggish movement is anticipated, this equalisation of expected returns can be achieved only by an immediate overappreciation of the currency to a level from which it then moves down (at least relative to trend) towards its equilibrium time path.

Now the possibility of overshooting arises from the impact effect that monetary contraction has on interest rates. To the extent that other variables can move to accommodate a smaller money supply, the chances of its occurring are reduced. Thus, if income falls when the money supply falls, or if agents simply allow their 'buffer stocks' of cash temporarily to shrink without taking remedial action, pressure is removed from the interest rate. Hence it would be more appropriate to speak of flexible exchange rates displaying a tendency to overshoot in response to monetary shocks than to speak of a definite propensity to do so. Even so, this tendency brings both benefits and costs. To the extent that the domestic price index is influenced by import and export prices, overshooting helps reduce inflation more rapidly than would otherwise be the case when monetary policy tightens up. However, overshooting has this effect while simultaneously imposing a competitive disadvantage upon the tradable-goods sector of the economy. Conventional wisdom has it that a slow-down in monetary growth takes between eighteen months and two years to have its first noticeable effects on domestic inflation; this disadvantage can, therefore, last quite long enough to do serious damage to the tradables sector. Though it is usual to analyse overshooting as a consequence of an attempt to slow down domestic inflation relative to that of the rest of the world, it should be noted that a step up in world monetary expansion imposes the same burden on the tradables sector of an economy which does not follow the world trend. Also, overshooting in response to monetary policy works in both directions; a tightening of monetary policy in the world economy designed to bring its inflation rate down can, therefore, lead to a temporary overdepreciation of the domestic currency and so to a tendency for the tradables sector to overexpand and the domestic inflation rate to rise temporarily to a rate higher than is ultimately compatible with domestic monetary policy.

The analysis of overshooting just discussed exemplifies a general characteristic of the properties of flexible exchange rates, and the characteristic in question may be described as follows. As Frenkel (1981b) and Mussa (1982) have stressed, the foreign-exchange market is an asset market, and the prices ruling there are highly flexible. At the same time, the agents operating in that market make their decisions on the basis of their expectations about the likely future course of the values of the currencies in which they deal. New information about anything that affects expectations about those future values will therefore influence the exchange rate the moment such information becomes available. Quite modest policy changes, for example, can have large effects on the exchange rate if these policy changes affect expectations. Moreover, to the extent that the domestic variables that might ultimately absorb the effects of such shocks are slow-moving, such effects will be further exaggerated. This conclusion is true of the consequences of a monetary policy change, which is what Niehans and Dornbusch analysed, but it also holds true for the consequences of any other event that can influence the exchange rate.

In the light of the foregoing discussion, it is small wonder that a completely free-floating exchange rate whose behaviour is completely ignored by the authorities is more often found in the writings of academic economists than in the real world. There, so-called dirty floating, under which the authorities intervene to influence the behaviour of the exchange rate in the hope of gaining the long-term advantages of flexibility while mitigating the short-term costs, is much favoured. Of course, the very concept of a dirty float is far from clear-cut. I use 'dirty float' here to refer to a policy regime in which the monetary authorities vary the quantity of money to influence the exchange rate *per se* rather than to pursue purely domestic goals. But to the extent that the behaviour of the exchange rate itself impinges upon domestic variables, the border between a clean and dirty float is certainly easier to define in principle than in practice. Though there has been some academic work on the principles that ought to underpin authorities' intervention in the foreign-exchange market, if such intervention is to be optimal in achieving its ends—see, for example, Boyer (1978c), Fortin (1979), Sparks (1979), or Frenkel and Aizenman (1982), all of whom build upon Poole's (1970) analysis of optimal monetary policy in a closed economy—it would seem that the knowledge needed to implement such principles systematically in the real world is simply not available. Dirty floating has in practice, therefore, been very much an *ad hoc* business.[16]

Monetary policy is difficult to implement smoothly under flexible exchange rates, but it can at least be expected to have sustainable long-run effects on prices, not to mention shorter-run impacts on output and employment. Fiscal policy is of limited use for demand management under such a regime. To the extent that fiscal expansion puts upward pressure on domestic interest rates and does not undermine international confidence in the future stability of a country's monetary policy, fiscal expansion will tend to cause an appreciation of the value of the domestic currency. This appreciation will in turn reduce exports and increase imports, with the net effect of government expenditure completely crowding out output in the tradable-goods sector of the economy. This result, which harks back to the Mundell–Fleming analysis of the 1960s does, of course, hinge upon an enlarged fiscal deficit affecting neither the price level nor confidence in the future stability of monetary policy. If the price level is affected, short-run output expansion becomes a possibility. At best, though, such effects are short-run, and any significant effect on confidence in the future stability of monetary policy stemming from fiscal deficits can have adverse consequences too obvious to need specifying here.

All in all, it is difficult to see more than a very limited scope for fiscal policy as a demand-management tool under flexible exchange rates. (This conclusion does not necessarily mean that specific job-creation schemes addressing structural labour-market problems and financed without in-creasing the overall deficit may not influence employment levels in particular times and places.) Nor can one be optimistic about wage and price controls as anti-inflation devices, particularly as long-term anti-inflation devices. As I have argued elsewhere (Laidler, 1982), to the extent that such controls are effective, they cause demand pressures, which might have been absorbed by domestic prices, to spill over into the foreign-exchange market and depreciate the currency. Thus controls divert inflationary pressures from one sector of the economy to another under flexible exchange rates and do not lower the overall inflation rate. One important qualification needs to be noted here, though. The above conclusion applies more clearly to the case where controls are used *instead* of more orthodox anti-inflation policies, and it does not rule out the possibility that controls deployed *as temporary supplements to* monetary contraction might help an economy make a transition to lower inflation at a smaller cost in unemployment than the economy might otherwise have to bear.

The implications of the analysis of the past few pages are easily enough stated. The economic basis of the case for flexible exchange rates is not as strong as it was once believed to be, even when the desirability of such a regime is judged solely from the viewpoint of the individual economy. That economic case rested in good measure on the postulate of a long-run inflation–unemployment trade-off, and this trade-off has turned out to be illusory. Nevertheless, this analysis does not mean that the case for flexible exchange rates can no longer be made. Rather, as Friedman (1953b) saw long ago, it means that there is a strong political element to the case. A flexible exchange rate perhaps confers on the domestic authorities a certain degree of short-run room to manœuvre in the conduct of stabilisation policy. But that is not the main point: a flexible rate also permits them to pick the path of the domestic inflation rate even in the long run. If the inflation rate is a variable of great political importance—and it seems to be—the relevant authorities can take responsibility for the inflation rate only if they operate (though not necessarily cleanly) a floating rate. Flexible exchange rates, therefore, are the natural institutional arrangement in a world in which political power is exercised at the level of the nation state and in which electorates expect their governments to make effective decisions about the inflation rate.

## The International Monetary System under Flexible Exchange Rates

The world economy does not cease to exist when a floating-rate regime is adopted. Even though there is nothing that may be defined unambiguously as a world money supply, goods and assets traded across international boundaries nevertheless have to be invoiced and paid for, and some national currency or currencies must play this specifically international role. These facts have recently come in for a good deal of analysis, much of which, in the current state of knowledge, must be regarded as controversial.[17]

It is a fundamental proposition of monetary theory that in a closed economy (considered over a period long enough for prices to be treated as fully flexible), the nominal quantity of money may be determined by the monetary authorities, but its real quantity will be decided by money holders. Their behaviour will ensure that, in the long run, the price level moves to convert the nominal quantity of money supplied to whatever real quantity is demanded. Provided that their liabilities are readily convertible into one another at guaranteed fixed rates, it does not matter whether there are multiple suppliers of nominal money in such a closed economy. The results of closed-economy monetary theory are therefore applicable to a world economy characterised by fixed exchange rates among national currencies.

An interesting theoretical question, first posed in 1972 by Boyer in an initially unappreciated paper not published until 1978 (Boyer, 1978b), concerns what happens in a system with multiple suppliers of nominal money when there are no rules governing the price at which a unit of one currency trades against another. There still exists a determinate aggregate demand for real money in such a system, but such a quantity of real balances can be made up in an infinity of ways, each involving different exchange ratios among currencies. At first sight, this indisputable fact seems to imply that under a system of flexible exchange rates, the value of any particular currency is indeterminate. Since a monetary system of multiple currencies with indeterminate exchange rates would not be viable, it might seem that, without direct government intervention, a flexible-exchange-rate system would evolve into one in which only one nominal currency was used in all transactions, with the values of all the other currencies being driven to zero—to a system, that is to say, in which one national currency served the entire world economy.[18]

The basic purpose of a monetary system is to provide an environment where trading can be carried on with a minimum of resource costs. From this point of view, there can be no doubt that a one-money system is more efficient than one which uses multiple monies; nor can there be much doubt that, left to themselves, market forces do tend to move a multiple-money system toward the use of a single money. However, we must not ignore certain important institutional facts which work against this tendency. In particular, it is just not the case that, in the world as it now exists, any currency is equally acceptable as a means of exchange in any transaction, regardless of where and between whom it is carried out. In our world, transactions carried on within the boundaries of a particular nation state must be carried out using (by force of custom often backed by law) that nation state's national currency. There is, therefore, a well-defined, real domestic demand for each national currency, derived from its domestic use; and underlying the conventional theory of flexible exchange rates is the idea that the nominal supply of each domestic currency, interacting with this real domestic demand for it, determines both the domestic price level in each country and—given that tradable goods must have the same price everywhere in the world—the exchange rates among domestic currencies.

This monetary theory of the exchange rate is undoubtedly too simple. Though the purchasing-power-parity doctrine that underlies it seems to hold up in long-run averages of data, it breaks down very badly in the short run, particularly where real as well as nominal shocks are disturbing the system.[19] Nevertheless, the fact that changes in the relative prices of tradable goods can undermine a purely monetary approach to explaining the exchange rate is not the point here. Even if these effects were absent, the approach as just sketched out ignores, according to the proponents of the currency-substitution idea, certain important phenomena. In particular they point out that not all transactions take place within national boundaries; those that do not, give their participants the opportunity to choose among currencies. To put it in the terminology of the academic literature, though perfect substitutability among currencies, which would lead to completely indeterminate exchange rates, is a figment of the economic theorist's imagination, there may well exist in the modern world a sufficient degree of substitutability among currencies in international transactions to imply that any analysis of flexible exchange rates which looks only at domestic issues and neglects the specifically international aspects of the international monetary system may be misleading.

Because there exists a demand for money which arises from international transactions and which must be met out of supplies of domestic currencies, McKinnon (1982) has suggested that it might be misleading to think of increases in the supply of a particular domestic money as influencing only the domestic price level of the country that emits it. He has argued that, to the extent that a particular domestic currency is used in international transactions, an increase in the nominal quantity of that national money will increase the nominal quantity of international money and will therefore raise prices measured in all currencies. This argument is correct if monetary authorities in other countries are involved in some kind of dirty float designed to maintain some target range for the exchange rates of their own currencies on the one in question, but not in the case of a clean float. If the real demand for a particular currency does not change in the wake of an increase in its supply, its purchasing power over everything, including other currencies, will fall equiproportionally. There is no reason to alter this conclusion just because some of the real demand for a particular currency stems from its international use.

There is a presumption that where different currencies compete with one another, the one that promises the most predictability in its purchasing power will come to be favoured. To the extent that predictability and constancy of purchasing power are related to each other—and they certainly are not identical—one might expect a speed-up in the creation rate of a particular nominal money to make it less desirable as a means of exchange in international transactions.[20] For this reason, currency substitution might have an independent influence on the demand for national monies, and exchange rates among currencies might be expected to move independently of the interaction of their supply and domestic demand. Such empirical work as has addressed this issue—for example, Brittain (1981)—though far from conclusive, suggests that this hypothesis might go a little way toward explaining the instability that has seemed to characterise demand-for-money functions over the past decade, particularly for the United States and West Germany. Currency substitution does not, however, seem to have been very important in the case of Canada—see, for example, Cuddington (1983) and Poloz (1981).

These arguments seem at first sight to imply that there is an irreducible element of volatility to the world monetary system under flexible rates which would be absent under a fixed rate regime. So there is, if a flexible-rate regime is compared with one of irrevocably fixed rates; but this comparison is not the only one to be made. One might also compare flexible rates with arrangements such as existed under the Bretton Woods system, whereby rates were fixed subject to the ability of member countries simultaneously to meet other policy goals. Under such an arrangement the same demand-for-money shifts arising from currency substitution that make flexible exchange rates potentially volatile can lead to 'hot money' movements and balance-of-payments instability, and can indeed undermine the ability of countries to maintain fixed exchange rates. To the extent that governments must be concerned to avoid sudden changes in their exchange rates, arguments about currency substitution imply that there exists some international discipline in the conduct of domestic monetary policy even under flexible exchange rates. These arguments do not imply that flexible rates are impracticable.

## The Bretton Woods System

So far, this chapter has expounded general principles of analysis rather than applied them to specific issues. However, these principles were developed largely in response to particular policy problems, and it is now time to discuss the international monetary system as it has evolved over the past quarter century or so. The history of international monetary arrangements over this period covers the heyday of the Bretton Woods system, its decline during the latter part of the 1960s, and its piecemeal replacement in the 1970s with the current *ad hoc* but predominantly floating-rate system.

By the mid-1950s the use, particularly by European countries, of quantitative restrictions on trade and capital flows for balance-of-payments purposes that marked the immediate post-war period of the so-called dollar gap, had greatly diminished. The Bretton Woods system was, therefore, becoming a system of fixed exchange rates among more or less convertible currencies. Exchange rates were not rigidly fixed because countries suffering from fundamental balance-of-payments disequilibria could alter their exchange rates. In practice, the rather vague term 'fundamental' came to refer to a state of affairs in which, to correct a balance-of-payments problem, a country would have had to engage in a degree of deflation that would have had a politically serious effect on domestic income and employment. As it was, exchange-rate realignments were few and far between under the Bretton Woods system. Even Canada, which adopted a nominally floating rate against the US dollar in 1950, pursued a domestic monetary policy that kept the exchange rate fluctuating within very narrow bounds throughout the 1950s. With the benefit of hindsight, we may judge Canada to have run something rather close to a fixed exchange rate during the 1950s and hence to have been *de facto* part of the Bretton Woods system for most of the period.[21]

A system of fixed exchange rates among national currencies requires an international money for use as a reserve currency and must provide for control of the reserve currency's creation. Keynes originally intended that in the post-war world, the International Monetary Fund (IMF) would play the role of a world central bank and that its paper liabilities—Bancor— would play a key role as an international means of exchange for the system; but this is not how the system was set up, let alone how it evolved. Instead of acting as a central bank, the IMF came to play, in essence, a supervisory function for countries in balance-of-payments difficulties. The IMF made credit available to such countries to enable them to maintain their exchange rates while corrective policies were put in place, and also periodically ensured that the policies in question were undertaken. In the rare cases where changes in exchange rates were deemed desirable, the IMF helped co-ordinate the changes with a view to avoiding the competitive rounds of devaluation that had plagued the 1930s.

Under the Bretton Woods system, the IMF was excluded from the all-important business of providing an international money—or was excluded at least until the introduction of the Special Drawing Rights (SDR) in 1970.[22] This task fell upon the monetary authorities of the United States, not entirely by conscious design (though the fact that the recipients of Marshall Plan aid were forbidden to use IMF facilities must certainly have inhibited that institution's development), but mainly because, in the wake of the Second World War, only the US dollar was able to provide the monetary foundation upon which a liberal international economic order could be rebuilt. The US dollar was convertible into gold at a fixed price of $35 per ounce, and gold also functioned as an international money; but gold did not influence money creation in the United States. The acid test here is whether United States monetary policy was conducted with a view to maintaining some link between the quantity of money in circulation and US holdings of gold. Darby and Lothian et al. (1983, Chapter 16) have studied this matter in considerable detail, and have found no such link. It is therefore a mistake to regard Bretton Woods as having provided a variation on the gold exchange standard. Although gold was an international money and remnants of the sterling area survived the war, Bretton Woods was a key currency system based on the US dollar.

Needless to say, all of this is much clearer with the benefit of two or three decades of hindsight than it was at the time, and from the mid-1950s onward there was much discussion of the roles of the US dollar and gold in the international monetary system. As the world economy grew in the post-war period and barriers to trade and capital flows were removed, so the demand for international liquidity naturally grew in countries other than the United States. Countries were able to satisfy this demand by collectively running a balance-of-payments surplus with the United States whereby they obtained either dollars or gold to add to their reserves. In either case, with a fixed dollar price of gold, the result was a continuous fall in the ratio of the value of US gold holdings to the value of US short-term foreign liabilities; this falling ratio in turn gave rise to doubts, expressed as early as 1960 by Robert Triffin (see Triffin, 1960), about the ability of the Bretton Woods system to continue to meet growing demands for world liquidity and even about the system's ultimate stability.[23]

Crudely put, Triffin's argument was as follows: the demand for the US dollar as a reserve currency derived from the dollar's convertibility into gold, the ultimate reserve currency; as that convertibility was undermined by a falling ratio of the value of gold to the value of US short-term liabilities, so was the demand for US dollars; as a result, a flight from the dollar became increasingly likely, and the Bretton Woods system was fundamentally unstable because it provided for no orderly means of devaluing the US dollar.

The pure logic of the argument is flawless, but its first premiss, that the demand for dollars was ultimately a demand for gold, is very much open to question. For those who believe the demand for dollars to have been a demand for a universally acceptable currency of stable and predictable purchasing power, convertibility into gold was an inessential property of the Bretton Woods system. In their view, gold could have been demonetised rather than, as some proposed, raised in price, and—subject only to appropriate behaviour on the part of the US monetary authorities—the world could have continued indefinitely on a dollar standard.

Although I agree with this latter interpretation of the roles of gold and the dollar in the Bretton Woods system, the case for this interpretation cannot be argued with complete confidence because the matter was never put to the test. Although US fiscal institutions provided built-in stabilisers from the 1940s onward and fiscal deficits were tolerated quite readily in practice during the 1950s, there can be no doubt that from the early 1960s onward, the rhetoric of American policy became more Keynesian. The practice of American policy also became more Keynesian, not only with the use of a tax-cut to promote employment goals, but—perhaps even more important—with a relatively small, nevertheless systematic increase in the rate of monetary expansion after 1962. By 1966, the Johnson administration was firmly committed to its 'war on poverty', and the Vietnam War had reached serious proportions. What had initially been a modest relaxation of the stance of US monetary policy developed into a steady increase in the US rate of monetary expansion as the decade progressed. One suspects that this increase was not a matter of conscious design, but a by-product of the fiscal pressures implicit in the administration's decision to fight both its wars without significant tax increases. This monetary expansion ultimately undermined the Bretton Woods system, but not before setting in motion the world-wide inflation from which the Western world has yet to recover.[24]

Under a fixed-exchange-rate system, where a particular national currency also plays the role of international money, the limits on the conduct of monetary policy are not the same in the key-currency country as they are in peripheral countries. In peripheral countries, the balance-of-payments mechanism ensures that monetary policy can have only short-term domestic effects and must ultimately be geared to maintaining the stock of foreign exchange reserves within an appropriate range. This is the sense in which the balance of payments constrains the pursuit of domestic goals. The balance of payments does no such thing in the centre country, whose balance-of-payments deficit will always be absorbed into the reserve holdings of the rest of the world. For a peripheral country, too expansionary a domestic monetary policy involves a balance-of-payments deficit and a need to reverse the policy; for the centre country, too expansionary a policy involves a deficit, but no requirement that policy be reversed, at least as long as the future of the country's currency as the base of the international monetary system can be taken for granted. Instead, the effects of too expansionary a policy wil work through to excessive growth in international reserves, thence to excessive growth in national money supplies, and so to an increase in the inflation rate throughout the system.

That is what happened to the Bretton Woods world as US monetary policy became steadily more expansionary during the 1960s. This trend steadily undermined what, with the benefit of hindsight, we can see was the key to the system's long-term viability, namely, stability in the purchasing power of the key currency. However, the above simple diagnosis was difficult to make at the time, and might be a matter of some controversy even now, because many factors complicated the monetary history of the late 1960s.[25] One such factor was the growth of the so-called Eurodollar market. In this market, banks located mainly in Europe, some of them subsidiaries of US resident banks, borrow and lend in US dollars, often at short term; in the process, liabilities viewed by many as good substitutes for national monies, including US national money, are created.

In principle, the development of the Eurodollar market in the 1960s could have been inflationary in its own right; in practice, it is doubtful that it was. First, Eurodollar deposits are overwhelmingly term deposits and are marketed in wholesale-sized lots. Second, even though Eurodollars might be substitutes on the demand side for money, on the supply side the providers of Eurodollars hold small reserves of US money against Eurodollars; this holding of reserves implies an increase in the demand for money, offsetting to some extent the influence of the existence of Eurodollars in the demand of ultimate wealth holders for US money. Third, and most important, had Eurodollars been an independent source of inflation in the late 1960s, there would have been otherwise unexplained downward shifts in national demand-for-money functions at that time. Such shifts did not appear until the early 1970s, after the Bretton Woods system had collapsed. Though Eurodollar interest rates can be shown to have influenced the demand for money in some countries, the influence was stable and predictable; it was the consequence of the growing internationalisation of short-term capital markets, not of some inflationary flight from national monies.[26]

The United States was not the only country whose domestic policy was inflationary under the Bretton Woods system: France had devalued and instituted a partial currency reform in 1959, and the government's response to the events of 1968 was to accommodate large nominal-wage increases; Britain's misconceived 'dash for growth' of 1963–4, based on fiscal and monetary expansion, culminated in devaluation in 1967, and the experiment was repeated with similar results in the early 1970s; Italy had become seriously inflation-prone by the early 1970s; and so on. Moreover, it is a mistake to attribute all fluctuations in inflation rates to monetary causes. As has been shown (Laidler, 1976b), social unrest ought to be accorded a role in the inflation of the 1960s and 1970s, if only as a factor determining the timing and magnitude of particular short-run, but nevertheless significant, fluctuations in national inflation rates relative to world-wide trends.

Nevertheless, as Genberg (1975) has shown, from the mid-1950s to 1970 the variability in the inflation rates of OECD countries was no greater than that among major US cities over the same period. This finding strongly suggests that the Bretton Woods world should be regarded as a single monetary system. More recently, Darby, Lothian *et al.* (1983) have presented theoretical and empirical arguments in support of the view that, under Bretton Woods, the United States was the only country whose domestic policy could and did create a long-run increase in inflation throughout the world economy. In doing so, the United States destroyed the background of monetary stability that peripheral countries had taken for granted in evolving the rules of thumb upon which their own domestic policies were based. Thus, national Phillips curves, which had seemed to promise stable trade-offs between inflation and unemployment, shifted as the inflation rate in the world economy began to move upward, and a balance-of-payments surplus could no longer be taken as a reliable indication that domestic policy could safely become more expansionary.[27]

The speed with which such changes were perceived by policy-makers varied from country to country, and 1969–72 was a period of considerable confusion in the conduct of macroeconomic policies in Western economies. Countries early to realise that their balance of payments was a source of inflationary pressure—for example, Canada and West Germany—began to permit their currencies to appreciate against the US dollar. These countries suffered less in the first round of inflation than they otherwise might have, but only at the cost of weakening their commitment to the Bretton Woods system. By mid-1971 the system was in a crisis, and the Smithsonian Agreement of December 1971 provided for a realignment of currencies within the system and a devaluation of the dollar against gold. Had the Smithsonian Agreement been accompanied by serious efforts among member nations to co-ordinate their domestic policies, it might have rescued the Bretton Woods system. However, no such attempts were made; indeed, in the summer of 1971, the Nixon administration attempted to combine wage and price controls with vigorous monetary expansion as a simultaneous cure for US inflation and unemployment. The US example was soon followed in the United Kingdom, but not elsewhere, with the result that the Smithsonian Agreement collapsed in mid-1972. Nothing replaced it and, *faute de mieux*, by 1973 a floating-rate regime had come into being.[28]

## The Experience with Floating Rates

The adoption of floating exchange rates is often characterised as one of a series of important exogenous shocks which propelled the world economy into the inflation and accompanying economic stagnation of the 1970s. This is the position taken by, for example, McCracken *et al.* (1977). The interpretation advanced here is very different: namely, that the adoption of floating rates was a consequence of long-standing and unevenly distributed inflationary pressures largely associated with a chronic divergence of domestic fiscal and monetary policies already present in the system. By 1971, when national governments began to take different positions about what domestic inflation rate was desirable and what policies were appropriate to achieve government ends, the fixed-rate system was no longer able to cope with the consequences. Countries which tried to combine wage and price controls and domestic monetary expansion—for example, the United States and Britain—found that their policies did not work, but they did not abandon them before their own inflation rates had risen considerably. Countries which relied on the traditional methods of tight money to control the price level—for example, West Germany and Switzerland—could not maintain those policies and their exchange rates simultaneously in the face of pressures from the balance of payments emanating particularly from the United States; and they had to allow their currencies to appreciate.

The world's experience with floating rates has been very different from what academic advocates expected. But with the benefit of hindsight and of the developments in economic theory discussed earlier, we can make some sense of that experience. The salient unexpected facts are the degree of volatility exchange rates have displayed and the sustained shifts in real exchange rates that have taken place since 1971, not to mention the extent to which, under floating rates, national monetary authorities have continued to hold and use foreign-exchange reserves. Some of the volatility displayed by the international monetary system in the 1970s undoubtedly had its origins in the series of real shocks that hit the world economy in the early 1970s. There *were* bad harvests; the anchovies *did* disappear for a while; there *was* a series of explosions in international commodity prices; OPEC *did* begin to exercise political and economic power, and so on.[29] It is important to keep these events in perspective though, for not all of them were necessarily exogenous to monetary developments. In particular, the monetary analysis underlying this essay forces us at least to consider the possibility that various booms in commodity prices were one particularly vivid manifestation of the failure of confidence in the future stability of the US dollar that accompanied the breakdown of the Bretton Woods system.

Commodity prices are set principally in terms of US dollars, and the adoption of floating rates did not change that convention. Moreover, being determined in something very close to continuous auction markets, many of these prices are essentially perfectly flexible. These prices can, therefore, change in response to new information much more rapidly than can the prices of most manufactured goods, not to mention the prices of services and money wages. In this respect, the US-dollar prices of commodities may overshoot their long-run equilibrium values in response to new information, not least about the conduct of US policy; such overshooting is essentially the same as that discussed in the section on domestic policies under flexible exchange rates. Therefore, in the early 1970s, inflation emanating from the United States might have been expected to cause the *relative* prices of commodities to rise even in countries pursuing rather tight monetary policies and appreciating their currencies against the US dollar.

Just how such a development ought to have affected different countries depended upon which commodities they consumed and produced and in what amounts. For many countries, not least Canada, the adoption of flexible exchange rates coincided with important 'temporary' changes in the terms of trade which, although here interpreted as having a common monetary cause, at the time seemed to be making independent contributions to the instability of the international economy. OPEC must stand somewhat apart from the above diagnosis; in this case, in 1973, a buyer's cartel lost its power to a seller's cartel made up of governments and in a strong political position to enforce its pricing policies. Nevertheless, the possibility that the first 1973 oil shock was partly a consequence of past monetary excesses among Western economies—not least the United States—must not be ignored; nor must the fact that the 1979 oil-price increase came in the wake of another increase in US money growth, set in motion during the first two years of the Carter administration.[30]

Before the 1970s, many critics of floating exchange rates feared that speculation in foreign exchange markets would render such a system inherently volatile, whereas proponents of floating rates argued that speculation would be stabilising because specialist traders capable of making profitable use of all available information would dominate the market and keep exchange rates at or near their equilibrium levels, those levels in turn being determined largely by purchasing-power-parity considerations. The example of the Canadian exchange rate in the 1950s, as studied, for example, by Poole (1967), or the German mark during the Weimar hyperinflation, as studied by Frenkel (1976), were cited in support of this latter position. As I have already remarked, the volatility of exchange rates in the 1970s took the proponents of flexible rates by surprise, prompting one of them (Frenkel, 1981a) to write of 'the collapse of purchasing power parities' during the decade. However, it is important to be clear about which of these proponents' prior beliefs turned out to be wrong in the light of experience.

It was not so much that the foreign-exchange market turned out to be fundamentally unstable in and of itself or highly inefficient in the narrow economic sense of proving unable to assimilate and act upon readily available information.[31] Rather, it was that the supporters of flexible rates had failed to appreciate the capacity of such a system to amplify and transmit internationally instabilities arising elsewhere through the overshooting inherent in the behaviour of any asset market. It is arguable, therefore, that if the floating rate system of the 1970s had been introduced into a world where monetary and fiscal tranquillity reigned, and in which stable monetary and fiscal policies would have been pursued thereafter, the system's performance might have borne out the expectations of its proponents.

However, floating was not so much introduced as forced upon the world by pre-existing disequilibria, and in retrospect it is not surprising that the international monetary system was so lively under floating rates. Nor is it surprising that countries found their monetary independence a good deal less than total after the adoption of floating rates, and their ability to avoid 'imported' inflation considerably circumscribed. After all, the explosions in commodity prices already referred to, though perhaps having a monetary origin, *did* involve changes in relative prices, and we have seen that flexible rates cannot insulate a country from relative-price changes. Moreover, we have also seen that temporary exchange-rate overshooting is to be expected whenever countries are subjected to divergent shocks, not least those imparted by divergent monetary policies, and we have also noted that 'temporary' might well denote a period better measured in years than in months.

Canadian experience in the early 1970s provides a particularly good example of both classes of effects at work. Commodity-price increases affected not only Canada's external terms of trade, but also the internal terms of trade between resource sector and manufacturing. Moreover, manufacturing's difficulties were bound to be compounded by any tendency of the Canadian dollar to overappreciate in the face of rising US inflation. Given a natural and quite understandable concern about unemployment, not to mention the political influence of the manufacturing areas, it is hardly surprising that, having floated the dollar in 1970, the Canadian authorities by 1973 were vigorously resisting its further appreciation and, in the process, were importing inflation.[32]

The Canadian example is an extreme one because not every country was quite as vulnerable to the instability of the US dollar as Canada, and though no one avoided inflation in the 1970s, it is inconceivable that countries like West Germany, Switzerland and, later in the decade, Japan, could have maintained their inflation as far below the world average as they did without floating exchange rates. Their insulating properties were far from perfect, but they were certainly significant even in the face of pressures associated with that other fact about the 1970s that so surprised advocates of flexible rates, namely, that countries continued to hold and use foreign-exchange reserves after the adoption of flexible rates.

The idea that, with no requirement to support the exchange rate, central banks would carry no foreign-exchange reserves was widely held before 1971 and indeed is built into many theoretical models of the operations of flexible rates. Taken literally, these models suggest that, with the adoption of flexible rates, the international monetary system can be reduced to nothing more than a series of national systems. However, as I have already stressed, under floating rates, goods and assets still get traded across national boundaries, and international units of account and means of exchange are still required. Moreover, the floating-rate system of the 1970s did not come into being *ab initio* but grew piecemeal out of the wreckage of the preceding fixed-rate system. Part of that wreckage was an existing stock of international reserve assets. Just as the removal of sterling from an important role in the international monetary system by the combined effects of the Depression and the Second World War left an overhang of sterling balances, so did the collapse of the Bretton Woods system leave a dollar overhang.[33]

The residual role of gold in the international monetary system effectively ended with the collapse, in 1972, of the 1971 Smithsonian Agreement, even though much gold remained and remains in central bank and IMF stocks as an asset of uncertain liquidity and unstable value. The international monetary role of the US dollar, however, did not cease in 1972, and it was natural that central banks would find it convenient to continue to hold inventories of liquid dollar assets. Moreover, though a central bank could control its domestic money supply by open-market operations in domestic securities in a world without foreign-exchange reserves, the existence of reserves in the real world of the 1970s provided central banks with a choice of markets of intervention. Given imperfect substitutability between domestic and foreign securities in capital markets, this choice also offered central banks the possibility of some limited and perhaps short-term control over the value of the exchange rate and the domestic interest rate for any given value of the money supply.[34]

Reasons, which I have already discussed, existed for foreign-exchange-market intervention after the formal adoption of floating rates, and the political significance of domestic interest rates is obvious. It ought not to be surprising, therefore, that central banks availed themselves of the opportunities presented by the pre-existing stock of foreign-exchange reserves and continued to use them. It should be noted explicitly, though, that the evidence presented by Boothe and Longworth (1984) on the high degree of capital mobility between Canada and the rest of the world suggests that such arguments as these can be of only limited relevance in the specific case of Canada.

The composition of foreign-exchange reserves began to change in the 1970s as the boundary between official liabilities and short-term private capital began to shift. Although the liabilities of certain apparently secure private borrowers, such as the US commercial banks, were potentially available for use as reserves in the 1960s, these liabilities came to play a much more important role in the 1970s and 1980s. The commodity-price boom and, in particular, the increase in the price of oil from 1973 onward generated large and persistent trade imbalances in the world economy. These imbalances were matched by a desire on the part of surplus countries to hold a significant fraction of their growing wealth in marketable forms. The official short-term liabilities of (trade) deficit countries were available directly to absorb this demand in part, but it was met in much larger part by the expansion of the liabilities of private commercial banks. This borrowing was offset by lending to trade-deficit countries, notably, but by no means exclusively, those of the Eastern bloc and of the Third World, many of which had been particularly hard hit by oil-price increases and whose official liabilities did not have a ready international market.[35]

This recycling had a number of important implications for how the international monetary system developed in the 1970s. First, liabilities of private commercial banks came to play a reserve role in the international monetary system such as had largely been filled under the Bretton Woods system by official US liabilities. Second, the ultimate security of those newly created 'reserves' rested upon the continuing willingness, not to mention ability, of a number of governments—notably in Eastern Europe and South America—to meet their obligations. The security of the international banking system, upon which stable economic relations among the advanced economies and the market economies of South-east Asia relied, became to a degree dependent upon the ability of the non-market economies of the world to service their debts. Finally, because these countries' liabilities were typically denominated in US dollars and were relatively short-term, these countries' abilities to support their debt came to rely in good measure upon the conduct of monetary policy in the United States, a factor over which neither the ultimate debtors nor the creditors involved had any control.

With the benefit of hindsight, it is not hard to see how these developments contributed to a growing fragility of the international banking system, and hence of the international monetary mechanism, or how they lent a critical international dimension to the consequences of the Reagan administration's attempts to restore domestic monetary stability to the United States, a dimension not at first clearly perceived. This is not to absolve the governments of debtor countries of any responsibility for their own plight. Had the proceeds of their borrowing been used to finance investment designed to diversify and improve the international competitiveness of their export sectors, their problems would have been less severe. All too often, however, these proceeds went instead to shore up existing industries which might better have been allowed to contract, or to cover public-sector deficits. Nor are the commercial banks blameless for their naïve belief that so-called sovereign risks were nevertheless essentially riskless: had these banks been less willing to act as intermediaries in the international short-term capital market, the market would not have grown in the dangerous way it did.[36]

The key fact remains that under the flexible-exchange-rate regime of the 1970s, the world financial system continued to develop in a manner which gave an increasingly important international dimension to US monetary policy. Simultaneously, the rules of the game of the system seemed to make it possible for US authorities to conduct their policy with purely domestic ends in view. I say 'increasingly important' deliberately, because under Bretton Woods, where international reserves were almost entirely official liabilities of one sort or another, it had been possible to treat the maintenance of a smoothly functioning international monetary system and the provision of loans to less developed and Eastern bloc countries as separate issues (despite the proposals heard from time to time in the 1960s to create SDR-like assets by allocating them initially as foreign aid). It was the activities of private banks in recycling OPEC surpluses that unintentionally led to these two matters being brought together in such a way as to render an important aspect of so-called North–South (but also East–West) relationships directly vulnerable to the conduct of US monetary policy for the first time.

The consequences of this vulnerability are well known. The onset of systematically tight money in the United States in 1980, aimed at reducing US inflation, produced high domestic interest rates and an associated dramatic appreciation of the US dollar on foreign exchange markets. That policy also generated a severe domestic recession which was transmitted to other industrialised countries not only because US demand for their exports fell, but also because those countries tried to resist the US dollar's appreciation by raising their own domestic interest rates. In turn, not just oil and commodity markets, but the export markets in general of debtor countries were weakened, so that their financial problems were compounded. By 1982, an international debt crisis was at hand, and it is hard to see at the time of writing what the precise outcome of this crisis will be. Suffice it to note that, in principle, the problems of indebtedness and of the maintenance of the international monetary system are logically independent of each other and ought to be tackled separately. There are many more ways of maintaining the solvency of the banking system and the continued viability of the monetary system than forcing the repayment of existing debts. Provided central banks in advanced countries are willing to guarantee the liabilities of private-sector banks, there is no reason why even a series of defaults by debtor nations should lead to a monetary collapse. I shall take it as my task for the balance of this chapter to outline lessons that can be drawn from the 1970s for the debate about reform of the international monetary system, which the 1980s and 1990s are bound to bring. Only passing reference will be made to the issue of international indebtedness.

## The Question of International Monetary Reform

The history of the international monetary system in the past decade has been much more turbulent than advocates of flexible exchange rates would have predicted before the fact, but it would be misleading to write off the experiment with flexible exchange rates as a failure. They have clearly permitted a much wider divergence among domestic inflation rates than would have been possible in their absence: here one very simple but important prediction about such a regime's properties has been confirmed by experience. Moreover, monetary economists have learned and are continuing to learn new things from the experience with floating rates.

The analyses of overshooting and of the role of currency substitution in the system discussed in this chapter were prompted by recent experience, and they enable us to argue that exchange-rate volatility in the past decade has arisen mainly from the regime's capacity for amplifying shocks originated elsewhere in the system. Here one must not lose sight of three simple propositions. First, without shocks to be amplified, there would have been no exchange-rate volatility. Second, it is arguable that, in very large measure, the shocks in question originated in national policies. Third, those shocks could not have been absorbed by the world economy under a regime of fixed exchange rates without immediate and extensive resort by national governments to direct intervention in international goods and capital markets by way of tariffs, quotas, 'voluntary' trade limitations, exchange controls, and so on. In the light of these propositions, advocates of flexible exchange rates can make a strong case that, during the past decade, the great achievement of the flexible-exchange-rate regime has been to permit the international monetary system to function despite national policies, and in the process to enable trade in goods, services, and capital to continue to flourish.[37] Stated so boldly, this conclusion is too optimistic. It is true that world trade continued to grow in the 1970s, apparently unhindered by exchange-rate fluctuations, and that international capital flows were on an unprecedented scale, but it is also true that the experience of recent years casts doubt upon the permanence of these trends.

The tightening of US monetary policy after 1980 caused an overshooting of that currency and of the Canadian dollar, which was *de facto* pegged to it, relative to the Japanese yen and to European currencies. In turn, that overshooting was associated with a build-up of protectionist pressures, particularly in North America. Once created, those pressures seem unlikely to disappear when their immediate cause is removed. Overshooting was also associated with a failure of North American export industries to expand their overseas investment in marketing organisations to the extent that they otherwise would, with a corresponding overexpansion by importers, whence the protectionist pressures already mentioned. Thus, the pattern of world trade may well have been distorted and its volume shrunk in a long-lasting way as a result of the monetary environment. As to capital markets, the ongoing international debt crisis demonstrates for all to see that recycling was not the unqualified success people once claimed it to be. Nevertheless, as far as capital mobility among market economies is concerned, there is no sign that the system has failed in any way. Southeast Asian economies, such as that of South Korea, have borrowed heavily and are not in trouble. It is in the area of providing economic links between more market-oriented and less market-oriented economies that the system has been less successful.

Whatever the source of the current debt crisis, however, no one would be very surprised if its effects on future patterns of borrowing and lending turned out to be severely contractionary, and so the system may not, after all, have coped quite so successfully with the stresses placed upon it as it seemed at first to have done. But this does not mean that any other conceivable set of arrangements could have coped better; it simply means that monetary disturbances have real consequences of lasting importance and that though a flexible-exchange-rate regime can mitigate and delay the onset of those consequences, it cannot ultimately prevent them. That is hardly a new lesson.

Now, to say that the volatility of the international monetary system over the past ten years has in good measure been a result of the volatility of domestic monetary policies in various countries is not to attribute any ultimate causal significance to monetary policy. In contemporary economies, the instability of monetary policy is usually a manifestation of deeper political problems.[38] Nevertheless, to return to a point made at the outset of this chapter, that political power in the modern world resides at the level of the nation state, does imply that it is the policies of nation states which must be changed if monetary stability is to be restored and maintained in the international economy. Proposals for reform which ignore this point and seek to create stability in the world economy by overhauling international monetary institutions are therefore deeply flawed. Such proposals seek to treat the most obvious symptoms of monetary instability but leave its causes untouched. Proposals such as those of Kemp and Mundell (1983) to put the international monetary system back on to some kind of gold standard are particularly vulnerable to criticism on this point.

The gold standard is the archetype of commodity-based fixed-exchange-rate systems, and it worked reasonably well in the years before the First World War, when governments by and large took it for granted that their role in economic life was, by modern standards, a very limited one. Precisely because the economic role of the state was limited, acceptance of the monetary discipline imposed by the gold standard did not usually present politicians with difficult choices. When difficult choices did turn up, however, the discipline exerted by the gold standard was never absolute; in particular, when the exigencies of war forced government into assuming a wider economic role, the gold standard often gave way.[39] As the political climate slowly became more favourable to government intervention in economic life, and as the economic role of the State grew, particularly after the First World War, gold convertibility began to be treated as an object of political choice, and hence debate, rather than as a binding constraint upon policy to be observed unquestionably by all concerned. Once it became possible to debate the desirability or otherwise of maintaining gold convertibility in particular circumstances, the gold standard ceased—even before its formal abandonment—to be a source of overriding discipline in the conduct of policy. The change in status of the maintenance of gold convertibility from an unquestioned principle of policy to an object of political debate and choice was thus a more important event than its ultimate abandonment.

The adoption now of a commodity standard for the international monetary system would certainly force domestic monetary policies to become disciplined, but it is precisely because this fact is well understood that proposals to set up such a standard are regarded by many (including this author) as beside the point. Political authorities who would be willing to accept such discipline do not, as that willingness demonstrates, need it, whereas those whose conduct might benefit from such discipline would not accept it in the first place. Discipline in the conduct of domestic monetary policy is undoubtedly desirable, not least because of the benefits discipline would bring to the international economy; but, in the world we live in, such discipline must be generated and enforced through the political processes of individual nation states. It cannot be imposed upon those nation states by international arrangements not backed up by genuine political power. Such arguments as these are relevant not only to the proposals for the introduction of some sort of commodity convertibility as a basis for the international monetary system, but also to other plans for the reintroduction, by way of international agreement, of fixed exchange rates based, say, on the SDR or some other paper asset rather than on a commodity.

Experience with the European Monetary System (EMS) illustrates the practical relevance of the above arguments and the difficulty of reaching any conclusion about their empirical validity. Under this system, the exchange rates of member currencies are normally supposed to move within rather narrow bounds in response to market forces. Larger movements are supposed to be rare, taking place only in response to disequilibria judged too large to be safely corrected by domestic policies and then only by agreement among member countries. The system, which has created its own international means of exchange and unit of account, the ECU, was superimposed on an already existing set of supranational economic arrangements, the European Economic Community.[40] At the time of the system's inception, though scepticism was expressed in some quarters—notably in the United Kingdom, which did not join—it was difficult to discount entirely the plausibility of the claims of supporters that the system's very creation would, in and of itself, provide an incentive toward policy co-ordination among member states. Early experience with the system supported the sceptics' position. Policy co-ordination among member countries did not improve after its creation, as the repeated and serious difficulties encountered by the French franc and Italian lira in particular showed. However, the system did provide a framework within which parity changes among European currencies could be managed in an orderly way, and its supporters also claim that the Mitterand government's reversal of its inflationary policies in 1983 marked the beginning of a move to better policy co-ordination within the system than has ruled in the past. On the other hand, sceptics might still argue that domestic political discipline generated by the manifest failure of those policies to deliver high employment and inflation-free growth had much more to do with their abandonment than any external discipline imposed by the EMS.

Whatever one's judgement on the EMS, it would be a mistake to jump to the conclusion that the international monetary experience of the 1970s will inevitably be repeated in the 1980s and 1990s. It was not just the international economy that was disrupted by monetary instability in the 1970s. Domestic economies, too, suffered, and the early 1980s in particular have seen a transformation in the general public's understanding of the sources of monetary instability and willingness to support policies designed to drive instability from the system. The disinflationary policies of the past few years have been just as much a product of political processes as were the inflationary policies that preceded them. Though it would be rash to predict with any degree of confidence that the domestic policies of the countries of the Western world will be responsibly executed in the next ten or twenty years, there seems more prospect of this now than one could have dared hope for even five years ago.

If domestic policies in a number of important countries do indeed turn out to be more stable in the 1980s and 1990s than they have been in the recent past, so will exchange rates among their currencies, with or without the intervention of explicit institutional reform. The international economy will then be well on its way to evolving a 'new Bretton Woods system', which, being based upon stable domestic policies whose co-ordination stems from harmony among domestic political processes, will be viable. The reserve currency of such a system, the role of the IMF in the system, the extent to which exchange rates might formally be fixed under such a system, and so on, are impossible to predict. However, even now, after nearly two decades of instability, the US dollar remains by far the most widely used international money, and it is therefore hard to believe that it would not play a key role in such a system. As under the old Bretton Woods system, so under the new, if it comes into being, the continuing stability of the international economy will be heavily dependent upon the 'good behaviour' of the US monetary authorities.

The weakness of the foregoing argument is that 'good behaviour' on the part of the US monetary authorities cannot be relied upon. I hasten to add that, in saying this, I do not intend to attribute any special weakness to the political system in the United States or any extraordinary degree of political and economic irresponsibility to US leaders. I have already stressed that we must look to political processes to produce the policies upon which international monetary stability must depend, and that in a world of nation states these political processes are likely to be driven by largely domestic concerns. It does not reflect badly on the United States to say that this is as true of their political processes as it is of, say, Canada's. Nevertheless, it is the case that US economic policies have altogether more important international consequences than do those of other countries, both because of the sheer size of the US economy and because of the critical international status of the US dollar. It is arguable that the political organisation of the Western world is flawed to the extent that many people directly affected by US policies must rely upon either American goodwill or a fortunate coincidence of interests for the promotion of their economic well-being, but it would take us far beyond the scope of this essay to consider this matter. Rather, I would note that the governments of countries other than the United States do have at their disposal certain limited means of insulating their economies from US policies, not least in the choice of exchange-rate arrangements.

The salient point about current US policy is that without either a major increase in taxes or a significant cut in expenditures in the near future, the federal deficit is going to put greater and greater pressure upon the domestic and indeed upon the world financial system. This fact must be borne in mind by policy-makers in other countries, not least Canada, as they lay their plans for the next decade. If the US federal government does regain control of its budget and hence is able to consolidate recent gains against inflation, the task of Canadian policy-makers will be relatively simple on the monetary and exchange-rate front. Provided Canada pursues responsible policies of moderate monetary growth, Canada's exchange rate on the US dollar will be well behaved whether conscious attempts are made to peg that exchange rate or not. The monetary environment for

Canada will be very much like that of the 1950s, and the choice of whether to run a fixed or flexible exchange rate on the US dollar will be an issue of secondary importance. On the other hand, if the US federal deficit persists and is indeed the serious problem I believe it to be, Canada is in for a difficult time regardless of how that deficit is financed.

It is at least logically possible that the United States will be able to sustain relatively low monetary growth rates while continuing to run a large deficit. However, in this case it is hard to see how real interest rates both in the United States and in the world in general can fail to remain at levels high enough to inhibit investment. It is unlikely that monetary and exchange-rate policy could do very much to stave off the consequences for Canada of a continuing US deficit. A high real interest rate abroad is after all a real factor whose long-run influence on Canada ought to be the same regardless of the exchange-rate regime. Although I have noted that less than perfect substitutability between domestic and foreign assets confers upon the authorities of an open economy the ability to trade off domestic-interest-rate and exchange-rate values, the degree of substitutability between such assets increases with the passage of time; so most of the advantages a flexible-rate regime might confer in this case are temporary.[41]

Nevertheless, even partial and temporary protection against high real interest rates is worth having, not least because it is far from clear that the United States will be able politically to sustain indefinitely a combination of fiscal ease and monetary restraint. If the United States cannot do so, a bout of renewed monetary expansion and hence inflation there becomes a distinct possibility. If, in the face of renewed inflation in the United States, the same degree of priority is given by Canadian policy-makers to maintaining the US-dollar price of the Canadian dollar as was given in the early 1970s, a repeat of the economic history of 1970–6, on a more dramatic scale, would be a virtual certainty. On the other hand, if the authorities were, in such circumstances, willing to allow the exchange rate to appreciate and to face the short-term, but possibly painful, terms-of-trade consequences that would be produced by overshooting, policy-makers would at least be able to avoid a resurgence of inflation in Canada and the recession that would eventually be needed to remove it from the system.

What all this implies for Canadian policy toward the exchange rate over the next few years is straightforward. One can envisage situations in which the choice between a formally fixed and a formally flexible exchange-rate regime is of minor importance; situations in which the choice of a flexible rate might give the authorities valuable, albeit short-term room to manœuvre; and situations in which important long-term advantages are to be had from a flexible rate. There seem no circumstances in which, from the point of view of domestic policy, there are any advantages from fixed rates. Nor is there any reason to believe that the adoption by Canada of a fixed rate of exchange on any currency would hasten the establishment of a fixed-rate international monetary system, which, from the viewpoint of the world economy, might be considered by some as preferable to a system of multilateral flexible rates. The case for Canada's conducting monetary policy with a view to achieving domestic ends and letting the exchange rate take care of itself would therefore seem a strong one.

## Notes

1 For pioneering expositions of the monetary approach see, for example, Courchene (1970), Mundell (1971), and Johnson (1972a).

2 It will suffice if the reader of this chapter thinks of money as consisting of those assets that are readily transferable as means of exchange (currency and chequable bank deposits in the context of Canada). The precise specification of money for empirical purposes is a difficult and controversial matter, which I have discussed in Laidler (1985). Sparks (1985) deals with these issues in the context of Canadian policy problems.

3 It should be noted that the stability of national demand-for-money functions is neither necessary nor sufficient for the existence of a stable world demand function. Unstable demand-shifts at the national level can cancel out upon aggregation, while differences in the structure of national demand functions can render their aggregation impossible. Hence the proposition that there exists a world demand function for money must be tested directly. For an early and largely successful test, see Gray, Ward, and Zis (1976). For a general overview of theoretical, econometric, and empirical issues bearing on the stability of the demand-for-money function, see Laidler (1985).

4 Strictly speaking, this definition is appropriate only when the rate of growth of the world money supply is zero. With nominal money growth, equilibrium would involve each country's running a surplus with the world monetary authorirty big enough to keep its own domestic money supply growing at the rate of inflation.

5 I beg the issue here of what plays the role of the international money. This matter is discussed later in the specific context of the Bretton Woods system.

6 This is an important issue in the context of the breakdown of the Bretton Woods system and will be discussed in that context. Early work on the monetary approach to balance-of-payments analysis took it for granted that such insulation was impossible. However, see Parkin (1974) and Laidler (1975) for early theoretical exercises in which this overly restrictive assumption was relaxed.

7 Important Scandinavian papers on this issue include Aukrust (1970) and Edgren, Faxen and Ohdner (1969).

8 Darby, Lothian et al. (1983) have paid careful attention to the question of the possibility of sterilisation under the Bretton Woods system. Their work shows that, beyond any reasonable doubt, sterilisation was possible over periods of a few quarters under the Bretton Woods system, but not over longer periods. Their work also shows that governments frequently resorted to sterilisation in the 1950s and 1960s. See Darby, Lothian et al. (1983, Chapters 10–11).

9 Chipman (1980) has—somewhat unfairly I believe—inferred from this work that those proponents believed the balance of payments to be unaffected by real variables.

10 The origins of the Mundell–Fleming model are to be found in Fleming (1962) and Mundell (1963). The model is essentially a version of the standard textbook IS–LM model and has now become a fixture in the literature of

international monetary economics. One potential weakness of this model is that it analyses the capital account in purely flow terms. However, Boyer (1978a), for example, has shown that its main results on the relative effectiveness of monetary and fiscal policy under different exchange-rate regimes continue to hold even when capital movements are explicitly analysed in portfolio-balance terms with careful attention being paid to stock-flow distinctions and wealth effects.

11 This is essentially the policy prescription of the so-called New Cambridge school for the United Kingdom. See, for example, Cripps and Godley (1976).

12 Chipman (1980) offers an elaborate theoretical analysis of the possibilities here.

13 See Chapter 9 below, and note that Purvis (1979) contains a rather elaborate analysis of this and related issues.

14 This vicious-circle argument has been elaborated by Claassen (1976), among others. Of course it is not the case that money-wage behaviour must necessarily respond always and everywhere to prices. Where relativities are important, it might be argued that specific wage bargains will be conditioned to the general behaviour of money wages elsewhere in the economy. Fortin and Newton (1981) have argued that this is the case in Canada, and, if they are correct, the vicious-circle argument is of relatively little relevance to Canadian experience.

15 The classic articles on the short-run nature of the inflation–unemployment trade-off are those of Phelps (1967) and Friedman (1968). See Sumner (1976) for an early and thorough development of the implications of the Phelps–Friedman insight in the context of the debate on fixed versus flexible exchange rates.

16 In recent Canadian experience, the main argument of the Bank of Canada for intervening in the foreign-exchange market has been that, left to itself, the Canadian dollar might overdepreciate in the face of pressures originating in US monetary policy and might in the process set up adverse expectations about the future time path of Canadian inflation among the Canadian labour force. Since the textbook-style overshooting analysis of Dornbusch depends upon agents having correct expectations of the future time path of domestic prices, one cannot simultaneously explain the behaviour of the Canadian exchange rate in terms of that analysis and defend the above justification for intervention in the foreign-exchange market. It does not, of course, follow that the Bank of Canada's reading of agents' expectations has been in error. It could just as easily be that the textbook overshooting model does not capture certain important real-world phenomena. However, the Bank of Canada's argument is a version of the vicious-circle arguments discussed earlier, and the evidence of Fortin and Newton (1981) does not support the Bank's position.

17 Ronald McKinnon, in particular, has been a strong advocate of taking seriously the fact that national currencies play a specifically international role. See, for example, McKinnon (1979, 1982). For a survey of the issues and evidence involved in the currency-substitution debate, see Spinelli (1983).

18 This extreme view may be found expressed most forcefully by Karekan and Wallace (1978). For a thorough critique of their oversimplified analysis, see Haberler (1981, pp. 42–6).

19 On all this see, for example, Frenkel (1981a), Gailliot (1970), and Myhrman (1976).

20 Arguments, such as those of Hayek (1976), that the provision of money could be left to the unregulated private sector rest upon ideas such as we are discussing here. See also Chapter 6 above.

21 The sterling devaluation of 1967 was one of the most important realignments, as was the rapid decline of the Canadian dollar in 1961, which was brought to an end by the pegging of the Canadian exchange rate in that year. The French

currency reform of 1959 was accompanied by a devaluation, and there was a small realignment of European currencies in 1961.

The view of the Royal Commission on Banking and Finance, the Porter Commission—see Canada (1964)—that the differences between a fixed and a flexible exchange-rate regime for Canada were rather minor, with the emphasis being on the different nature of the signals that the regime gave to the domestic authorities about the appropriateness of their policies, is strong evidence in favour of the proposition that until the devaluation that marked its end, the Canadian float of 1950–62 really amounted to little more than a widening of the interval in which an otherwise pegged rate was allowed to fluctuate. Empirical work by Caves and Feige (1976) confirms that Canadian monetary policy was responsive to the exchange rate during this floating period, thus suggesting that there was indeed a target value for the exchange rate.

22 The SDR (Special Drawing Rights) is an IMF liability whose value is pegged against a basket of representative currencies. It has been issued in limited amounts since 1970, when it was intended to provide an alternative internationally tradable liquid asset to the US dollar and gold. The SDR is in some respects similar to Keynes's Bancor concept, but it is far from being a key reserve currency in an international monetary system.

23 The concept of world liquidity is a difficult one. In theory at least, any quantity of nominal international assets is adequate for providing for liquidity because the price of those assets in terms of goods may change. In practice, under Bretton Woods, the problem was to meet the demands of various member nations for international reserves without putting downward pressure on the world price level. For a survey of the extensive literature on this issue that grew up in the 1950s and 1960s, see Williamson (1973).

24 It is important to note that US monetary expansion did begin to increase before the Vietnam War became a serious matter. However, war finance had a good deal to do with the later acceleration of monetary expansion. It is clearly simplistic to blame the Vietnam War alone for the inflation of the 1960s, but it is yet more simplistic to ignore the war altogether and blame 'Keynesian' policies. Darby, Lothian et al. (1983, Chapter 16), provided evidence of the steady growth in the US rate of monetary expansion during the 1960s and early 1970s, and its role in generating world-wide inflation is the subject-matter of their whole book, as its title suggests.

25 Note, however, that Parkin, Richards and Zis (1975) and Swoboda (1973) provided early analyses of the role of US monetary expansion in fuelling world inflation that have, in all their essential outlines, been borne out by the detailed work of Darby, Lothian et al. (1983). For a dissenting view on this, see Feige and Johannes (1982). Note, though, that the time-series tests for causality conducted by Feige and Johannes did not permit them to reject the hypothesis that world inflation was largely a result of US monetary expansion. Their tests simply did not enable them to reject the alternative, 'no causation' hypothesis.

26 On this evidence, see, for example, Hamburger (1977).

27 In the case of Canada, under a flexible exchange rate, upward pressure on the exchange rate took the place of a balance-of-payments surplus as an indicator that domestic policy could become more expansionary, and vice versa.

28 For more detailed accounts of this period, see Argy (1981, Chapter 6), and Williamson (1977, Chapters 2–3).

29 On the role of all these matters in generating inflation in the early 1970s, see McCracken et al. (1977). As I have already remarked, I believe that McCracken et al. pay insufficient attention to the role of earlier monetary policy in generating inflation in the 1970s.

30 The argument of this paragraph is very different from that advanced by McCracken *et al.* (1977), who took it for granted that such commodity-price explosions as I discuss were exogenous events. As far as I am aware, the careful empirical work that would settle the disagreement implicit here remains to be done. However, Darby, Lothian *et al.* (1983, Chapter 8), explicitly investigated the contribution made by OPEC to world inflation in the 1970s, with inconclusive results. McKinnon (1983) is one source of the suggestion that oil prices should be regarded as being at least partially endogenous with respect to US monetary policy.

31 There has been a great deal of empirical work on the efficiency of the foreign-exchange market. Some studies, such as that of Boothe (1983), find evidence which suggests that the market is not entirely efficient. There do appear to be runs of data in which knowledge of past errors in the forward rate as a forecaster of the spot rate would have enabled agents to speculate profitably.

32 The *locus classicus* for the analysis of Canadian monetary policy in the 1970s is Courchene (1977).

33 The Radcliffe Report (Committee on the Working of the Monetary System, 1959) paid considerable attention to the problem of the sterling balances.

34 Williamson (1976) was one of the first to analyse the continued use of reserves under floating rates.

35 Not all borrowing nations were without oil. The cases of Mexico, Nigeria, and Venezuela come to mind here.

36 For a more detailed account of these developments, see Helleiner *et al.* (1983),

37 Balassa (1980) provided convincing evidence that at least before the late 1970s, flexible exchange rates and their associated exchange-rate fluctuations did not interfere with the growth of world trade.

38 The work of Assar Lindbeck (1976) on the 'political business cycle' ought to be cited in this context. However, Alt and Chrystal (1983) argued forcefully that the political business cycle is, at best, a transitory phenomenon.

39 Britain suspended the gold standard in 1797 and did not restore it until several years after the Napoleonic wars had ended. The United States fought the Civil War on a paper currency and, of course, most countries abandoned gold during the First World War.

40 The European Monetary System was much less ambitious, at least in its immediate scope, than the so-called Werner Plan, which envisaged complete European monetary union. Nevertheless, some of the supporters of the European Monetary System did see it as a first step toward more complete union. For an ingenious proposal for achieving European monetary union with an indexed money, see the 'All Saints Day Manifesto', published in Fratianni and Peeters (1978), along with a useful collection of essays debating the merits of a European currency.

41 Such temporary relief is not available under a fixed rate because pegging the price of domestic currency in terms of foreign currency removes from the authorities the ability to choose in which market to intervene in order to change the money supply.

# 9

# On Currency Unions

## Introduction

It is probably true to say that in the 1950s and 1960s the majority of economists favoured one form or another of exchange-rate flexibility between individual countries. However, the 'fixed exchange rate' system to which various forms of exchange-rate flexibility were regarded as superior was, in fact, usually an 'adjustable peg' system of the Bretton Woods variety. The merits of a system of rigidly and perpetually fixed exchange rates or, what amounts to the same thing, a common international currency, were less frequently discussed. Matters are now very different. An influential body of opinion once again exists to the effect that just such a system would provide the best of all possible means of organising the international monetary system. Robert Mundell and Arthur Laffer pioneered the revival of this view—see Wanniski (1975)—and some of its adherents, notably the signatories of the 'All Saints Day Manifesto', have argued that it is a practical possibility that such a system can be established, if not on a world-wide basis, then at least within the European Economic Community—see Fratianni and Peeters (1978). In this chapter I shall argue that, although this body of opinion is to be taken seriously, there is room for considerable doubt about certain aspects of the case that underlie it.

The case for a currency union is closely related to that loose-knit body of doctrine known as 'monetarism' without being an integral part of it, but it is not my purpose here to attack that case by launching a general assault on its theoretical foundations. I accept many, indeed probably most, of the theoretical preconceptions and empirical judgements that underlie it. Hence the first task I shall undertake in the pages that follow is to sketch out the case, and to discuss those aspects of it with which I agree. Only when this common ground is clearly identified does it become possible to deal with substantial areas of disagreement. As we shall see, the issues at stake, which are at least as much political as economic, hinge upon analysis of situations of both long-run equilibrium and short-run disequilibrium; these aspects of the question will be dealt with in turn in the following pages.

172

## *The Case for a Currency Union*

The essence of the case for a currency union between any group of countries is simply stated. The use of money as a means of exchange, a store of value, and a unit of account enables agents to economise on the use of scarce resources in the generation and transmission of the information upon which consumption, production, and employment decisions are based. If national monies exist, and if rates of exchange between them can fluctuate, those engaged in international transactions must either generate for themselves information about the likely course of such fluctuations, face the risks inherent in taking decisions in the light of incomplete information about them, or pay specialised agents to take such risks on their behalf. One way or another, real resources must be devoted to dealing with such problems: problems which would not exist if exchange rates between national monies were rigidly and perpetually fixed or one money were to circulate freely throughout a group of countries. As Johnson (1963) put it, without accepting the argument as a compelling one, the formation of a currency union extends, to economic relations between the countries making it up, the advantages achieved within a national economy by the use of a common currency.

Such arguments as these have long been understood, and they do not represent a novel element in contemporary debates. What is new is the fresh light cast by recent work on the advantages that would be lost if countries gave up on national monetary autonomy by abandoning their own currencies, and on the possibility of altering, or allowing to vary, the prices at which these exchange against one another. It used to be argued frequently that the most important such advantage involved the ability to use monetary policy actively to pursue domestic real-income and employment targets. Experience of the last decade has made us much less sanguine than we were about just what can be achieved by such 'fine-tuning'. Acceptance of the desirability of adopting some sort of a rule, or at least medium-term target, to determine the behaviour of a country's money supply is now more widespread than it was.

In the past, and notably in the work of Friedman (e.g. 1960), advocacy of a monetary rule has been closely associated with advocacy of national monetary autonomy and freely floating exchange rates. After all, the money supply of any one country in a currency union, or even under pegged exchange rates, is an endogenous variable. The only way in which a country can guarantee its own ability to adhere to a self-imposed rule for the monetary expansion rate, independently of what policies are being pursued elsewhere, is to have its own currency and adopt exchange-rate flexibility. Contemporary advocates of currency unions understand and accept this line of reasoning, but they go on to argue that to consider the matter in this way is to take too narrow a view of the issues at stake. They argue that the matter should be considered from the viewpoint of the international economy as a whole, rather than from that of the individual country.

If each potential member of a currency union has its own currency, and if each adopts its own monetary policy geared solely to the achievement of domestic ends, whether based on targets or on fine tuning, then exchange-rate *stability*, let alone fixity, is going to be impossible to maintain between them except by the most extraordinary coincidence. If short-term capital is highly mobile among the countries in question, any divergence of domestic monetary policies is bound to cause exchange rates to fluctuate, no matter what the formal institutional arrangements of the foreign-exchange market, and the international monetary system is going to be inefficient in its operation. Thus, so the argument goes, if from the point of view of each individual country it is desirable that 'rules' to govern the behaviour of the money supply be adopted in order to enhance domestic stability, from the point of view of the international economy there are extra gains to be realised by co-ordinating those 'rules' so as to achieve exchange-rate constancy.

If each of a group of countries adopts a monetary expansion rule, then it will enjoy a long-run, stable domestic inflation rate. Given that the purchasing-power-parity doctrine is a reasonable explanation of the long-run behaviour of exchange rates, this should lead to stable long-run rates of change in equilibrium exchange rates as well.[1] Though stable rates of change in the pattern of exchange rates are much to be preferred to instability, *constancy* of exchange rates will provide even greater efficiency in the international economy. If éach of a group of countries has independently chosen to adopt money-supply growth targets or rules, then it is an apparently short step to go on to argue that those countries may as well pick their monetary expansion rates so that they are compatible with long-run constancy of exchange rates.

To pick monetary expansion rates which generate exchange-rate constancy requires international agreement. Moreover, it cannot be guaranteed that a given set of rules for monetary expansion rates in various countries can forever be compatible with constant exchange rates among their currencies. If the real rate of growth of any country were to change, relative to those ruling elsewhere, or if the real-income elasticity of demand for money in any economy were to alter, or if institutional evolution were to affect the demand-for-money function in any other way, a rate of monetary expansion previously compatible with a zero rate of exchange-rate change, given the monetary rules being followed abroad, would no longer be so.[2] Thus to opt for long-run, constant exchange rates, in conjunction with governing money-supply behaviour, either by long-run rules or by medium-term targets, involves more than having individual countries attempting to adopt compatible domestic policies. Rather it involves the adoption of a rule or target for the behaviour of their aggregate money supply, to be implemented by some international authority or another, with the operation of the price–specie flow mechanism determining the manner in which that world money supply is then allocated between individual countries. In short, it involves the formation of a currency union.

I have already noted that there is much in the foregoing case that I accept. I agree that short-term capital is now so highly mobile internationally that divergent fine-tuning monetary policies are bound to lead to damaging exchange-rate fluctuations. For this reason, as well as for reasons stemming from a general pessimism about the effectiveness of monetary fine tuning, I too would advocate the adoption of a rule, or better still medium-term targets, to govern the monetary expansion of any country.[3] I would expect such a step to lead to stable long-run rates of inflation and, if other countries adopted similar policies, to a stable rate of exchange-rate change for the country concerned. Moreover, I agree that the exchange-rate stability that would arise if all countries adopted such domestic monetary policies would have desirable results for the efficiency of the international economy, and that exchange-rate constancy does have advantages over mere stability as far as that efficiency is concerned.

That, however, is as far as I go with the advocates of currency union. The subsequent steps in their argument seem to me to hinge on the implicit assumption that, given that it has already adopted a monetary rule or medium-term target, there is nothing for a country to lose if it abandons its own currency, joins a currency union and thereby gives up its ability to select its own long-term inflation rate. I do not accept this. I believe that there are long-run losses involved in giving up this ability. More important, I also believe that there are potentially important gains to be had from maintaining individual currencies and permitting exchange rates between them to fluctuate about their long-term trends in the short run. I will take up these matters in turn.

## Long-run Issues

It has already been remarked that the principal advantages of a currency union stem from the greater economy in the use of scarce resources that can be achieved by having the same means of exchange and unit of account in use in both foreign and domestic transactions. On the other hand, a system of national monies linked by flexible rates permits monetary policy to be used to achieve domestic ends. The key question that must be resolved in any attempt to choose between these alternative regimes from the point of view of long-run analysis is just what domestic variables can have their long-run equilibrium values influenced by an autonomous monetary policy. The development of macroeconomics in the 1970s has led to a marked change in perspective on this issue.

It has never been a matter of controversy that the principal long-run effect of monetary independence is that it confers on an individual economy the ability to choose its own inflation rate. This ability has never been highly regarded, at least from an economic viewpoint; instead, other gains which allegedly could be had as a result of the ability to select an inflation rate have been stressed. In particular, the Phillips curve once seemed to imply that, if an inflation rate could be chosen independently of that ruling in the rest of the world, so also could a domestic unemployment rate. Thus, so the argument went, a system of national monetary autonomy permits different economies, whose populations have different tastes *vis-à-vis* inflation and unemployment, to indulge those tastes. However, modern macro-theory has it that, in the long run, the expected and actual price levels are equal to one another, as are the expected and actual rates of change of the price level. One particular application of this view yields the 'natural unemployment rate' hypothesis, whose major policy implication is that any trade-off between inflation and unemployment which policy-makers can exploit, if it exists at all, is only transitory.

The 1970s have generated a considerable body of evidence in favour of the proposition that the inflation–unemployment trade-off vanishes in the long run. Even if that evidence is such as to leave some disinterested observers in doubt about the empirical truth or falsity of the proposition in question, this very doubt is sufficient to undermine an important element in the traditional case for monetary autonomy. If we do not know the extent to which we can improve the unemployment situation in the long run by the use of inflationary monetary policy, and if attempts to do so carry with them the risk of ever-accelerating inflation should it in fact not be possible to achieve any long-run improvements in this way, then the policy freedom that is sacrificed by joining a currency union is illusory. Policy-makers who cannot be sure whether an inflation–unemployment trade-off exists, let alone what its nature may be if it does exist, are in no position to take advantage of any freedom to exploit such a trade-off that the maintenance of monetary independence might confer upon them.[4]

It would be easy to jump from the foregoing argument to the conclusion that the ability to choose its own inflation rate confers no long-run benefits on an individual country. Such a conclusion would be valid only if variations in the long-run, and hence fully anticipated, inflation rate had no effect on the equilibrium values of other economic variables, only if money were superneutral. Unless all money balances, including high-powered money, bear a competitive rate of return, we know that money is not superneutral. The seigniorage accruing to the monetary authority will vary with the rate of inflation, as will the allocation of resources between consumption and capital accumulation, not to mention between work, leisure, and trading activities. Seigniorage is, of course, just an old-fashioned name for the tax that is levied on cash balances when a competititve rate return is not paid on them, and the resource allocation effects of varying the rate of seigniorage are but manifestations of the welfare consequences of raising tax revenue in that particular way.[5]

Harry Johnson (1966) was among the first to recognise the relevance of what we might call the 'inflation tax' literature to international monetary questions such as I am discussing here, and once its relevance is noted, it becomes clear, as Sumner (1976) has pointed out, that to be able to choose the amount of seigniorage it collects gives a national government an extra degree of freedom in designing its tax structure. Unless the tax rate to be applied to cash balances within an optimal tax structure is the same for all countries linked together in a currency union, there is a potential benefit to be realised by each of them from the ability individually to generate a different long-run inflation rate which the maintenance of national monetary independence would confer. Given that tastes, technology, and the availability of resources are inevitably going to differ between countries, and given that such differences will influence the relative collection costs of different taxes as well as the structure of the economy upon which they are going to be levied, the presumption must be that the optimal seigniorage rate will vary, and that there are therefore gains to be made, even in the long run, from maintaining national monetary independence.

Now the foregoing argument is certainly not as weighty as one based on the ability to control the level of employment in the long run would have been, had it proved valid. If the inflation rate for a currency union were chosen so as to produce a 'second best' tax structure, designed subject to the constraint that the tax rate levied on cash balances be the same for each country, one would have to agree with Sumner (1976) that it would be difficult to get very excited about the welfare losses that might arise for any economy as a result of being a member of such a union. But is it any easier to get excited about the long-run gains from having a common currency? Does it really take up a significant amount of resources to deal with the extra costs of trading in a world in which exchange rates between national monies, though not remaining fixed, stably and predictably adjust to long-run differences in inflation rates? The most sensible conclusion to draw from the foregoing discussion is surely that the arguments we have considered so far are unlikely to be crucial to the choice between joining a currency union and maintaining national monetary autonomy.

Nevertheless, we have not yet finished with our discussion of seigniorage. The possibility of raising revenue by taxing cash balances raises two closely related issues which must be settled among countries that seek to form a currency union. These issues are more political than narrowly economic, but that in no way diminishes their importance. As Grubel (1966) pointed out, before such a union is viable the countries involved in it must agree on how much seigniorage is to be collected, and the manner in which it is to be distributed among them. Neither of these questions is a matter for international negotiation when countries maintain their monetary independence. What we have already said about the significance of the welfare losses arising from a non-optimal rate of seigniorage for the individual country might seem to imply that there would be little to gain or lose for the individual country in having to accept a non-optimal rate of taxation on money balances, and hence that such a tax rate would be easy to negotiate. However, our earlier discussion was premissed on a 'second best' tax structure being in force.

If seigniorage were the *only* tax to be levied on an across-country basis, it would be politically difficult to have its rate chosen with a view to providing a second-best solution to the optimal tax problems of the countries involved in a currency union. This is because it is possible to gear the arrangements adopted for the collection and distribution of seigniorage in order to effect international transfers of income. Potential recipients of such transfers would certainly have every incentive to press for a revenue-maximising rather than a welfare-maximising rate of seigniorage, and the extent to which they would be successful would depend critically upon the institutional framework set up to administer the working of the union's monetary system. Recent history provides at least two illustrations of how such problems can arise and of how important they can be. The debate about the creation and allocation of Special Drawing Rights, and whether to use their allocation as a means of aiding poor countries, is the first of these. The second is the behaviour of the United States, as the producer of the major reserve currency under the Bretton Woods system, in using that position to extract seigniorage from the rest of the world during the Vietnam War, with economic and political consequences too obvious to need further discussion here.

It is well known that even if their assessment is confined to the conventional 'triangle under the demand-for-money function' measure, the welfare costs of overutilising taxation of cash balances are relatively severe, but the formation of a currency union, according to the foregoing argument, carries with it the danger that such taxation would be overutilised. To be sure, there are methods of organising matters so that the operation of the monetary system could not be used to effect international redistributions of income, thus eliminating this danger. An agreement to pay competitive interest on all components of the money supply, or the adoption of commodity money as a reserve base for the system, would accomplish this end, although the first of these solutions would involve a non-optimal tax rate on money and the second the incurring of unnecessary real-resource costs. Even so, the key question here is not the technical one of how to organise the monetary system of a currency union so that it would generate a zero rate of seigniorage, but the political one of how to ensure that it would not in fact be organised with the aim of providing a means of income redistribution, an aim whose implementation might then result in an inefficiently high rate of inflation for the union.

Moreover, even if the danger of overutilising a tax on cash balances were to be initially avoided when a currency union was first formed, the very existence of seigniorage would provide a continuing source of potential conflict among member countries about its distribution. Within a currency union, the amount of seigniorage which any country would contribute would be equal to domestic money holdings times the difference between the market nominal-interest rate and any rate of return that money might bear. Anything that might alter the distribution of the money supply among countries over time would cause variation in an individual country's payments of seigniorage and hence alter the distributional consequences of any simple formula for the allocation of receipts. The rules for such allocation would thus in practice be open to continuous pressure for renegotiation.

The best guarantee against the problems that we have here raised becoming matters of practical importance would be the existence of relatively small disparities of income between currency union members and, more generally, the existence of alternative means of effecting cross-country redistribution of income. Thus they do not amount to a general case against currency unions, but do suggest that some unions would be more likely to be politically feasible than others. I will come back to this point later, but now turn to dealing with short-run issues.

## *Short-run Issues*

This essay is addressing the question whether a group of countries, each of which would adopt medium-term money-supply targets or long-run rules, would, under a system of national monetary autonomy, be better off to form a currency union. Thus, although we know a great deal about the consequences for domestic variables of nominal shocks—alterations in the domestic rate of monetary expansion, or the rate ruling in the rest of the world—under alternative exchange-rate schemes, that knowledge is not relevant to the issues under debate here.[6] Such shocks are ruled out if monetary targets or rules are in force, and if they are adhered to. But this does not mean that real shocks are ruled out. Changes in tastes do sometimes occur as they do in available technology; natural resources do get depleted; and so on. If there is no money illusion, the long-run consequences of such happenings as these for an individual country can in no way be made different by having a different monetary system, except, of course, to the extent that the nature of the long-run equilibrium depends upon the path that the economy takes to get there. Even so, if a country's rate of productivity-growth falls, or the real terms of trade move against it, the effects of such an event on real income cannot be offset by an exchange-rate change. However, it is conceivable that the path whereby an economy moves from the original long-run equilibrium to the new one required by such a change (and therefore perhaps the nature of that equilibrium) can differ, depending upon monetary arrangements, and that one path may be preferable to another.

Consider the case of an economy which, for some reason, suffers a fall in its real income and in its equilibrium level of real wages as a result of a deterioration in its terms of trade. If that country is a member of a currency union of which it makes up a relatively small part, its equilibrium price level and inflation rate will be given by those ruling in the union as a whole, so that a lower real wage means a lower money wage. If, instead, that country combines a constant rate of growth for its own nominal money supply with a flexible exchange rate, the requirement that lower levels of real income and real wages prevail would be met by the establishment of a higher price level and a lower exchange rate. To make matters as clear as possible, let us think for a moment of a very special case where equilibrium real income and the equilibrium real wage in each industry are affected in equal proportions by the change in question and in which the real income elasticity of demand for money is unity. In this case, under a currency union, a uniform fall in money wages would re-establish equilibrium, while, with national monetary autonomy, a currency depreciation with no change in money wages would suffice. If either change could be implemented with equal ease, then it would not matter which happened. The real effects of either change would be the same. However, it cannot be taken for granted that one of these changes could occur as easily as the other, and in those circumstances it might matter very much indeed which adjustment mechanism was relied upon, for reasons which I shall now discuss.

Wages, prices and exchange rates do not set themselves. Economic agents set their values, and real resources are used up both in taking decisions to adjust those values and in the actual process of adjustment. Once this is recognised, it should be clear why it is not necessarily a matter of indifference whether a country relies on money wages or the exchange rate to adjust to changed circumstances. At the very least, the alternatives might involve the economy incurring different resource costs. Of course, the example we are considering here is a very special case indeed. Real shocks that change income, and/or the terms of trade, typically require changes in relative prices and real wages as well as changes in their economy-wide average levels, and, as Purvis (1979) shows, there is nothing that can be said in general about these matters because much depends upon the precise nature of the shock. If this is so, given a currency union, adjustment to some real shock will certainly impose the costs involved in changing prices and wages; but, with national monetary autonomy, such costs will still be incurred, with that of changing the exchange rate being added to them. However, this does not mean that the currency-union alternative is the more attractive of the two; because it is not the cost of making one sort or another of price change *per se* that is of central importance in the present context, but rather what the existence of such costs implies for the speed at which prices adjust, and hence for the length of time it takes for a new equilibrium to be established after the economy is shocked.

This is a matter of particular importance when the re-establishment of equilibrium requires that the overall level of real wages be reduced (or rise less rapidly than in the past), since the persistence of disequilibrium in such a case will involve an abnormally high level of unemployment. If we could rely upon money wages and the exchange rate to adjust with equal speed, there would be nothing to choose between a currency union and monetary autonomy; but if the process of money-wage adjustment were less rapid than exchange-rate adjustment, then that would be an important point in favour of maintaining monetary autonomy. Causal empiricism suggests that exchange rates are potentially a great deal more flexible than money wages. Furthermore, there are good *a priori* reasons, arising from the nature of the foreign exchange and labour markets, why this should be so.

When there are autonomous national monies, there exists a foreign-exchange market operated by specialist dealers whose explicit role is to set the exchange rate and to hold inventories of currencies with which they stand ready to deal with the public at large at the prices they set. The costs to them of generating the information upon which to base their pricing decisions, and of changing the prices that they set, are small relative to the gains and losses available to them. In such a market it is not unreasonable to expect that something very close to 'rational expectations' will underlie the prices that actually rule. This is but another way of asserting that speculative behaviour will typically be such as to take the foreign-exchange market rapidly towards, rather than away from, equilibrium. That market has all the essential characteristics of what Sir John Hicks (1974) has termed a 'flex price' market.

The labour market, on the other hand, is Hicks's archetypical 'fix price' market. It is decentralised, and contains no agents whose specialised task is to set money wages and hold inventories of labour. In the labour market, the costs to the relevant agents of generating the extra information that would lead them closer to a market clearing price are likely to be high relative to the benefits accruing to them from so doing. Moreover, the widespread existence of long-term wage contracts, which are themselves a response to the costs of gathering and processing information, makes it prohibitively expensive for agents bound by them to respond rapidly to new information about changed circumstances, except by altering unemployment levels. And this is not to mention the rigidities introduced by the presence of monopoly elements in the market. One does not have to go all the way with Hicks, who argues that the behaviour of money wages is to all intents and purposes independent of the behaviour of the supply and demand for labour, in order to recognise that the labour market is for all these reasons likely to be sluggish in generating changes in money wages in response to changed market conditions.

If the foregoing arguments are valid, then the overall level of real wages can be changed more rapidly by allowing the exchange rate and the price level to vary than by holding the price level fixed and putting the burden of adjustment solely on to money wages. This is not to say that national monetary autonomy carries with it a guarantee of perpetual full employment, because we have already noted that the circumstances in which an exogenous shock requiring a fall in the real wage could be met by having all the adjusting done by the exchange rate, and none at all by money wages, are very special indeed. However, it is to argue that, given such autonomy, the economy will adjust more rapidly towards equilibrium in response to any shock that requires a fall in the level of real wages and hence will experience less transitional unemployment than it would under a currency union.

Not all shocks require that real wages fall—some cause equilibrium real wages to rise. Anyone who believes that the labour market behaves so that money wages can react more rapidly in an upward direction than downward will be less concerned with the advantages of flexible exchange rates in such a case. Even if there is symmetry in the slowness of money wages to adjust upwards and downwards, unemployment would not be a key problem if such slow adjustment kept the economy out of equilibrium at too low a real wage. Nevertheless, there would still be resource-allocation costs to be borne in such circumstances, costs that could be mitigated by the more rapid adjustment to equilibrium than we have argued is promised by exchange-rate flexibility.

Now the truth or falsity of the foregoing arguments cannot be settled on purely *a priori* grounds. They rest on the empirical proposition that those involved in the wage-bargaining process are, relative to those operating in the foreign-exchange market, slow to perceive the need for a price change and slow to implement it, so that the average level of real wages can be kept closer to its equilibrium level by permitting the exchange rate to fluctuate than by relying on money-wage fluctuations. In earlier literature, for example Corden (1972), on exchange rates and currency unions it was frequently argued that a small and specialised economy, importing most of its consumer goods, would not benefit from maintaining a flexible exchange rate precisely because those involved in wage bargaining would be unlikely to suffer from money illusion when the exchange rate changed, and because in the limit they might even resort to bargaining in terms of some foreign currency rather than their own. But this is really to say that, for such an economy, so much of its trading is carried out externally as opposed to internally that a separate domestic money is not in any case viable. Nevertheless, in the case of an economy in which there is a real choice to be made between national monetary autonomy and membership of a currency union, there exists an argument closely related to the one just cited that merits consideration.

If those involved in the labour market are slow to see the need for a change in real wages, but rapid both in recognising when real wages have changed and in moving to restore their level, then the advantages that we have been claiming for a system of national monetary autonomy will not exist. Under such circumstances, an exchange-rate change which lowers the real wage would be met at once by a compensatory money-wage increase, and a classic 'cost-push'-generated wage–price spiral accompanied by unemployment would result. In short, if wage rigidity is *real-wage rigidity* stemming from slowness in economic agents to perceive the need for real wages, or their rate of growth to change, rather than *money-wage rigidity* arising from short-run money illusion and/or from high costs of money-wage adjustment, then the foregoing arguments against currency unions are not valid. Though it must be clear from my arguments that I believe money-wage rigidity to be important, it is nevertheless the case that, in the present state of knowledge, there seems to be no formal empirical evidence either to support or to undermine that belief.

Now in the last few pages I have concentrated on arguments about the short-run behaviour of the economy, but I have also noted in passing that they may in fact have implications for the long-run as well. It has been argued that the maintenance of monetary independence by individual countries would lead to smaller short-term fluctuations in output and employment. Given the asymmetry of the relationship between the excess demand for labour and the level of unemployment, this immediately implies that the average level of unemployment over time will, for a similar pattern of shocks, be higher in a country which belongs to a currency union. To the extent that human capital deteriorates more rapidly when it is unemployed, and to the extent that less investment in new human capital takes place in the presence of unemployment, this could have long-term effects in terms both of raising the natural unemployment rate of the economy, and of reducing the level of output associated with it. Despite Phelps's (1972, Chapter 3) theoretical discussion of these issues, we have next to no formal empirical knowledge about the extent to which the evolution of an economy's long-run equilibrium characteristics is affected by short-run fluctuations, so that there is no way of assessing the importance, if any, to be placed upon the arguments just advanced. To the extent that they are given credence, they add to the case against currency unions.[7]

One caveat concerning international fiscal co-operation should be noted before this discussion is brought to a close. If mechanisms exist whereby real-income transfers can be made between countries which belong to a currency union, then they can be used either to offset permanently the effects of terms-of-trade changes on real-income output, and employment, or to subsidise employment during the transition to a new equilibrium structure of real wages. As with the long-run arguments, so also the amount of weight to be attached to the short-run arguments against currency unions is lessened if we conceive of such a union being adopted as part of a process of more general international economic integration. Once again then, the debate about currency unification turns out to hinge upon matters that are as much political as economic.

## Conclusions

The arguments of the last four sections of this chapter stop far short of making a case that, for *any* group of countries, a currency union is *a priori* less desirable than the maintenance of national monetary autonomy. The hypothesis of the existence of a long-run inflation–unemployment trade-off, combined with the observation that different nations have different tastes *vis-à-vis* these variables, was the key element in earlier versions of the case for flexible exchange rates, but it can no longer be regarded as valid. Nevertheless, there are other advantages to maintaining national monetary autonomy, and the fact that Phillips's trade-off has been discredited does not immediately imply that a world-wide currency union is desirable. The arguments that I have presented suggest that some groups of countries stand to gain more—or lose less—by forming such a union than others, and that some currency unions are more feasible than others.

First, a group of countries whose governments are unable to agree about the merits of using monetary policy to 'fine-tune' macroeconomic activity are not going to be able to form a union, although if one regards attempts at monetary fine-tuning as misguided, then the ability to indulge in it can hardly be counted as an advantage of maintaining national monetary independence. Indeed, many advocates of currency unions regard the fact that indulging in irresponsible domestic monetary policies is rendered impossible by members in a currency union as one of the principal advantages conferred by that membership. Laffer and Mundell—see Wanniski (1975)—and the authors of the All Saints Day Manifesto—see Fratianni and Peeters (1987)—lay great stress on this matter. However, I would argue that the true implication of the argument is not that irresponsible governments ought to join a currency union, but that they will not do so. A recognition of the need for monetary discipline must precede its acceptance, and this seems to me to imply that only those governments that do not need currency-union membership to discipline their policies are going to commit themselves to it in the first place. Hence, I regard this argument for currency unification as irrelevant.

Secondly, I have noticed the possibility that, with the formation of a currency union, seigniorage would become a potentially ready source of revenue for international redistribution, and that the resulting pressures towards inflation would be less in a currency union made up of countries whose levels of income were rather similar than in one where great disparities existed. Thus, it is much harder, for example, to see inflation as a danger in a currency union made of the EEC countries than in a world-wide currency union. Arguments that SDRs be put into circulation by distributing them initially to poor countries are precisely arguments that seigniorage be used to redistribute income internationally; they are not uncommon, and they do carry with them the threat that world liquidity might be overexpanded for the sake of redistributing income if a world-wide currency union were formed.

Thirdly, I have noted that the maintenance of national monetary autonomy might help a country cushion the employment effects of certain real shocks, but of course it will do so only if the other potential members of a currency union do not also suffer from the same shocks at the same time. If, as I have suggested, the relevant shocks are likely to involve changes in tastes and technology, then a currency union between countries of similar industrial structure is going to be more feasible than one which involves very disparate economies. It is also worth noting that such similarity between countries might make it easier for them to solve the political problem of deciding on the rate of seigniorage to be levied within the currency union, since the optimal tax structure for each country will be similar in such a case.

Finally, and most important of all, I have stressed that all the arguments against currency unions that I have advanced are weakened if the existence of some degree of fiscal unity is postulated. If there exist fiscal means for redistributing income between countries, the tendency to overindulge in money creation for such purposes is lessened. If unaffected countries can be taxed in order to subsidise transition costs imposed on other countries by real shocks, then the desirability of maintaining monetary independence is reduced. Indeed, we can look at this matter from the opposite viewpoint. Suppose a group of countries do form some kind of political or fiscal union, but each maintains its own currency with flexible exchange rates between them. In what currency then are taxes to be collected? In what currency are tax calculations to be made? In what currency are subsidies to be fixed? And so on. Clearly a fiscal union with a common currency would be much easier to administer than would one without.

In short, these arguments lead us to a not very original conclusion about currency unions, and one that was clearly stated in more than one place by Harry Johnson (cf 1963, 1969b). The formation of a currency union extends to the international economy the advantages gained within a national economy by having a common currency. National economies,

however, have other institutions to help them counteract the difficulties
that particular regions from time to time experience as a result of belonging
to a national currency area. If such institutions can be extended to the
international economy along with the adoption of a common currency, the
case against forming a currency union becomes much weaker. In the last
resort then, what is or is not a feasible currency union is more a political
than an economic matter.

## Notes

1 See Gailliot (1970) and Myhrman (1976) for evidence on the long-run validity
of purchasing-power parity.

2 Evidence gathered by Bordo and Jonung (1987), after this paper was written,
suggests that such institutional change is an important long-run influence on
velocity.

3 And as the reader of Chapter 7 above will realise, I would nowadays be much
more comfortable defending medium-term targets rather than long-run rules here.

4 See Sumner (1976) for an early and thorough discussion of this and related
issues.

5 This is not to say that the analysis of seigniorage in an optimal tax structure is
straightforward. See Marty (1976) for a pioneering effort to deal with these
questions.

6 Thus Dornbusch's (1976b) analysis of exchange rate overshooting in response
to money-supply disturbances would not be relevant to a world in which such
shocks did not occur. The issue of overshooting is discussed in Chapter 8 above.

7 Since this passage was written in 1976, of course, a considerable empirical
literature on 'hysteresis' effects has grown up. See, for example, Cross (1988). The
phenomenon does seem to be important, at least in Western Europe.

# 10

# Fiscal Deficits and International Monetary Institutions

## *Introduction*

The early 1970s were marked by two striking changes in the economic-policy environment of the Western world, one quite obvious at the time and the second, no less important, only clearly visible with the benefit of hindsight. The first of these changes was the break-up of the Bretton Woods system of fixed exchange rates and its replacement by an *ad hoc* array of floating exchange-rate mechanisms; the second was the beginning of a period of chronic fiscal deficits in a number of countries, notably but by no means uniquely the United States, on a scale unprecedented in peacetime.

It is natural to enquire about the interconnectedness of institutional change in the international monetary system and such a fundamental shift in the stance of fiscal policy, coming as they did at about the same time, and this chapter addresses aspects of this issue. It begins with a general discussion of whether deficits are indeed something to be concerned about, and concludes that they are. It then goes on to consider the role of the Bretton Woods system as a constraint upon fiscal policy in earlier times, and argues that the system could act as a constraint for only so long as this was not fully apparent to those who believed in the beneficial effects of deficit finance. Finally, it considers the interaction of the United States deficit with the special role played by the US dollar in the current international monetary system, and suggests that this interaction poses special and crucial problems for the conduct of US fiscal policy which do not arise from other countries' deficits.

## Deficits and the Ricardian Equivalence Theorem

Any essay dealing with government debt and deficits must first take a position about the effect, if any, that they have upon the economy both in the present and in the future. Robert J Barro (1974) sets out conditions under which the economic effects of tax- and bond-financed government expenditure are equivalent. Though it is one thing to point out that such equivalence may hold in principle, and quite another to argue that it does hold in practice, Barro's analysis is surely the intellectual source of widespread unconcern about the current stance of fiscal policy in the United States and elsewhere.

To put matters in their simplest possible terms, the 'Ricardian equivalence' theorem, as, following Buchanan (1976) it has come to be called, tells us that the choice between tax and bond finance for current government expenditure is of no real consequence if: taxes now and in the future have no allocative effects; all agents perceive that the substitution of current-debt issue for current taxation represents the substitution of future taxes for present taxes; and those same agents evaluate future taxes as having exactly the same present value as the current taxes they replace, because they discount future tax liabilities at the same rate as they discount the coupon payments borne by the government bonds that they purchase instead of paying current taxes.[1] If these conditions hold, the choice between financing current government expenditure by taxes or borrowing will have no effect upon agents' evaluation of their own wealth, and hence no effects upon the rate at which the economy accumulates capital.

There is a certain irony in the fact that this analysis, advanced by a leading proponent of 'new-classical' macroeconomics, should resemble one much used by 'Keynesian' proponents of deficit finance, notably Abba Lerner (1943), in earlier times. For the typical Keynesian of forty years ago, and for some even now, the national debt is no burden because 'we owe it to ourselves'. How, the rhetorical question was asked (and sometimes still is) can we impose a burden upon ourselves by writing IOUs to ourselves? Of course, if that is all deficit finance amounts to, we cannot; and a moment's reflection will convince the reader that Barro's assumptions that the current generation may be modelled as a simple aggregate of identical representative agents in whose utility functions the welfare of unknown members of future generations gets exactly the same weight as does their own future welfare, is logically equivalent to assuming that the economy under analysis consists of one representative infinitely lived individual. In such an economy the creation of government debt is exactly equivalent to that individual writing IOUs to himself, and an immortal Robinson Crusoe obviously could write IOUs to himself to his heart's content with no real consequences of any sort. That, stripped to its basics, is what Barro's Ricardian equivalence theorem amounts to saying.[2]

Now the representative agent assumption certainly obscures many issues in the analysis of public debt, but it does not lie at the heart of Barro's result. Rather it is the assumption that the individuals who are now faced with a choice between tax and debt finance for government expenditure both care about the welfare of their descendants, and realise that this welfare can only be provided for by endowing them with the appropriately chosen stock of capital, regardless of methods of government finance currently in force, that accounts for his conclusions. Nevertheless, anyone who believes that the representative-agent assumption does not distract attention from important questions presumably also believes that an immediate repudiation of the existing domestically held debt of the United States government or any other government would be an event of no more importance than Robinson Crusoe's destroying his existing stock of IOUs. Obviously important wealth redistributions would stem from such a repudiation, and their analysis would require ethical questions, beyond the boundaries of positive economics, to be addressed. However, the perfect altruism towards future generations on the part of the representative members-of-the-current-generation assumption of Barro's analysis, if extended towards other members of the current generation, would produce just the case in which such distribution effects are irrelevant. The fact that we would regard it as highly unlikely that society would tolerate with equanimity debt repudiation by government, because of its redistributive effects *within* a generation, should alert us to the possibility that the assumptions, about altruism *between* generations, from which the Ricardian equivalence theorem follows, involve propositions of dubious validity about the attitudes of individuals now living towards the welfare of anonymous members of future generations.[3]

Another reason for doubting Ricardian equivalence arises, as Buchanan (1976) has pointed out, from the fact that a society made up of agents so altruistic that the theorem in question holds would not be one in which democratic processes were systematically biased in favour of debt-, as opposed to tax-, financed government expenditure. Altruistic agents who cared equally about all members of future generations would be indifferent between tax- and bond-financed government expenditure and would have no systematic incentive to vote for one rather than the other. They would recognise that they could make provision for the welfare of those future generations only by reducing their own current consumption and that the means used to finance current government expenditure should not be allowed to impinge upon their choice here. For such agents, the choice between debt and tax finance only becomes determinate when the welfare costs imposed by non-lump-sum taxation are taken into account. Debt finance then opens up the possibility of smoothing out such welfare burdens over time in the face of fluctuating government expenditure. Though Barro (1979b) shows that such considerations explain much of the variation in the

US public debt between 1917 and 1976, a period in which expenditure fluctuations are dominated by war-time requirements, and in which tax-smoothing motives might well have been important, it is hard to reconcile the steadily increasing deficits of the last ten years with this analysis.

It is at least plausible that the apparently strong bias towards deficit finance recently displayed by democratic processes in the US stems from a desire on the part of individual members of society to provide for their own futures, and perhaps those of their own descendants, without sacrificing current consumption. How better to do this than to endow themselves and those descendants with enforceable claims on the incomes of others? And what does the creation of government debt accomplish if not that? This highly plausible explanation of deficit financing of government expenditure offered by the public-choice literature is, of course, logically inconsistent with the Ricardian equivalence theorem.

The foregoing arguments do not prove that Barro's celebrated theorem is wrong: given its assumptions it is patently correct. However, they strongly suggest that those assumptions do not hold in the real world, and that, therefore, the choice between taxation and debt issue made by the current generation does indeed matter for the welfare of future generations, and does so precisely because it matters for that of the current generation. Those arguments further suggest that our proclivity to choose debt finance implies that (at least in a closed economy) future generations will be endowed with a smaller capital stock than would be theirs in the absence of such debt financing. Now in a fully employed economy, future generations taken as a whole may enjoy a higher level of consumption only if the current generation tolerates a lower one, and vice versa. In the absence of some market imperfection or outright failure, the choice between tax and debt finance is therefore, of its very essence, a choice about the inter-generational distribution of economic welfare.[4] This does not mean that there is nothing to be said about the issue however, but rather that its nature is at least as much ethical as it is economic. An economist must be wary when he discusses such an issue, and the reader of his discussion should be doubly so, but it is hard to see how the discussion can be avoided.

If the choice between tax and debt finance for government expenditure fundamentally concerns the inter-generational distribution of consumption, it is also one in which some of the affected parties are not, and by the very nature of things cannot be, consulted. There must therefore, be a presumption that, if left to choose on its own account, a less than perfectly altruistic current generation will tend to tip the scales further in its own direction than a dispassionate spectator, who weighed the utilities accruing to individuals independently of the time at which they happened to be born, would think appropriate. If this argument is accepted, then not only does debt finance have real consequences, but those consequences are ethically questionable. It would then follow that limits on the extent to which the current generation can choose debt finance are desirable.

## Deficits in Keynesian Analysis

In the light of the foregoing arguments we might helpfully think of the present generation as a political interest group which, when it comes to decisions about debt and tax financing of current government expenditure, acts so as to extract rents from future generations whose interests are underrepresented in the political process. Such rent-seeking behaviour through political processes is hardly unique, and a well-known approach to the problems it generates involves the creation of new, or the defence of existing, institutional constraints upon agents' activities.[5] Such institutional constraints may be formally constitutional and *de jure*, incapable of being set aside by simple fiat of any legislature, or informal but nevertheless powerful manifestations of social and political conventions which *de facto* prevent a legislature taking, or indeed even contemplating, particular acts.

Constraints on debt finance have in the past typically been of the latter kind. Adam Smith's dictum, quoted with disapproval and scandalous disregard for context by Keynes (1936, p. 361), that 'What is prudence in the conduct of every private family can scarce be folly in that of a great Kingdom' occurs in the context of a discussion of free trade, and not of deficit finance as the unwary reader of the *General Theory* might think; but, it is nevertheless the case that, outside of war-time, the notion that budgets should be balanced dominated the conduct of fiscal policy in much of the Western world throughout the nineteenth century and into the twentieth. An idea whose wisdom is universally taken for granted is a powerful constraint upon policy for just as long as it is not subjected to careful criticism; but it will only remain such if it turns out to be logically coherent when analysed. Though 'sound finance', as Abba Lerner (1943) was to term it, may be judged desirable in the light of arguments advanced earlier in this chapter, any defence of it, based on a transparently false analogy between the individual and the nation, was bound to crumble in the face of Keynesian attacks on behalf of 'functional finance' (again the phrase is Lerner's).

But we must be careful here, because when Keynes, and most of his disciples, attacked the conventional wisdom of the 'balanced budget', they did not base their arguments on any Ricardian equivalence theorem, nor would they have regarded the arguments advanced earlier in this chapter as being of the slightest relevance to their concerns. We have so far discussed the pros and cons of debt finance in a full-employment situation in which current consumption has an opportunity cost in terms of current capital accumulation and hence of future consumption, but they did not. Rightly or wrongly, their vision of the world was one in which a failure of market mechanisms created involuntary unemployment so that output produced in response to current government expenditure had a zero opportunity cost. Modern commentators on Keynes such as Johnson (1961), Clower (1965) and Leijonhufvud (1968) are surely right in arguing that, to the extent that this vision is relevant, it refers to the depression phase of a business cycle rather than to the economy's secular behaviour—*pace* Hansen (1938) and the secular stagnationists.[6]

Most early Keynesian advocates of debt-financed expenditure cast their arguments in the context of an explicitly cyclical analysis which envisaged deficits accumulated during the depression phase being offset by surpluses generated during prosperous times, with the whole thrust of policy being to mitigate cyclical instability, while maintaining rough secular balance in the budget. Thus, though the rhetoric of Keynesian economics has been used to defend the chronic secular deficits that so many governments are now running, it probably ought not to have been. Lerner (1943) was something of an exception among early Keynesians in being willing to entertain the idea of essentially perpetual deficit finance should it prove necessary to maintain full employment, and he also advocated monetising those deficits to maximise their impact on aggregate demand. As Colander (1984) has recorded, Keynes himself was unwilling to face up to these apparent implications of his own theory when Lerner drew his attention to them. Thus, when Keynes and most Keynesians attacked the principles of 'sound finance', it was their application on a year-by-year basis, regardless of the cyclical state of the economy, that they had in mind, and not their validity as guides to the appropriate long-run stance of fiscal policy. In an economy whose cyclical fluctuations are about a full-employment secular trend, the zero-opportunity-cost doctrine may be a valid defence of deficits during the depression phase, but it is not relevant to secular questions.

There is no inherent logical contradiction in expressing concern about the current fiscal deficits of the United States and Canada, while still conceding a role to fiscal policy as a short-run stabilisation device. Such a position is, however, politically awkward to maintain, and perhaps risky too. There can be little doubt that, having undermined the constraints placed upon fiscal policy by an unthinking adherence to the principles of sound finance by showing that there might be circumstances to which those principles are inappropriate, Keynesian economics has rendered those constraints totally ineffective in the political arena, even in those situations in which the logic of Keynesian analysis itself might suggest that deficits are undesirable.

## Keynesian Policy and the Bretton Woods System

The *General Theory* was published some fifty years ago, and in only ten or fifteen years came to dominate thinking about fiscal policy. Furthermore, by the late 1940s a number of countries, notably the United Kingdom, had governments and bureaucracies firmly committed to Keynesian policy. It has only been since the late 1970s that fiscal deficits have been widely perceived as a problem, and it is difficult to make the case that they represented any kind of unrecognised problem much before the early 1970s, even in countries where policy had been avowedly Keynesian for two decades. It is instructive to ask why it was that Keynesian policies apparently 'worked' in countries such as the UK for close on two decades without creating problems; to ask why active fiscal stabilisation policies did not lead to chronic secular budget imbalances. An answer to this question which this author, Laidler (1976a), has offered in the past lies in the operation of the international monetary system, and in particular the constraints imposed upon domestic policies of countries such as the United Kingdom by their adherence to the Bretton Woods arrangements.[7]

So-called 'Gladstonian' ideas about the appropriateness of balanced budgets were not the only informal though powerful constraints upon policy which the twentieth century inherited from the nineteenth. It also inherited a deeply held conviction that a gold or gold exchange standard was the right way to organise the international monetary system. The international gold standard was in fact a rather short-lived affair, because, until Gresham's Law began to operate in the wake of the gold discoveries of the 1840s and 50s, most of the world other than Britain was on a silver standard. What with the financial disruptions associated with the US civil war and the Franco-Prussian war, it was not until the late 1870s that a gold standard was at all widely established in the international economy, and it was brought to an end by the outbreak of war in 1914, the best (and worst) efforts of governments to restore it in the 1920s notwithstanding. However, the idea that it was the moral duty of those responsible for monetary policy to preserve constancy in the purchasing power of money, and the notion that compelling convertibility of bank liabilities into specie was a good way of ensuring this, both pre-dated and long outlasted the gold standard as a functioning set of institutions. Indeed, belief in the inherent wisdom of these principles was strengthened rather than weakened by the monetary experiences of the inter-war years.[8]

The Bretton Woods system represented a conscious effort to rebuild a stable international monetary environment after the Second World War on the basis of rather fixed exchange rates and gold convertibility, while permitting latitude to governments to utilise short-term Keynesian policies to counter any cyclical instabilities to which their economies might be prone; although, in cases of chronic difficulties, it was supposed to permit exchange rates to be changed rather than force governments to impose severe deflationary policies. As is well known, the system did not evolve in practice quite as it had been designed. For countries other than the United States (and we will come to the US in due course) it grew into something more akin to a dollar standard than a gold exchange standard, and, of particular importance in the current context, it was characterised by rather more exchange-rate fixity than its founders, particularly Keynes, had intended.

It is surely no accident that in the post-war world, the period of successful Keynesian macro-policy in peripheral countries of the system, such as the United Kingdom, coincided with a period of rather conservative and distinctly unKeynesian policies in the United States. To maintain a fixed exchange rate on the United States dollar, a peripheral country had to permit its monetary policy to be made in the United States, and in the 1950s and early 1960s this involved accepting policy which was widely understood to be, and expected to remain, non-inflationary. In effect the monetary institution of a fixed exchange rate on the stable United States dollar provided an essential prerequisite for a successful regime of Keynesian fiscal fine-tuning which avoided the chronic fiscal deficits, not to mention inflation, that have plagued the world in more recent years.

In a closed economy, current consumption undertaken because government expenditure is bond- rather than tax-financed, to the extent that it employs resources which have alternative uses, must come at the cost of reduced capital accumulation. In an open economy such as the UK's, it can, and under the Bretton Woods system it did, generate deficits in the current account of the balance of payments which the international capital markets of that time did not automatically and willingly finance. The balance-of-payments effects of fiscal deficits implicit here were exacerbated by the then-prevalent practice of making nominal interest rates the centre-piece of monetary policy. Increased government borrowing tends, under such a monetary policy regime, to lead to increased domestic-credit expansion and hence ensures that current-account difficulties quickly become overall balance-of-payments problems. So long therefore as the central country of the Bretton Woods system pursued responsible policies, fiscal deficits in a peripheral country such as the UK generated balance-of-payments problems for that country, and any government seriously committed to maintaining a fixed exchange rate on the US dollar found its freedom to run such deficits severely curtailed by that commitment.

In the UK the phenomenon popularly known as 'stop–go'—a sequence of events involving fiscal and monetary restraint, sluggish domestic activity and an improving balance of payments, followed by fiscal and monetary expansion, a buoyant domestic economy, and balance-of-payments problems, followed by a return to restraint, and so on—was the natural outcome of the interaction of Keynesian domestic policies and a firm commitment to Bretton Woods. So long as the exchange rate was fixed on the stable non-inflationary US dollar, and so long as international capital markets would not lend freely in unlimited amounts at given nominal-interest rates, fiscal deficits could not become chronic. Under 'stop–go', moreover, the economy performed well, though this last judgement is made with benefit of much hindsight. In the 1950s and 60s, 'stop–go' was perceived as anything but satisfactory, and the exchange-rate regime came to be viewed, not as inhibiting chronic and undesirable fiscal deficits (not to mention monetary expansion) but as standing in the way of policies that could lead to a permanent increase in the economy's long-run growth rate; for if balance-of-payments problems were the 'cause' of the 'stop' phase of the policy, would it not be possible to prolong the 'go' phase indefinitely by removing that cause?

Perhaps, as has already been argued, the type of chronic, secular fiscal deficits which currently infect the world's economies should not really be laid at the door of Keynesian economics, because they do not result from the type of anticyclical fiscal policies whose desirability Keynes's macro-theory seemed, to most of his followers, to imply. Nevertheless, there arose amongst some of those followers from the 1950s onwards a tendency to neglect the all-important cyclical-secular distinction and to argue that policies with a proven ability to generate cyclical expansion could also be relied upon to provide demand-led secular growth. The fundamental resource constraint on the economy which ensures that, in a secular setting, the extra consumption generated by debt-financed government expenditure has an opportunity cost, in terms of current capital accumulation, was lost sight of; and the manifestation of that constraint under the Bretton Woods system, namely balance-of-payments problems, came to be interpreted as the result of an artificial, self-imposed, and 'merely financial' constraint implicit in the fixed exchange rate.

Hence there developed the doctrine that growth could be sustained if only exchange-rate depreciation were permitted to maintain international competitiveness. As is usually the case, there was a germ of truth in this doctrine. If the component of aggregate demand relied upon to lead growth was exports, and if these expanded because of a real shift in world demand towards them, then the home country would indeed become genuinely better-off as a result. It was of course a different matter altogether to try to promote growth by fiscal expansion and devaluation, but the all-important distinction here was lost sight of by policy-makers at some time in the late 1960s.[9]

Economists are accustomed to distinguish rather sharply between ends and means, and the foregoing argument has been cast implicitly in terms of this distinction. The size and duration of the fiscal deficit have been treated as objects of choice for policy-makers, and a fixed-exchange-rate regime has been presented as a factor constraining choices about them. Though this treatment has, it is hoped, facilitated the narrative, there is a sense in which it has been fundamentally misleading. Social institutions are not like physical characteristics of the environment. They are not given factors, but are themselves the outcome, often unintended to be sure, of agents' choices. As we have already seen in the context of the principles of 'sound finance', when a particular institution ceases to be taken for granted and is subjected to analysis, it also ceases to be a constraint upon political choice and becomes one of its objects.

Thus it was also with the fixed exchange rate in the United Kingdom. Once it was believed that it prevented the authorities using continuous fiscal and monetary expansion to promote growth, the choice between 'stop–go' along with a fixed exchange rate on the one hand, and perpetual growth accompanied by a flexible exchange rate on the other, was entered upon the political agenda; and the decision was made, quite explicitly, to choose fiscal expansion rather than exchange-rate fixity.[10] The resource constraint facing the economy was not removed by changing the exchange-rate regime, however. When debt-financed government expenditure began to divert resources from capital accumulation to consumption by putting upward pressure on the interest rate, this effect too was resisted by the authorities. The fundamental resource constraint then manifested itself in inflation instead, and the current generation ended up paying for its own extra consumption from the proceeds of tax on cash balances and a not-immediately-perceived capital levy on already existing stocks of nominal debt.[11] By the late 1970s, policies to bring both inflation and deficits under control were coming into place in the UK, and by now it is possible to argue that deficits there are too small, rather than too large. This is hardly the case in the United States, to which we now turn.

As noted earlier, the position of the United States under the Bretton Woods system was different from that of other nations. The obligation to design policies so as to maintain a balance-of-payments position compatible with maintaining a fixed exchange rate on the US dollar, that the system imposed upon peripheral countries, could not, by its very nature, affect the policies of the key-currency country. Indeed, it is debatable whether the Bretton Woods system imposed any institutional constraint at all upon the United States. At the outset the US had assumed the responsibility of maintaining the convertibility of the dollar into gold at a fixed price, and the designers of the system intended this measure to ensure the ultimate restoration of a gold exchange standard; but institutions have a way of evolving in unexpected directions.

It is at least arguable that the evolution of the US dollar into the key currency of the Bretton Woods system had little if anything to do with its gold convertibility.[12] As we have seen, policy in peripheral countries was influenced by dollar convertibility considerations; but Darby, Lothian *et al.* (1983, Chapter 16) report no evidence that the conduct of short-run domestic policy in the United States in the 1950s and 1960s was in any similar way influenced by the gold-convertibility commitment. This of course is not to deny the obvious fact that, although US policy was becoming increasingly lax from the early 1960s onwards, the recent and truly alarming growth of US fiscal deficits dates from the early 1970s—the very time at which gold convertibility was abandoned—but we must be careful how we interpret this fact.

Perhaps the abandonment of gold convertibility did indeed represent the inadvertent removal of a constraint upon US fiscal policy and 'caused' the latter to become less responsible, but it may also be that the maintenance of gold convertibility came to be seen as standing in the way of a fiscal-policy stance which for other reasons was regarded as desirable, so that its abandonment was 'caused' by fiscal-policy decisions. The data will hardly permit us to discriminate between these two quite contradictory explanations of a single event, consisting as they do of the facts that the alternative explanations are designed to deal with in the first place. Be that as it may, gold convertibility was abandoned as a matter of conscious policy and the only issue in doubt is whether, when this was done, the implications for future fiscal and monetary policy were understood and taken into account in the decision. There can be no debating the conclusion that, as in the case of the UK fixed exchange rate, an institutional factor which might have acted as a constraint upon political choices in the United States in fact became one of the objects of such choices, and was removed in 1972.

It would be wrong to end any account of the demise of the Bretton Woods system without drawing explicit attention to the elementary fact that a system of fixed exchange rates need not be given up if all of its members decide to indulge in expansionary policies. Such a system requires long-run compatibility among the domestic macroeconomic policies of its members; it does not also require those policies to be responsible. At the end of the 1960s the policies of countries such as West Germany and Japan did not involve fiscal or monetary expansion, and, given what was by then happening elsewhere, those countries found themselves with ever-increasing balance-of-payments surpluses. Had they accepted the 'discipline' imposed by fixed exchange rates they would have had to import inflation. Their unwillingness to do so led them to give up their wholehearted commitment to Bretton Woods and made its own contribution to that system's collapse.

Presumably these countries' decisions to maintain responsible macro-economic policies, when other nations were abandoning them, are explicable in terms of domestic political and institutional factors having to do with 'tastes' vis-à-vis inflation and unemployment, such as were analysed by Fried (1973b), but it would take us beyond the scope of this essay to discuss them. However, the implications of all this as far as they concern constraints imposed upon domestic policies by international monetary institutions under Bretton Woods are surely clear: in the case of responsible governments, as with their irresponsible counterparts, it was domestic factors which determined the conduct of macroeconomic policy in the 1960s and 1970s; and when those domestic factors began to work to produce an array of policies incompatible with a system of fixed exchange rates, that system did not provide a quasi-constitutional institutional constraint upon policy; instead it collapsed.

## After Bretton Woods

It has been argued that policy choices based upon erroneous economic analysis, involving a confusion between short- and long-run responses of the economy to fiscal expansion, lay at the root of the problems encountered by such countries as the UK (and perhaps also the United States) as the Bretton Woods system was abandoned, though old-fashioned problems of war finance associated with the Vietnam conflict must not be neglected in the United States case. However, those choices did not immediately involve deficit and debt problems of the type that we now face. Rather they led on to inflation which actually eroded real government debt. Increased consumption provided through the government sector must, as we have repeatedly said, be paid for, and in the 1970s it was typically paid for, not by reducing capital accumulation and hence the consumption of future generations, but from the proceeds of an inflation tax on cash balances and an inflation-imposed capital levy on existing nominal wealth.

It would be a mistake to argue literally that this was the outcome of a carefully considered choice made and imposed through political processes by a self-conscious and well organised pro-inflation coalition. Nevertheless the specific brand of erroneous economics, which holds that fiscal expansion accommodated by money growth can lead to real secular growth in the economy, must have seemed particularly attractive to the large cohort of young voters to whom, in the early 1970s, inflation redistributed a substantial portion of the wealth of older people, largely through the housing and mortgage markets.[13] With the passage of time, in the United States as elsewhere, the inflation tax has become as unpopular as other taxes, while government-provided consumption has retained or even increased its popularity; and that same generation which first financed its consumption by imposing inflationary redistributions on its elders, having exhausted that source, is now maintaining its living standards by imposing costs, through fiscal deficits, on future generations of American taxpayers— or is this really so?[14]

In a closed economy, any increase in current consumption, to the extent that it requires resources with alternative uses, must be at the expense of capital accumulation and hence of future consumption; but in an open economy there is an alternative source of supply for such resources, namely capital inflow associated with a balance-of-payments current-account deficit. The United States is, of course, an open economy, but at first sight it may seem that this complication does not change the essential trade-off already discussed. It should make no difference to their consumption opportunities whether future generations inherit a smaller or larger capital stock, if the latter is accompanied by an obligation to make payments to foreigners equal in value to the return on the extra capital in question. The critical point in the latter case, however, is how binding upon future generations are the commitments to foreign creditors entered into upon their behalf by their predecessors.

If foreign debt is unquestionably collectible, and is denominated in a unit of account of stable purchasing power, then indeed its existence and growth do nothing more than complicate the mechanisms whereby debt-financed government expenditure reduces the consumption of future generations inhabiting the country whose government emits the debt in question. However, neither of these conditions can be taken for granted in the case of the United States government debt. As Buchanan (1987) argues, moral constraints against default are not in general particularly strong when applied to the debt of a nation state. To borrow, consume, and then repudiate debt must be tempting for any country, though, for most, difficulties of borrowing again after outright repudiation—Kindleberger (1985, Chapter 12) suggests, on the basis of historical experience, a hiatus of about thirty years—inhibit this ultimate step. Nevertheless there are many degrees of default short of outright repudiation, and with recent experience in eastern Europe, Africa, and Latin America to reflect upon, no one can take it for granted that loans made to a so-called 'sovereign risk', even the US government, are completely secure; nor, with two decades of inflationary experience behind us, can anyone be confident that inflation might not break out again in the US and erode existing debt.

Valid though these two points may be, neither taken by itself is quite central. The key point rather is that in the case of the United States, unlike any other country, the two factors interact to offer its citizens a choice not available elsewhere.[15] The current generation of United States citizens, in accumulating foreign debts denominated in US dollars, is leaving open to its successors the option of repudiating that debt by *choosing* to inflate it away; and of all the methods of defaulting on its obligations open to an electorate, inflation is the one against which moral sanctions seem to be the weakest. This option, uniquely available to citizens of the United States, is created by the special role played by the US dollar in the international monetary system.

Under Bretton Woods, the world was to all intents and purposes on a dollar standard. This did not come about by conscious design, but rather because the expanding international economy of the period following the Second World War required means of exchange and units of account. As with any economy in which such things are left to the collective outcome of a myriad of individual choices, the international economy converged on the use of a single money that was cheap to use and stable and secure in its purchasing power. Perhaps the convertibility of the US dollar into gold was initially an important factor in generating widespread confidence in its security, but, as has already been argued, once established as the international money *par excellence*, the dollar's link with gold became progressively less relevant to its ability to play that role. When the Bretton Woods system broke down, and the dollar's link with gold was severed, the international economy did not disappear, nor did an internationally acceptable means of exchange and unit of account cease to be required. Thus the US dollar continued to play the role of international money in the face of instability in its purchasing power of a degree which, if experienced earlier, would surely have prevented it assuming that role. The dollar's complete dominance has been eroded, to be sure, but it remains far and away the most important international money.

The point of all this is that governments which borrow abroad usually do so in US dollars. The United States government is now doing precisely that, and is thereby creating incentives, which increase over time, for its electorate to vote for inflation as a means of repudiating its debt; and though the federal reserve system is nominally independent, and hence insulated from direct political pressures, Weintraub (1978) shows only too clearly that such insulation in the past has never prevented the electorate, through the influence of the President, ultimately having its way with monetary policy. Moreover, the very institutional fact that makes this option available also implies that, if it is exercised, the resulting damage will go far beyond that inflicted by a capital levy upon the United States' creditors. All the damage that inflationary monetary policy can do to the functioning of any economy will, in the case of an inflation of the United States dollar, be inflicted on the international economy.[16] Already the international economy is showing signs of the stresses imposed both by past Eastern European and Third World borrowing and by current United States borrowing, in ways too well known to merit discussion here. It is not going too far to say that, particularly given the fragile state of the international monetary system, implicit in current United States fiscal policy is a threat to the continued existence of the liberal international economic order whose creation was the great political achievement of the post-war period.

The 'Ricardian equivalence' theorem discussed at the beginning of this chapter contributes nothing to our understanding of this issue. It would have it that either no problem exists, because agents in the United States are accumulating capital out of whose income debt interest will be paid, and because agents in the rest of the world did the same when their governments were borrowing; or that if a problem does exist it must be the result of some random error in expectations about which economics has nothing to say. On the other hand, the 'public choice' approach which underlies this essay tells us that a problem does indeed exist, first because governments face incentives to increase their citizens' current consumption by emitting public debt, and second because, later, if debt is held abroad, they face other incentives to seek means of defaulting on it in order to maintain domestic consumption levels. Many debtor countries are already acting in this way, and the United States differs from them only in lagging behind in its foreign borrowing, and having open to it domestic inflation as a means to default on foreign debt.

It is small wonder that, among thoughtful commentators, a search is on for a set of institutional constraints which will prevent political processes in the United States generating so destructive an outcome as that just envisaged. Because the establishment of a set of international monetary arrangements based upon fixed exchange rates and some form of commodity convertibility would provide just such a set of constraints, it is equally small wonder that calls are being heard for a return to gold or the establishment of a 'new Bretton Woods'. Much as I sympathise with its aims, it should be clear from the preceding discussion that such advocacy seems to me to be beside the point. After all we *had* the old Bretton Woods, and it lasted just so long as the electorates of certain key member countries refrained from attempting to secure for themselves through government activities increased consumption at no extra current cost. The Bretton Woods system stood in the way of such political choices being made. It had to be given up if those choices were to be exercised, and given up it was. It did not prevent them.

Surely it is wishful thinking to believe that any electorate in hot pursuit of a free lunch will deliberately act so as to close down the counter at which such meals are available, but that is what attempting to constrain domestic fiscal imprudence by the establishment of a new set of international monetary institutions would require. The problem, that is to say, is not how to design the international economic order in order to curb domestic policies. Rather it is how to curb domestic policies in order to preserve international economic order.

## Concluding Comment

The underlying theme of this chapter is easily stated. The political decisions from which deficits stem are taken by the governments of nation states, and international monetary institutions link the economies of those same nation states. It may be regrettable, but it is hardly surprising, that, when the maintenance of a set of institutions, which by their very nature inhibited the growth of deficits, came into conflict with the domestic political forces tending to produce them, it was the international institutions which gave way. It follows that the re-establishment of a stable international monetary order must await the re-establishment of prudent domestic policies in individual nations, and that any attempt to impose prudence surreptitiously by prior reform of international monetary institutions would be bound to fail.

To discuss in detail the nature of the domestic institutional reforms that might accompany and encourage the fundamental changes in fiscal policy which seem so desirable would be to go far beyond the assigned bounds of this chapter, but a few concluding comments on this issue are in order. First and foremost, when institutional constraints on a particular type of action are missing in the political structure of any country, it is necessary first to convince its electorate that the action in question is undesirable before such constraints can be imposed. Indeed, a widely held conviction of its undesirability is surely the most important and binding limit that can be placed upon any specific course of government action. No electorate is going to impose upon its representatives restrictions which will prevent them undertaking desirable policies, but it is unlikely to resist restrictions on what it regards as undesirable.

The key task for opponents of chronic deficit finance then, is to persuade electorates that it is undesirable, at least on its current scale, and there are some grounds for hoping that this can be done. It has been argued above that deficit, as opposed to tax, finance of government expenditure is undertaken because individuals now living wish simultaneously to maintain their own consumption levels while providing for their descendants' well-being by endowing them with enforceable claims upon the incomes of others. It has also been suggested that, collectively, this action is self-defeating to the extent that it results in those descendants as a group inheriting a lower capital stock than would otherwise be theirs. There is, therefore, an element of 'public bad' about deficit finance which once understood might be harnessed to make a case against it.

In the case of the United States however, matters are, as we have seen, more complex. Because of the critical role of the US dollar in the international monetary system, current United States deficits do not necessarily impose a lower standard of living upon future generations of Americans. Instead they offer them a choice between putting up with lower living standards on the one hand and legally repudiating their inherited debts by way of inflation on the other. That inflation is a public bad is not, of course, in dispute, but in the case of the US dollar the constituency that would be adversely affected by its inflation is far bigger than the electorate that would pass judgement on the issue. To say that this is worrisome is not to say that the US electorate is somehow more short-sighted and self-interested than any other, but merely to say that it must be persuaded to display more foresight and public-spiritedness than any other if the US is to be expected to put its fiscal house in order.

## Notes

1 It is worth pointing out for the record that, though the theorem in question may have originated with Ricardo, he rejected it as a practical guide to policy. The analysis of this theorem presented here is brief. It is dealt with in much greater detail by Brennan and Buchanan (1986).

2 It is to Barro's credit that he at least is consistent in his treatment of debt finance, arguing both that it creates no long-term burden and also that it has no current real effects. Lerner of course claimed short-run benefits with no long-run costs, at least in a closed economy. However, Lerner's analysis, unlike Barro's, was premissed on the Keynesian assumption of involuntarily unemployed resources being available. This matter is discussed on pp. 191–2. And foreign-debt considerations are discussed on p. 200 *et seq.*

3 For a rigorous analysis of the way in which the combination of self-interest and mortality undermine the Ricardian theorem, see Blanchard (1984).

4 Note that Lerner (1961) was well aware of the logical possibility of deficit finance affecting capital accumulation, thereby placing a burden upon future generations. He noted this possibility while attacking the views of Buchanan (1958), but attached no empirical relevance to it.

5 For an excellent survey of the literature on constitutional constraints upon rent seeking, see Rowley (1985).

6 This is not to deny that Keynes himself toyed with the notion of secular stagnation, because he clearly did, but only to point out that, if the stagnationist thesis fails, his model still maintains potential validity as a device for analysing certain properties of the depression phase of the business cycle.

7 Canada, of course, was one of those countries that adopted Keynesian policies at a very early date, but she opted more-or-less simultaneously for a flexible exchange rate. However, since the exchange rate remained a policy target, balance-of-payments considerations exercised a restraining influence on other aspects of policy even there.

8 Mints (1945) remains a classic source of information on the development of monetary thought over the period in question.

9 It would be unfair to attribute the fallacies involved here to all British Keynesians. Sir Alec Cairncross, for example, is nothing if not a Keynesian, but he was very critical of attempts to generate demand-led growth. See Cairncross (1975).

10 Fixed exchange rates were repudiated in the 1972 budget speech. On all this see Laidler (1976b).

11 Moreover, there were considerable wealth redistributions between members of that generation inherent in the policies in question. This issue is discussed below, p. 198.

12 This is by no means a universally held view. Robert Triffin (e.g. 1960) was a persuasive advocate of the position that the gold convertibility of the dollar was a vital component of the Bretton Woods system.

13 I am indebted to Michael Parkin for long ago suggesting to me the importance of demographic factors in generating a political climate favourable to inflation in the late 1960s and early 1970s. This matter would be well worth a careful study.

14 I have already commented on the ironical similarity of the arguments of Robert J. Barro to those of Abba Lerner. It is also worth pointing out that the nominally 'conservative' arguments of supply-side economics, often used to justify US fiscal policy, are remarkably similar to 'liberal' demand-side Keynesian analysis.

15 A Canadian economist should be careful about criticising US fiscal policy, when Canadian fiscal policy is, relatively speaking, much more irresponsible. For a first-rate Canadian perspective on questions having to do with deficits, see Purvis (1985).

16 And let it be noted that this author is not one of those who believe that the costs of inflation can be reduced to a few insignificant welfare triangles. See Chapter 3 above, and Leijonhufvud (1977).

# References

Akerlof, G. A. (1973) 'The Demand for Money: A General-Equilibrium Inventory-Theoretic Approach', *Review of Economic Studies*, 40 (Jan.), 115–30.

Akerlof, G. A. and Yellen, J. L. (1986) 'A Near-Rational Model of the Business Cycle with Wage and Price Inertia', *Quarterly Journal of Economics*, 100 (Supplement), 823–38.

Alchian, A. A. (1970) 'Information Costs, Pricing and Resource Unemployment' in E. S. Phelps *et al.* (eds.) *The Microeconomic Foundations of Employment and Inflation Theory*, Norton.

Alchian, A. A. (1977) 'Why Money?', *Journal of Money, Credit, and Banking*, 9 (Feb., pt. 2), 133–40.

Alt, J. G. and Chrystal, K. A. (1983) *Political Economics*, University of California Press.

Archibald, G. C. and Lipsey, R. G. (1958) 'Monetary and Value Theory: A Critique of Lange and Patinkin', *Review of Economic Studies*, 26 (1), 1–22.

Argy, V. (1981) *The Postwar International Monetary Crisis*, Allen & Unwin.

Artis, M. J. and Lewis, M. K. (1976) 'The Demand for Money in the United Kingdom', *Manchester School*, 44 (June), 147–81.

Artis, M. J. and Lewis, M. K. (1981) *Monetary Control in the United Kingdom*, Philip Allan.

Artis, M. J. and Lewis, M. K. (1984) 'How Unstable is the Demand for Money in the United Kingdom?', *Economica*, 51 (Nov.) 473–6.

Aukrust, O. (1970) 'PRIM I: A Model of the Price and Income Distribution Mechanism of an Open Economy', *Review of Income and Wealth*, 16 (Mar.) 51–78.

Bagehot, W. (1873) *Lombard Street: A Description of the Money Market*.

Bailey, M. J. (1956) 'The Welfare Cost of Inflationary Finance', *Journal of Political Economy*, 64 (Feb.), 93–110.

Balassa, B. (1980) 'Flexible Exchange Rates and International Trade', in J. S. Chipman and C. P. Kindleberger (eds.) *Flexible Exchange Rates and the Balance of Payments, Essays in Memory of Egon Sohmen*, North-Holland.

Barro, R. J. (1972) 'A Theory of Monopolistic Price Adjustment', *Review of Economic Studies*, 39, 17–26.

Barro, R. J. (1974) 'Are Government Bonds Net Wealth?', *Journal of Political Economy*, 82 (Nov.–Dec.), 1095–117.

Barro, R. J. (1977a) 'Unanticipated Money Growth and Unemployment in the United States', *American Economic Review*, 67 (Mar.), 101–15.

Barro, R. J. (1977b) 'Long-term Contracting, Sticky Prices and Monetary Policy', *Journal of Monetary Economics*, 3 (July), 305–16.

Barro, R. J. (1978) 'Unanticipated Money, Output, and the Price Level in the United States', *Journal of Political Economy*, 86 (Aug.), 549–81.

Barro, R. J. (1979a) 'Second Thoughts on Keynesian Economics', *American Economic Review*, 69 (May: Papers and Proceedings), 54–9.

Barro, R. J. (1979b) 'On the Determination of the Public Debt', *Journal of Political Economy*, 87 (Oct.), 960–71.

Baumol, W. J. (1952) 'The Transactions Demand for Cash—An Inventory Theoretic Approach', *Quarterly Journal of Economics*, 66 (Nov.), 545–56.

Bergstrom, A. R. and Wymer, C. R. (1974) 'A Model of Disequilibrium Neoclassical Growth and its Application to the United Kingdom', LSE mimeo.

Black, F. (1970) 'Banking and Interest Rates in a World Without Money: The Effects of Uncontrolled Banking', *Journal of Banking Research* (Autumn), 8–28.

Blanchard, O. P. (1984) 'Current and Anticipated Deficits, Interest Rates and Economic Activity', *European Economic Review*, 25 (June), 7–28.

Boothe, P. (1983) 'Speculative Profit Opportunities in the Canadian Foreign Exchange Market 1974–78', *Canadian Journal of Economics*, 16 (Nov.), 603–11.

Boothe, P. and Longworth, D. (1984) 'International Capital Mobility', Ottawa: Bank of Canada mimeo.

Bordo, M. D. and Jonung, L. (1981) 'The Long-run Behaviour of the Income Velocity of Money in Five Advanced Countries 1879–1975—An Institutional Approach', *Economic Inquiry*, 19 (Jan.), 96–116.

Bordo, M. D. and Jonung, L. (1987) *The Long-Run Behaviour of the Velocity of Circulation*, Cambridge University Press.

Boschen, J. and Grossman, H. I. (1982) 'Tests of Equilibrium Macroeconomics Using Contemporaneous Data', *Journal of Monetary Economics*, 10, 309–33.

Boyer, R. S. (1978a) 'Financial Policies in the Open Economy', *Economica*, 45 (Feb.), 39–57.

Boyer, R. S. (1978b) 'Currency Mobility and Balance of Payments Adjustment', in B. H. Putnam and D. S. Wilford (eds.) *The Monetary Approach to International Adjustment*, Praeger.

Boyer, R. S. (1978c) 'Optimal Foreign Exchange Interventions', *Journal of Political Economy*, 86 (Dec.), 1045–52.

Brennan, H. G. and Buchanan, J. M. (1986) 'The Logic of the Ricardian Equivalence Theorem', in J. M. Buchanan, C. K. Rowley and R. D. Tollison (eds.) *Deficits*, Basil Blackwell.

Brittain, B. (1981) 'International Currency Substitution and the Apparent Instability of Velocity in Some European Economies and in the United States', *Journal of Money, Credit, and Banking*, 13 (May), 135–55.

Brittan, S. (1982) *How to End the 'Monetarist' Controversy*, IEA.

Brunner, K. and Meltzer, A. H. (1963) 'Predicting Velocity: Implications for Theory and Policy', *Journal of Finance*, 18 (May), 319–54.

Brunner, K. and Meltzer, A. H. (1971) 'The Uses of Money: Money in the Theory of an Exchange Economy', *American Economic Review*, 61 (Dec.), 784–805.

Brunner, K. and Meltzer, A. H. (1976a) 'An Aggregative Theory for a Closed Economy', in J. L. Stein (ed.) *Monetarism*, North-Holland.

Brunner, K. and Meltzer, A. H. (1976b) 'Reply', in J. L. Stein (ed.) *Monetarism*, North-Holland.

Brunner, K. and Meltzer, A. H. (1987) 'Money and the Economy: Issues in Monetary Analysis', the 1987 Raffaele Mattioli lectures, Carnegie–Mellon University mimeo.

Buchanan, J. M. (1958) *Public Principles of Public Debt*, Homewood IL: Richard Irwin.
Buchanan, J. M. (1976) 'Barro on the Ricardian Equivalence Theorem', *Journal of Political Economy*, 84 (Apr.), 337–42.
Buchanan, J. M. (1987) 'The Ethics of Default', in Charles Rowley (ed.) *Towards a Political Economy of Deficits*, Blackwell.
Buchanan, J. M., Tulloch, R. D. and Tollison, G. (eds.) (1980) *Towards a Theory of the Rent Seeking Society*, College Station: Texas A & M Press.
Burton, D. (1980) 'Expectations and a Small Open Economy with Flexible Exchange Rates', *Canadian Journal of Economics*, 13 (Feb.), 1–15.
Cairncross, A. (1975) *Inflation, Growth and International Finance*, Allen & Unwin.
Canada (1964) Royal Commission on Banking and Finance (Porter Commission) *Report*, Ottawa.
Carr, J. and Darby, M. (1981) 'The Role of Money Supply Shocks in the Short-Run Demand for Money', *Journal of Monetary Economics* (Sept.), 183–200.
Carr, J., Darby, M. and Thornton, D. (1985) 'Monetary Anticipations and the Demand for Money: A Reply', *Journal of Monetary Economics*, 8 (Sept.), 251–58.
Caves, D. W. and Feige, E. L. (1976) 'Efficient Foreign Exchange Markets and the Monetary Approach to Exchange Rate Determination', University of Wisconsin Social Systems Research Institute mimeo.
Chick, V. (1973) *The Theory of Monetary Policy*, Blackwell.
Chick, V. (1983) *Macroeconomics after Keynes*, Philip Allan; MIT Press.
Chipman, J. S. (1980) 'Exchange Rate Flexibility and Resource Allocation', in J. S. Chipman and C. P. Kindleberger (eds.) *Flexible Exchange Rates and the Balance of Payments, Essays in Memory of Egon Sohmen*, North-Holland.
Chow, G. (1966) 'On the Long-Run and Short-Run Demand for Money', *Journal of Political Economy*, 74 (Apr.), 111–31.
Claassen, E. (1976) 'World Inflation under Flexible Exchange Rates', *Scandinavian Journal of Economics*, 78, 346–65.
Clower, R. W. (1965) 'The Keynesian Counter-Revolution—a Theoretical Appraisal', in F. H. Hahn and E. R. P. Brechling (eds.) *The Theory of Interest Rates*, Macmillan for the IEA.
Clower, R. W. (1967) 'A Reconsideration of the Microfoundations of Monetary Theory', *Western Economic Journal*, 6 (Dec.), 1–8.
Clower, R. W. and Howitt, P. W. (1978) 'The Transactions Theory of the Demand for Money: A Reconsideration', *Journal of Political Economy*, 86 (June), 449–66.
Coase, R. (1937) 'The Nature of the Firm', reprinted (1952) in AEA *Readings in Price Theory*, Homewood IL: Richard Irwin.
Coats, W. L. (1982) 'Modeling the Short-Run Demand for Money with Exogenous Supply', *Economic Inquiry*, 20 (Apr.), 222–39.
Coghlan, R. (1981) *Money, Credit and the Economy*, Allen & Unwin.
Colander, D. (1984) 'Was Keynes a Keynesian or a Lernerian?', *Journal of Economic Literature*, 22 (Dec.), 1572–5.
Committee on the Working of the Monetary System (the Radcliffe Committee) (1959) *Report*, HMSO.
Corden, W. M. (1972) 'Monetary Integration', *Princeton Essays in International Finance*, 93 (Apr.).
Courchene, T. J. (1970) 'General Equilibrium Models and the World Payments System', *Southern Economic Journal*, 26 (Jan.), 309–22.
Courchene, T. J. (1977) *Money Inflation and the Bank of Canada*, Montreal: C. D. Howe Institute.
Cowen, T. and Krozner, R. (1987) 'The Development of the New Monetary

Economics', *Journal of Political Economy*, 95 (June), 567–90.

Cripps, F. and Godley, W. (1976) 'A Formal Analysis of the Cambridge Economic Policy Group Model', *Economica*, 43 (Nov.) 335–48.

Cross, R. (ed) (1988) *Unemployment, Hysteresis, and the Natural Rate of Hypothesis*, Blackwell.

Cuddington, J. (1983) 'Currency Substitution, Capital Mobility, and Money Demand', *Journal of International Money and Finance*, 2 (Aug.), 111–33.

Cuthbertson, K. and Taylor, M. P. (1986) 'Monetary Anticipations and the Demand for Money in the UK: Testing Rationality in the Shock Absorber Hypothesis', *Journal of Applied Econometrics*, 1, 355–65.

Cuthbertson, K. and Taylor, M. P. (1987) 'Monetary Anticipation and the Demand for Money: Some Evidence for the UK', *Weltwirtschaftliches Archiv*, 183 (3), 509–20.

Darby, M., Lothian, J. *et al.* (1983) *The International Transmission of Inflation*, University of Chicago Press for the National Bureau of Economic Research, Inc.

Diamond, P. A. (1984) *A Search Equilibrium Approach to the Microfoundations of Macroeconomics*, MIT Press.

Diewert, W. E. (1974) 'Intertemporal Consumer Theory and the Demand for Durables', *Econometrica*, 42 (May), 497–516.

Dornbusch, R. (1976a) 'Comments on Brunner and Meltzer', in J. Stein (ed.) *Monetarism*, North-Holland.

Dornbusch, R. (1976b) 'Expectations and Exchange Rate Dynamics', *Journal of Political Economy*, 84 (Dec.), 1161–76.

Dowd, K. (1985) *The Demand for Money, Consumption and Real Wages*, University of Western Ontario mimeo.

Drazen, A. (1987) 'Reciprocal Externality Models of Low Employment', *European Economic Review*, 31 (Feb.–Mar.), 436–43.

Dutton, D. S. and Gramm, W. P. (1973) 'Transactions Costs, the Wage Rate, and the Demand for Money', *American Economic Review*, 63 (Sept.), 652–65.

Edgeworth, F. Y. (1888) 'The Mathematical Theory of Banking', *Journal of Royal Statistical Society*, 51, 113–26.

Edgren, G., Faxen, K. O. and Ohdner, G. E. (1969) 'Wages, Growth and the Distribution of Income', *Swedish Journal of Economics*, 71 (3), 133–60.

Fama, E. (1980) 'Banking in the Theory of Finance', *Journal of Monetary Economics*, 6 (Jan.), 39–57.

Feige, E. L. and Johannes, J. M. (1982) 'Was the United States Responsible for Worldwide Inflation Under the Regime of Fixed Exchange Rates?', *Kyklos*, 35 (2), 263–77.

Feige, E. L. and Parkin, J. M. (1971) 'The Optimal Quantity of Money, Bonds, Commodity Inventories and Capital', *American Economic Review*, 61, 335–49.

Feige, E. L. and Pearce, D. K. (1976) 'Economically Rational Expectations', *Journal of Political Economy*, 84 (3), 499–522.

Feige, E. L. and Pearce, D. K. (1977) 'The Substitutability of Money and Near-Monies: A Survey of the Time-Series Evidence', *Journal of Economic Literature*, 15 (June), 439–69.

Fischer, S. (1977) 'Long-Term Contracts, Rational Expectations and the Optimal Money Supply Rule', *Journal of Political Economy*, 85 (1), 191–206.

Fisher, D. (1971) *Money and Banking*, Homewood IL: Richard Irwin.

Fisher, I. (1911) *The Purchasing Power of Money*, Macmillan Publishing Company, Inc.

Fleming, J. M. (1962) 'Domestic Financial Policies under Fixed and Floating Exchange Rates', *IMF Staff Papers*, 9, 369–79.

Floyd, J. (1985) *World Monetary Equilibrium*, Philip Allan.

Fortin, P. (1979) 'Monetary Policy and Monetary Targets in Canada: A Critical Assessment', *Canadian Journal of Economics*, 12 (Nov.), 625–46.

Fortin, P. and Newton, K. (1981) 'Labour Market Tightness and Wage Inflation in Canada', (Quebec: Université Laval) Département d'Économique, Cahier 8108, mimeo.

Foster, J. I. (1987) *Evolutionary Macroeconomics*, Allen & Unwin.

Fratianni, M. and Peeters, T. (eds.) (1978) *One Money for Europe*, Macmillan.

Frenkel, J. (1976) 'A Monetary Approach to the Exchange Rate, Doctrinal Aspects and Empirical Evidence', *Scandinavian Journal of Economics*, 78 (2), 200–24.

Frenkel, J. (1981a) 'The Collapse of Purchasing Power Parities During the 1970s', *European Economic Review*, 16 (Feb.), 145–65.

Frenkel, J. (1981b) 'Flexible Exchange Rates, Prices, and the Role of "News": Lessons from the 1970s', *Journal of Political Economy*, 89 (Aug.), 665–705.

Frenkel, J. and Aizenman, J. (1982) 'Aspects of Optimal Management of Exchange Rates', *Journal of International Economics*, 13 (Nov.), 231–57.

Fried, J. (1973a) 'Money, Exchange and Growth', *Western Economic Journal*, 11 (Sept.), 285–301.

Fried, J. (1973b) 'Inflation Unemployment Trade-offs under Fixed and Floating Exchange Rates', *Canadian Journal of Economics*, 6 (Feb.), 43–52.

Friedman, M. (1953a) 'The Methodology of Positive Economics', in *Essays in Positive Economics*, University of Chicago Press.

Friedman, M. (1953b) 'The Case for Flexible Exchange Rates', in *Essays in Positive Economics*, University of Chicago Press.

Friedman, M. (1956) 'The Quantity Theory of Money—A Restatement', in *Studies in the Quantity Theory of Money*, University of Chicago Press.

Friedman, M. (1957) *A Theory of the Consumption Function*, Princeton University Press for the NBER.

Friedman, M. (1959) 'The Demand for Money—Some Theoretical and Empirical Results', *Journal of Political Economy*, 67 (June), 327–51.

Friedman, M. (1960) *A Program for Monetary Stability*, Fordham University Press.

Friedman, M. (1968) 'The Role of Monetary Policy', *American Economic Review*, 58 (Mar.), 1–17.

Friedman, M. (1969) *The Optimum Quantity of Money*, Macmillan.

Friedman, M. (1974) *Milton Friedman's Monetary Framework*. R. J. Gordon (ed.), University of Chicago Press.

Friedman, M. (1975) *Unemployment Versus Inflation*, IEA.

Friedman. M. (1984) 'Lessons from the 1979–82 Monetary Policy Experiment', *American Economic Review*, 74 (May) papers and proceedings, 397–400.

Friedman, M. and Meiselman, D. (1963) 'The Relative Stability of Monetary Velocity and the Investment Multiplier in the United States 1898–1958', in *Commission on Money and Credit: Stabilization Policies*, Prentice-Hall.

Friedman, M. and Schwartz, A. J. (1963) *A Monetary History of the United States 1867–1960*, Princeton University Press for the NBER.

Friedman, M. and Schwartz, A. J. (1970) *The Monetary Statistics of the United States*, NBER.

Friedman, M. and Schwartz, A. J. (1982) *Monetary Trends in The United States and the United Kingdom: Their Relation to Income, Prices and Interest Rates, 1867–1975*, University of Chicago Press for the NBER.

Gailliot, H. J. (1970) 'Purchasing Power Parity as an Explanation of Long Term Changes in Exchange Rates', *Journal of Money, Credit and Banking*, 2 (Aug.), 348–57.

Galbraith, J. W. (1988) 'Modelling Expectations Formation with Measurement

Errors', *Economic Journal*, 98 (June), 412–28.

Geary, P. and Kennan, J. (1982) 'The Employment Real Wage Relationship: An International Study', *Journal of Political Economy*, 90 (Aug.), 854–71.

Genberg, H. (1975) *World Inflation and the Small Open Economy*, Swedish Industrial Publications.

Goldfeld, S. M. (1973) 'The Demand for Money Revisited', *Brookings Papers on Economic Activity*, 577–638.

Goldfeld, S. M. (1976) 'The Case of the Missing Money', *Brookings Papers on Economic Activity*, 683–730.

Goldman, S. M. (1974) 'Flexibility and the Demand for Money', *Journal of Economic Theory*, 9 (Oct.), 203–22.

Goodfriend, M. (1985) 'Reinterpreting Money Demand Regressions', in K. Brunner and A. H. Meltzer (eds.) *Understanding Monetary Regimes* (Carnegie– Rochester Conference Series on Public Policy, 22), North-Holland.

Goodhart, C. A. E. (1975) *Money, Information and Uncertainty*, Macmillan.

Goodhart, C. A. E. (1982a) 'Monetary Trends in the United States and the United Kingdom: A British Review', *Journal of Economic Literature*, 20 (Dec.), 1540–51.

Goodhart, C. A. E. (1982b) 'Disequilibrium Money—a Note', Bank of England mimeo.

Gordon, R. J. (1983) 'The Conduct of Domestic Monetary Policy', NBER working paper 1221.

Gordon, R. J. (1984) 'The Short-Run Demand for Money: A Reconsideration', *Journal of Money, Credit and Banking*, 16 (1), 403–34.

Gramley, L. and Chase, S. B. (1965) 'Time Deposits in Monetary Analysis', *Federal Reserve Bulletin*, 51 (Oct.), 1380–406.

Gray, M. and Parkin, J. M. (1973) 'Portfolio Diversification as Optimal Precautionary Behaviour', in M. Morishima *et al.*, *Theories of Demand, Real and Nominal*, Oxford University Press.

Gray, M., Ward, R. and Zis, G. (1976) 'World Demand for Money', in J. M. Parkin and G. Zis (eds.) *Inflation in the World Economy*, Manchester University Press.

Grubel, H. G. (1966) 'The Distribution of Seigniorage from International Liquidity Creation', in R. Mundell and A. K. Swoboda (eds.) *Monetary Problems of the International Economy*, University of Chicago Press.

Gurley, J. and Shaw, E. (1960) *Money in a Theory of Finance*, Brookings Institution.

Haberler, G. (1981) 'Flexible Exchange Rate Theories and Controversies Once Again', in J. S. Chipman and C. P. Kindleberger (eds.) *Flexible Exchange Rates and the Balance of Payments, Essays in Memory of Egon Sohmen*, North-Holland.

Hahn, F. H. (1965) 'On Some Problems of Proving the Existence of Equilibrium in a Monetary Economy', in F. H. Hahn and F. R. P. Brechling (eds.) *The Theory of Interest Rates*, Macmillan for the IEA.

Hahn, F. H. (1971) 'Professor Friedman's Views on Money', *Economica*, 38, 61–80.

Hall, R. (1980) 'Employment Fluctuations and Wage Rigidity', *Brookings Papers on Economic Activity*, 1, 91–123.

Hall, R. (1982) 'Monetary Trends in the United States and the United Kingdom: A Review from the Perspective of New Developments in Monetary Economics', *Journal of Economic Literature*, 20 (Dec.), 1552–5.

Hall, T. E. and Noble, N. R. (1987) 'Velocity and the Variability of Money Growth: Evidence from Granger Causality Tests', *Journal of Money, Credit and*

*Banking*, 19 (Feb.), 112–16.

Hamburger, M. (1977) 'The Demand for Money in an Open Economy: Germany and the United Kingdom', *Journal of Monetary Economics*, 3 (1), 25–40.

Hansen, A. H. (1938) *Full Recovery or Stagnation?*, Norton.

Hansson, B. A. (1983) *The Stockholm School and the Development of Dynamic Method*, Croom Helm.

Hartley, P. (1988) 'The Liquidity Services of Money', *International Economic Review*, 29 (Feb.), 1–24.

Hawtrey, R. (1913) *Good and Bad Trade*, Constable.

Hayek, F. A. von (1928) 'Intertemporal Price Equilibrium and Movements in the Value of Money', translated and reprinted (1984) in F. A. Hayek, *Money Capital and Fluctuations—Early Essays*, R. McCloughry (ed.), University of Chicago Press.

Hayek, F. A. von (1937) 'Economics and Knowledge', *Economica*, NS 4 (Feb.), 33–54.

Hayek, F. A. von (1976) *Denationalising Money*, IEA.

Helleiner, G. *et al.* (1983) *Towards a New Bretton Woods*, The Commonwealth Secretariat.

Hicks, J. R. (1935) 'A Suggestion for Simplifying the Theory of Money', *Economica*, 2 (Feb.), 1–19.

Hicks, J. R. (1937) 'Mr. Keynes and the Classics: a Suggested Interpretation', *Econometrica*, reprinted in J. R. Hicks (1967) *Critical Essays in Monetary Theory*, Clarendon Press.

Hicks, J. R. (1956) 'Methods of Dynamic Analysis', reprinted in J. R. Hicks (1982) *Money, Interest and Wages: Collected Essays in Economic Theory*, II, Harvard University Press.

Hicks, J. R. (1967) 'The Two Triads', in *Critical Essays in Monetary Theory*, Clarendon Press.

Hicks, J. R. (1974) *The Crisis in Keynesian Economics*, Blackwell.

Hicks, J. R. (1982) *Money, Interest and Wages: Collected Essays in Economic Theory*, II, Harvard University Press.

Holland, A. S. (1988) 'The Changing Responsiveness of Wages To Price-Level Shocks: Explicit and Implicit Indexation', *Economic Inquiry*, 26 (Apr.), 265–79.

Howitt, P. W. (1974) 'Stability and the Quantity Theory', *Journal of Political Economy*, 82 (Jan.–Feb.), 133–51.

Howitt, P. W. (1979) 'Evaluating the Non-Market Clearing Approach', *American Economic Review*, 69 (May) papers and proceedings, 60–4.

Howitt, P. W. (1981) 'Activist Monetary Policy under Rational Expectations', *Journal of Political Economy*, 89 (Apr.), 249–69.

Howitt, P. W. (1985) 'Transactions Costs in the Theory of Unemployment', *American Economic Review*, 75 (Mar.), 88–100.

Howitt, P. W. (1986a) 'Conversations with Economists—A Review Essay', *Journal of Monetary Economics*, 18, 103–18.

Howitt, P. W. (1986b) *Monetary Policy in Transition: A Study of Bank of Canada Policy 1982–85*, Toronto: C. D. Howe Institute.

Howitt, P. W. (1987) 'Wicksell's Cumulative Process as Non-convergence to Rational Expectations Equilibrium', UWO mimeo.

Howitt, P. W. and Laidler, D. (1979) 'Recent Canadian Monetary Policy—a Critique', in R. Wirick and D. Purvis (eds.) *Issues in Canadian Public Policy*, 11, Kingston: Queen's University mimeo.

Johnson, H. G. (1951–2) 'Some Cambridge Controversies in Monetary Theory', *Review of Economic Studies*, 19 (2), 90–104.

Johnson, H. G. (1961) 'The *General Theory* After 25 Years', *American Economic Review*, 51 (May), papers and proceedings, 1–17.

Johnson, H. G. (1962) 'Monetary Theory and Policy', *American Economic Review*, 52 (June), 335–84.

Johnson, H. G. (1963) 'Equilibrium Under Fixed Exchange Rates', *American Economic Review*, 53 (May), 112–19.

Johnson, H. G. (1966) 'A Note on Seigniorage and the Social Saving from Substituting Credit for Commodity Money', in R. Mundell and A. K. Swoboda (eds.) *Monetary Problems of the International Economy*, University of Chicago Press.

Johnson, H. G. (1968) 'Problems of Efficiency in Monetary Management', *Journal of Political Economy*, 76 (Sept.–Oct.), 971–90.

Johnson, H. G. (1969a) 'Inside Money, Outside Money, Income, Wealth and Welfare in Monetary Economics', *Journal of Money, Credit and Banking*, 1 (Feb.), 30–45.

Johnson, H. G. (1969b), 'The Case for Flexible Exchange Rates 1969', *Federal Reserve Bank of St. Louis Review* (June), 12–24.

Johnson, H. G. (1970) 'Recent Developments in Monetary Theory—A Survey', in D. Croome and H. G. Johnson (eds.) *Money in Britain*, Oxford University Press.

Johnson, H. G. (1971) 'The Keynesian Revolution and the Monetarist Counter-Revolution', *American Economic Review*, 61 (May), 9–22.

Johnson, H. G. (1972a) *Inflation and the Monetarist Controversy*, North-Holland.

Johnson, H. G. (1972b) 'The Monetary Approach to the Balance of Payments', in *Further Essays in Monetary Economics*, Allen & Unwin.

Johnson, H. G. (1972c) 'Notes on Incomes Policy and the Balance of Payments', in J. M. Parkin and M. Sumner (eds.) *Incomes Policy and Inflation*, Manchester University Press.

Johnson, H. G. (1974) 'Major Issues in Monetary Economics', *Oxford Economic Papers* 26 (July), 212–25.

Jones, R. A. (1976) 'The Origin and Development of Media of Exchange', *Journal of Political Economy*, 84 (Aug.), Part 1, 756–75.

Jonson, P. D. (1976a) 'Money, Prices and Output—an Integrative Essay', *Kredit und Kapital*, 4 (2), 499–518.

Jonson, P. D. (1976b) 'Money and Economic Activity in the Open Economy: The United Kingdom 1880–1970', *Journal of Political Economy*, 84 (Sept./Oct.), 979–1012.

Jonson, P. D. and Kierzkowski, H. I. (1975) 'The Balance of Payments: an Analytic Exercise', *Manchester School*, 43 (June), 105–33.

Jonson, P. D., Moses, E. and Wymer, C. R. (1976) 'A Minimal Model of the Australian Economy', Reserve Bank of Australia discussion paper 7601.

Jonson, P. D. and Rankin, R. W. (1986) 'On Some Recent Developments in Monetary Economics', *Economic Record*, 62 (Dec.), 257–67.

Jonson, P. D. and Trevor, R. G. (1980) 'Monetary Rules: A Preliminary Analysis', Reserve Bank of Australia research discussion paper 7903, mimeo.

Jorgenson, D. W. (1967) 'The Theory of Investment Behaviour', in R. Ferber (ed.) *The Determinants of Business Behaviour*, NBER.

Judd, J. and Scadding, T. (1982a) 'The Search for a Stable Money Demand Function: A Survey of the Post-1973 Literature', *Journal of Economic Literature*, 20 (Sept.), 993–1023.

Judd, J. and Scadding, T. (1982b) 'Dynamic Adjustment in the Demand for Money: Tests of Alternative Hypotheses', Federal Reserve Bank of San Francisco mimeo.

Kaldor, N. (1980) 'Memorandum of evidence . . .', Treasury and Civil Service

Committee, Session 1979–80, *Memoranda on Monetary Policy*, HMSO.

Kanniainen, V. and Tarkka, J. (1983) 'The Role of Capital Flows in the Adjustment of Money Demand: The Case of Finland', University of Helsinki working paper 188, mimeo.

Karekan, J. and Wallace, N. (1978) 'International Monetary Reform, the Feasible Alternatives', *FRB of Minneapolis Quarterly Review*, (Summer), 2–7.

Karni, E. (1974) 'The Value of Time and the Demand for Money', *Journal of Monetary Economics*, 6 (Feb.), 45–64.

Kawasaki, S., McMillan, J. and Zimmerman, K. F. (1983) 'Inventories and Price Inflexibility', *Econometrica*, 51 (May), 599–610.

Kemp, J. and Mundell, R. (1983) *A Monetary Agenda for World Growth*, Boston: Quantum.

Keynes, J. M. (1930) *A Treatise on Money*, Macmillan.

Keynes, J. M. (1936) *The General Theory of Employment, Interest and Money*, Macmillan.

Kindleberger, C. P. (1985) *Keynesianism vs Monetarism, and Other Essays in Financial History*, Allen & Unwin.

Klamer, A. (1984) *Conversations with Economists*, Romand and Allanheld.

Klein, B. (1977) 'The Demand for Quality Adjusted Cash Balances: Price Uncertainty in the US Demand for Money Function', *Journal of Political Economy*, 85 (Nov.), 691–716.

Knight, M. and Wymer, C. (1975) 'A Monetary Model of an Open Economy, with Particular Reference to the United Kingdom', International Monetary Research Project discussion paper, mimeo.

Knoester, A. (1979a) 'Theoretical Principles of the Buffer Mechanism, Monetary Quasi-equilibrium and its Spillover Effects', Institute for Economic Research discussion paper series 7908/9/M, Rotterdam: Erasmus University.

Knoester, A. (1979b) 'On Monetary and Fiscal Policy in an Open Economy', *De Economist*, 127 (1), 105–42.

Kohn, M. and Manchester, J. (1985) 'International Evidence on Misspecification of the Standard Money Demand Equation', *Journal of Monetary Economics*, 16 (Mar.), 87–94.

Konieczny, J. (1987) *Inflation and Costly Price Adjustment*, unpublished Ph.D. thesis, University of Western Ontario.

Kydland, F. and Prescott, E. (1982) 'Time to Build and Aggregate Fluctuations', *Econometrica*, 50 (Sept.), 1345–70.

Laidler, D. (1969) *The Demand for Money—Theories and Evidence*, Scranton PA: International Textbook Co.; 3rd edn (1985), Harper & Row.

Laidler, D. (1975) *Essays on Money and Inflation*, Manchester University Press; University of Chicago Press.

Laidler, D. (1976a) 'Inflation in Britain: A Monetarist Perspective', *American Economic Review*, 66 (Sept.), 485–500.

Laidler, D. (1976b) 'Inflation—Alternative Explanations and Policies: Tests on Data Drawn from Six Countries', in K. Brunner and A. H. Meltzer (eds.) *Institutions, Policies and Economic Performance* (Carnegie-Rochester Conference Series on Public Policy, 4), North-Holland.

Laidler, D. (1980) 'The Demand for Money in the United States: Yet Again', in K. Brunner and A. H. Meltzer (eds.) *The State of Macroeconomics* (Carnegie-Rochester Conference Series on Public Policy, 12), North-Holland.

Laidler, D. (1981) 'Inflation and Unemployment in an Open Economy', *Canadian Public Policy*, 7 (Apr., special supplement), 179–88.

Laidler, D. (1982) *Monetarist Perspectives*, Philip Allan; Harvard University Press.

Laidler, D. (1984) 'Did Macroeconomics Need the Rational Expectations

Revolution?', in G. Mason (ed.) *Macroeconomics: Theory, Policy and Evidence*, Winnipeg: Institute for Social and Economic Research.

Laidler, D. (1985) 'Comment on Money Demand Predictability', *Journal of Money, Credit, and Banking*, 17 (Nov., Part 2), 647–52.

Laidler, D. (1987) 'Fisher and Wicksell on the Quantity Theory and the Backing of Money: a Comment on the Debate between Bruce Smith and Ronald Michener', in K. Brunner and A. H. Meltzer (eds.) *Empirical Studies of Velocity, Real Exchange Rates, Unemployment and Productivity* (Carnegie–Rochester Conference Series on Public Policy, 27), 325–34, North-Holland.

Laidler, D. and Bentley, B. (1983) 'A Small Macro-Model of the Post-War United States', *The Manchester School*, 51/4, 317–340.

Laidler, D., Bentley, B., Johnson, D. and Johnson, S. T. (1983) 'A Small Macro-Economic Model of an Open Economy—The Case of Canada', in E. Claassen and P. Salin (eds.) *Recent Issues in the Theory of Flexible Exchange Rates*, North-Holland.

Laidler, D. and Parkin, J. M. (1975) 'Inflation—A Survey', *Economic Journal*, 75 (Dec.), 741–809.

Lane, T. (1983) *Essays on Monetary Control*, unpublished Ph.D. thesis, University of Western Ontario.

Leijonhufvud, A. (1968) *On Keynesian Economics and the Economics of Keynes*, New York: Oxford University Press.

Leijonhufvud, A. (1973) 'Effective Demand Failures', *Swedish Journal of Economics*, 75 (Mar.), 27–48.

Leijonhufvud, A. (1977) 'On the Costs and Consequences of Inflation', in G. C. Harcourt (ed.) *The Microeconomic Foundations of Macroeconomics*, Macmillan for the IEA.

Leijonhufvud, A. (1981) *Information and Coordination*, Oxford University Press.

Leijonhufvud, A. (1986) 'Real and Monetary Factors in Business Fluctuations', *The Cato Journal*, 6 (Fall), 409–20.

Leijonhufvud, A. (1987) 'Rational Expectations and Monetary Institutions', in M. de Cecco and J.-P. Fitoussi (eds.) *Monetary Theory and Economic Institutions*, Macmillan.

Lerner, A. P. (1943) 'Functional Finance and the Federal Debt', *Social Research*, 10 (Feb.), 38–51.

Lerner, A. P. (1951) *The Economics of Employment*, McGraw-Hill.

Lerner, A. P. (1961) 'The Burden of the Debt', *Review of Economics and Statistics*, 43 (May), 139–41.

Lewis, M. (1978) 'Interest Rates and Monetary Velocity in Australia and the United States', *Economic Record*, 54 (Apr.), 111–26.

Lindbeck, A. (1976) 'Stabilization Policies in Open Economies with Endogenous Politicians' (the 1975 Richard T. Ely lecture), *American Economic Review*, 66 (May, papers and proceedings), 1–19.

Lipsey, R. G. (1981) 'Presidential Address: The Understanding and Control of Inflation—Is There a Crisis in Macroeconomics?', *Canadian Journal of Economics*, 14 (Nov.), 545–76.

Lucas, R. E. Jr. (1972) 'Expectations and the Neutrality of Money', *Journal of Economic Theory*, 4 (2), 115–38.

Lucas, R. E. Jr. (1973) 'Some International Evidence of Output–Inflation Tradeoffs', *American Economic Review*, 63 (June), 326–34.

Lucas, R. E. Jr. (1975) 'An Equilibrium Model of the Business Cycle', *Journal of Political Economy*, 83 (Nov./Dec.), 1113–44.

Lucas, R. E. Jr. (1976) 'Econometric Policy Evaluation' in K. Brunner and A. H. Meltzer (eds.) *The Phillips Curve and the Labor Market* (Carnegie–

Rochester Conference Series on Public Policy, 1), North-Holland.

Lucas, R. E. Jr. (1977) 'Understanding Business Cycles' in K. Brunner and A. H. Meltzer (eds.) *Stabilization of the Domestic and International Economy* (Carnegie–Rochester Conference Series on Public Policy, 5), North-Holland.

Lucas, R. E. Jr. (1980) 'Methods and Problems in Business Cycle Theory', *Journal of Money, Credit, and Banking*, 12 (Nov., pt. II), 696–715.

Lucas, R. E. Jr. (1984) 'Money in a Theory of Finance', in K. Brunner and A. H. Meltzer (eds.) *Essays on Macroeconomic Implications of Financial and Labour Markets and Political Processes* (Carnegie–Rochester Conference Series on Public Policy, 21), North-Holland.

Lucas, R. E. Jr. (1986) 'Adaptive Behaviour and Economic Theory', *Journal of Business*, 59 (Oct., pt. 2), s401–s426.

Lucas, R. E. Jr. (1988) 'Money Demand in the United States: A Quantitative Review', in K. Brunner and B. T. McCallum (eds.) *Money, Cycles and Exchange Rates: Essays in Honour of Allan Meltzer* (Carnegie–Rochester Conference Series on Public Policy, 29), North-Holland.

Lucas, R. E. Jr. and Rapping, L. A. (1970) 'Real Wages, Employment and Inflation', in E. Phelps *et al.*, *The Microeconomic Foundations of Employment and Inflation Theory*, Norton.

Lucas, R. E. Jr. and Sargent, T. J. (1978) 'After Keynesian Economics', in *After the Phillips Curve: Persistence of High Inflation and High Unemployment*, FRB of Boston.

McCallum, B. T. (1980) 'Rational Expectations and Macroeconomic Stabilization Policy—An Overview', *Journal of Money, Credit, and Banking*, 12 (Nov., pt. 2), 716–46.

McCallum, B. T. (1983) 'The Role of Overlapping-Generations Models in Monetary Economics', in K. Brunner and A. H. Meltzer (eds.) *Money, Monetary Policy and Financial Institutions* (Carnegie–Rochester Conference Series on Public Policy, 18), North-Holland.

McCallum, B. T. (1985) 'On Consequences and Criticisms of Monetary Targeting', *Journal of Money, Credit, and Banking*, 17 (Nov., pt. 2), 570–97.

McCallum, B. T. (1986), 'On "Real" and "Sticky Price" Theories of the Business Cycle', *Journal of Money, Credit, and Banking*, 18 (Nov.), 397–414.

McCallum, B. T. (1987) 'The Optimal Inflation Rate in an Overlapping-Generations Model with Land', in W. A. Barnett and K. J. Singleton (eds.) *New Approaches to Monetary Economics*, Cambridge University Press.

McCallum, J. (1988) 'The Persistence of Output Fluctuations', McGill University mimeo.

McCloughry, R. (1984) Editorial Introduction to F. A. Hayek, *Money Capital and Fluctuations: Early Essays*, ed. R. McCloughry, University of Chicago Press.

McCracken, P. *et al.* (1977) *Towards Price Stability and Full Employment*, OECD.

McKinnon, R. L. (1979) *Money in International Exchange*, Oxford University Press.

McKinnon, R. L. (1982) 'Currency Substitution and Instability in the World Dollar Standard', *American Economic Review*, 72 (Sept.), 320–33

McKinnon, R. L. (1983) 'Declining American Monetary Autonomy within the World Dollar Standard', Stanford University mimeo.

Marcet, A. and Sargent, T. J. (1987) 'Convergence of Least Squares Learning in Environments with Hidden State Variables and Private Information', Carnegie–Mellon University mimeo.

Marshall, A. (1890) *Principles of Economics*, Macmillan.

Marty, A. L. (1969) 'Inside Money, Outside Money, and the Wealth Effect', *Journal of Money, Credit and Banking*, 1 (Feb.), 101–11.

Marty, A. L. (1976) 'Real Cash Balances and the Optimal Tax Structure', in M. J. Artis and A. R. Nobay (eds.) *Essays in Economic Analysis*, Cambridge University Press.

Melitz, J. (1974) *Primitive and Modern Money*, Addison-Wesley.

Melvin, M. (1985) 'Currency Substitution and Western European Monetary Unification', *Economica*, 52 (Feb.), 79–92.

Meltzer, A. H. (1963) 'The Demand for Money: the Evidence from the Time Series', *Journal of Political Economy*, 71 (June), 219–46.

Menger, C. (1871) *Principles of Economics* tr. and ed. (1950) J. Dingwall and B. Hoselitz, The Free Press.

Milbourne. R. (1988) 'Disequilibrium Buffer Stock Models: A Survey', Kingston: Queen's University mimeo.

Minford, P. (1980) 'A Rational Expectations Model of the United Kingdom under Fixed and Floating Exchange Rates', in K. Brunner and A. H. Meltzer (eds.) *On the State of Macroeconomics* (Carnegie–Rochester Conference Series on Public Policy, 12), 293–355, North-Holland.

Mints, L. (1945) *A History of Banking Theory in Britain and the United States*, University of Chicago Press.

Mishkin, F. (1982) 'Does Anticipated Monetary Policy Matter? An Econometric Investigation', *Journl of Political Economy*, 90 (Feb.), 22–51.

Modigliani, F. (1977) 'The Monetarist Controversy or, Should We Forsake Stabilization Policies', *American Economic Review*, 67 (Mar.), 1–19.

Modigliani, F. and Brumberg, R. (1954) 'Utility Analysis and the Consumption Function: An Interpretation of the Cross-Section Data', in K. K. Kurihara (ed.) *Post Keynesian Economics*, Rutgers University Press.

Montgomery, E. and Shaw, K. (1985) 'Long-Term Contracts, Expectations and Wage Inertia', *Journal of Monetary Economics*, 16 (Sept.), 209–26.

Mundell, R. (1963) 'Capital Mobility and Stabilisation Policy under Fixed and Flexible Exchange Rates', *Canadian Journal of Economics and Political Science*, 29, 475–85.

Mundell, R. (1971) *Monetary Theory*, Goodyear.

Mundell, R. and Swoboda, A. K. (eds.) (1972) *Monetary Problems of the International Economy*, University of Chicago Press.

Mussa, M. (1982) 'A Model of Exchange Rate Dynamics', *Journal of Political Economy*, 90 (Feb.), 74–104.

Myhrman, J. (1975) *Monetary Policy in Open Economies*, Stockholm: Institute for International Economic Studies.

Myhrman, J. (1976) 'Experiences of Flexible Exchange Rates in Earlier Periods: Theories, Evidence and a New View', *Scandinavian Journal of Economics*, 78 (2), 169–96.

Nelson, C. R. and Plosser, C. I. (1982) 'Trends and Random Walks in Macro-economic Time Series', *Journal of Monetary Economics*, 10, 139–62.

Niehans, J. (1971) 'Money and Barter in General Equilibrium with Transactions Costs', *American Economic Review*, 61 (Dec.), 773–83.

Niehans, J. (1975) 'Some Doubts about the Efficiency of Monetary Policy under Flexible Exchange Rates', *Journal of International Economics*, 5 (Aug.), 348–56.

Niehans, J. (1978) *The Theory of Money*, Johns Hopkins University Press.

Okun, A. (1981) *Prices and Quantities: A Macroeconomic Analysis*, Brookings Institution.

Olson, M. (1982) *The Rise and Decline of Nations*, Yale University Press.

Olson, M. (1984) 'Microeconomic Incentives and Macroeconomic Decline', *Weltwirtschaftliches Archiv*, 120, 631–45.

Orr, D. (1970) *Cash Management and the Demand for Money*, Praeger.

Ostroy, J. M. (1973) 'The Informational Efficiency of Monetary Exchange', *American Economic Review*, 63 (Sept.), 597–610.

Parkin, J. M. (1974) 'Inflation, the Balance of Payments, Domestic Credit Expansion and Exchange Rate Adjustment', in R. Z. Aliber (ed.) *National Monetary Policies and the International Monetary System*, University of Chicago Press.

Parkin, J. M. (1977) 'The Transition from Fixed Exchange Rates to Money Supply Targets', *Journal of Money, Credit, and Banking*, 9 (Feb., pt. 2), 228–42.

Parkin, J. M. (1982) *An Introduction to Modern Macroeconomics*, Prentice-Hall.

Parkin, J. M. (1986a) 'The Output Inflation Trade-Off When Prices are Costly to Change', *Journal of Political Economy*, 94 (Feb.), 200–24.

Parkin, J. M. (1986b) 'Essays on and in the Chicago Tradition: a Review Essay', *Journal of Money, Credit, and Banking*, 18 (Feb.), 104–15.

Parkin, J. M. (1987) 'What Do We Know about Business Cycles?' (the 1987 Timlin Lecture), University of Saskatchewan.

Parkin, J. M., Richards, I. and Zis, G. (1975) 'The Determination and Control of the World Money Supply Under Fixed Exchange Rates', *Manchester School of Economic and Social Studies*, 43 (Sept.), 293–316.

Patinkin, D. (1948) 'Price Flexibility and Full Employment', *American Economic Review*, 38 (Sept.), 543–64.

Patinkin, D. (1956) *Money, Interest and Prices* (1st edn), Harper & Row.

Patinkin, D. (1965) *Money, Interest and Prices* (2nd edn), Harper & Row.

Patinkin, D. (1967) *On the Nature of the Monetary Mechanism: The 1967 Wicksell Lectures*, Stockholm: Almqvist & Wicksell.

Patinkin, D. (1969a) 'Money and Wealth—A Review Article', *Journal of Economic Literature*, 7 (Sept.), 1140–50.

Patinkin, D. (1969b) 'The Chicago Tradition, the Quantity Theory, and Friedman', *Journal of Money, Credit, and Banking*, 1 (Feb.), 46–70.

Patinkin, D. (1986) 'A Reply', *Journal of Money, Credit, and Banking*, 18 (Feb.), 116–21.

Perron, P. (1987) 'The Great Crash, the Oil Price Shock and the Unit Root Hypothesis', Université de Montréal mimeo.

Pesek, B. and Saving, T. R. (1967) *Money, Wealth, and Economic Theory*, Macmillan Publishing Company, Inc.

Phelps, E. (1967) 'Phillips Curves, Expectations of Inflation and Optimal Unemployment Over Time, *Economica*, NS 34 (Aug.), 254–81.

Phelps, E. (1970) 'Introduction: The New Microeconomics in Employment and Inflation Theory', in E. S. Phelps *et al.*, *The Microeconomic Foundations of Inflation and Employment Theory*, Macmillan.

Phelps, E. (1972) *Inflation Policy and Unemployment Theory: The Cost–Benefit Approach to Monetary Planning*, Macmillan.

Phelps, E. and Taylor, J. B. (1977) 'Stabilizing Powers of Monetary Policy Under Rational Expectations', *Journal of Political Economy*, 85 (Feb.), 163–90.

Phelps, E. *et al.* (1970) *Microeconomic Foundations of Employment and Inflation Theory*, Norton.

Phillips, A. W. (1954) 'Stabilisation Policy in a Closed Economy', *Economic Journal*, 64 (June), 290–323.

Phlips, L. (1978) 'The Demand for Leisure and Money', *Econometrica*, 46 (Sept.), 1025–43.

Poloz, S. (1981) *Unstable Velocity: Volatile Exchange Rates, and Currency Substitution: The Demand for Money in a Multi-Currency World*, Ph.D. dissertation, University of Western Ontario.

Poole, W. (1967) 'The Stability of the Canadian Flexible Exchange Rate 1950–1962', *Canadian Journal of Economics and Political Science*, 33 (2), 205–17.

Poole, W. (1970) 'Optimal Choice of Monetary Policy Instruments in a Simple Stochastic Macroeconomic Model', *Quarterly Journal of Economics*, 84 (May), 197–216.

Purvis, D. D. (1978) 'Dynamic Models of Portfolio Behavior: More on Pitfalls in Financial Model Building', *American Economic Review*, 68 (June), 403–9.

Purvis, D. D. (1979) 'Wages, the Terms of Trade and the Exchange Rate Regime', *Zeitschrift für Wirtschafts und Sozialwissenschaften*, 99 (1/2), 9–39.

Purvis, D. D. (1985) 'Innis Lecture—Public Sector Deficits, International Capital Movements, and the Domestic Economy: The Medium Term is the Message', *Canadian Journal of Economics*, 18 (Nov.), 723–42.

Robbins, L. C. (1935) *An Essay on the Nature and Significance of Economic Science* (2nd edn), Macmillan.

Rowe, N. (1989) *Rules and Institutions*, Philip Allan.

Rowley, C. K. (1985) 'Rules Versus Authorities in Constitutional Design', in D. Laidler (ed.) *Responses to Economic Change*, University of Toronto Press for the Royal Commission on the Economic Union and Development Prospects for Canada.

Rymes, T. K. (1979) 'Innis Lecture—Money, Efficiency, and Knowledge', *Canadian Journal of Economics*, 12 (Nov.), 575–89.

Samuelson, P. A. (1958) 'An Exact Consumption-Loan Model of Interest With or Without the Social Contrivance of Money', *Journal of Political Economy*, 66 (Dec.), 467–82.

Samuelson, P. A. and Solow, R. M. (1960) 'Analytical Aspects of Anti-Inflation Policy', *American Economic Review*, 50 (May, papers and proceedings), 177–94.

Sargent, T. J. (1976) 'A Classical Macroeconomic Model for the United States', *Journal of Political Economy*, 84 (Apr.), 207–38.

Sargent, T. J. (1984) 'Autoregressions, Expectations, and Advice', *American Economic Review*, 74 (May, papers and proceedings), 408–15.

Sargent, T. J. and Wallace, N. (1973) 'Rational Expectations and the Dynamics of Hyperinflation', *International Economic Review*, 14 (Apr.), 328–50.

Sargent, T. J. and Wallace, N. (1976) 'Rational Expectations and the Theory of Economic Policy', *Journal of Monetary Economics*, 2 (May), 169–83.

Sargent, T. J. and Wallace, N. (1982) 'The Real Bills Doctrine and the Quantity Theory: A Reconsideration', *Journal of Political Economy*, 90 (Dec.), 1212–36.

Smith, A. (1776) *An Inquiry into the Nature and Causes of the Wealth of Nations.*

Sparks, G. R. (1979) 'The Choice of Monetary Policy Instruments in Canada', *Canadian Journal of Economics*, 12 (Nov.), 615–25.

Sparks, G. R. (1985) 'The Theory and Practice of Monetary Policy in Canada, 1945–83', in J. Sargent (ed.) *Fiscal and Monetary Policy*, University of Toronto Press for the Royal Commission on the Economic Union and Development Prospects for Canada.

Spinelli, F. (1983) 'Currency Substitution, Flexible Exchange Rates and the Case for International Monetary Cooperation—A Discussion of a Recent Proposal', IMF mimeo.

Stigler, G. C. (1961) 'The Economics of Information', *Journal of Political Economy*, 69 (June), 213–25.

Sumner, M. (1976) 'European Monetary Union and the Control of Europe's Inflation Rate', in M. Parkin and G. Zis (eds.) *Inflation in the World Economy*, Manchester University Press.

Svensson, L. E. O. (1985) 'Money and Asset Prices in a Cash-in-Advance

Economy', *Journal of Political Economy*, 93 (Oct.), 919–44.

Swoboda, A. K. (1973) 'Eurodollars and the World Money Supply: Implications and Control', in *Europe and the Evolution of the International Monetary System*, Geneva: A. W. Sijthoff-Leiden.

Taylor, J. B. (1979) 'Staggered Wage Setting in a Macro Model', *American Economic Review*, 79 (May, papers and proceedings), 108–13.

Tobin, J. (1956) 'The Interest Elasticity of Transactions Demand for Cash', *Review of Economics and Statistics*, 38 (Aug.), 241–7.

Tobin, J. (1969) 'A General Equilibrium Approach to Monetary Theory', *Journal of Money, Credit, and Banking*, 1 (Feb.), 15–29.

Tobin, J. (1977) 'Inflation Control as a Social Priority', Yale University mimeo.

Tobin, J. (1981) 'The Monetarist Counter-Revolution Today—An Appraisal', *Economic Journal*, 91 (Mar.), 29–42.

Triffin, R. (1960) *Gold and the Dollar Crisis: The Future of Convertibility*, Yale University Press.

Tsiang, S. C. (1956) 'Liquidity Preference and Loanable Funds Theories, Multiplier and Velocity Analysis: A Synthesis', *American Economic Review*, 46 (Sept.), 539–64.

Tsiang, S. C. (1966) 'Walras' Law, Say's Law and Liquidity Preference in General Equilibrium Theory', *International Economic Review*, 7 (Sept.), 329–45.

Tsiang, S. C. (1982) 'Stock or Portfolio Approach to Monetary Theory and the Neo-Keynesian School of James Tobin', *IHS Journal*, 6, 149–71.

Tucker, D. (1971) 'Macroeconomic Models and the Demand for Money Under Market Disequilibrium', *Journal of Money, Credit, and Banking*, 3 (Feb.), 57–83.

Turnovsky, S. (1979) 'On the Insulating Properties of Flexible Exchange Rates', *Revue Économique*, 30 (4), 719–46.

Vaubel, R. (1986) 'Currency Competition versus Governmental Money Monopolies', *The Cato Journal*, 5 (Winter), 927–42.

Wallace, N. (1981) 'A Modigliani–Miller Theorem for Open-Market Operations', *American Economic Review*, 71 (June), 267–74.

Wallace, N. (1982) 'Panel Discussion', in *Interest Rate Deregulation and Monetary Policy*, Federal Reserve Bank of San Francisco.

Wallace, N. (1988) 'A Suggestion for Oversimplifying the Theory of Money', *Conference Papers*, supplement to *The Economic Journal*, 98 (Mar.), 25–36.

Wanniski, J. (1975) 'The Mundell–Laffer Hypothesis', *Public Interest* (Spring).

Weinrobe, M. D. (1972) 'A Simple Model of the Precautionary Demand for Money', *Southern Economic Journal*, 39 (July), 11–18.

Weintraub, R. E. (1978) 'Congressional Supervision of Monetary Policy', *Journal of Monetary Economics*, 4 (Apr.), 341–62.

Weldon, J. C. (1973) 'On Money as a Public Good', McGill University mimeo.

White, L. (1984) *Free Banking in Britain: Theory, Experience and Debate 1800–1845*, Cambridge University Press.

White, W. H. (1981) 'The Case for and Against "Disequilibrium Money"', *IMF Staff Papers* (Sept.), 534–72.

Wicksell, K. (1906) *Lectures on Political Economy*, Vol. 2, tr. (1935) E. Claassen, Routledge & Kegan Paul.

Williamson, J. (1973) 'International Liquidity', *Economic Journal*, 83 (Sept.), 685–746.

Williamson, J. (1976) 'Exchange Rate Flexibility and Reserve Use', *Scandinavian Journal of Economics*, 78 (2) 327–39.

Williamson, J. (1977) *The Failure of World Monetary Reform 1971–74*, Nelson.

# Author Index

# Subject Index

224